WITHDRAWN

KING ZOG'S ALBANIA

Zog I, King of the Albanians

(*Frontispiece*)

KING ZOG'S

ALBANIA

By
J. SWIRE
Commander of the Order of Skenderbeg
Fellow of the Royal Geographical Society
Member of the Royal Institute of International Affairs

Author of
"ALBANIA: THE RISE OF A KINGDOM"
"ALBANIA: (NEAR EAST YEAR BOOK)"

Liveright Publishing Corporation
NEW YORK

COPYRIGHT, 1937 BY
LIVERIGHT PUBLISHING CORPORATION

ALL RIGHTS RESERVED

MANUFACTURED
IN THE UNITED STATES OF AMERICA

"Land of Albania! Let me bend mine eyes
On thee, thou rugged nurse of savage men!
The cross descends, thy minarets arise,
And the pale crescent sparkles in the glen,
Through many a cypress grove within each city's ken.

"Yet in famed Attica such lovely dales
Are rarely seen; nor can fair Tempe boast
A charm they know not; loved Parnassus fails,
Though classic ground and consecrated most,
To match some spots that lurk within this lowering coast."

(Childe Harold's Pilgrimage : **Byron**).

AUTHOR'S NOTE

THESE pages are written for all those who travel—whether by sea, by air, by land or by arm-chair—and would know something of Albania, her self-made king, her clansmen and antique towns, her heroes and her rascals; for there are few countries so accessible which have so much that is picturesque or unusual for the traveller's delight. There are regular sailings from Bari to Durrës, there is an air service from Italy to Tirana and all parts of Albania, and there now exists in Tirana an organisation to assist travellers, while the British Automobile Association can provide facilities for motorists wishing to tour this beautiful land in their own cars.

Nominally under the Turks from the days of her national hero Skenderbeg until 1912, Albania's independence has been brief and hardly kept. Overrun by seven different armies during the World War, she barely escaped partition. Then she joined the League of Nations; but Great Britain, France and Japan admitted Italy's special interest in the maintenance of her territorial integrity as a buffer state. That has always caused grave misgivings in Yugoslavia, where Italian influence in Albania is held to be a menace; but relations between Yugoslavia and Albania are improving as both grow more mature, while Italy has, until now, acted towards her small protégée with reason and restraint. The Italian advisers departed in 1934—during a temporary rift in Italo-Albanian relations—then came again; and Albania had, perforce, to stand by her ally in the Abyssinian crisis. The abortive rising at

Fieri last year cost the life of my good old friend General Ghilardi; but it warned the rogues of Tirana that they must mend their ways. Albania is now looking forward to brighter days under the government of that enlightened Bektash, Mehdi Frashëri, who has for his collaborators several of the younger school, progressive men.

For the correct pronunciation of Albanian names these rules should be remembered:

The Albanian letter c = ts in English—as in bits.
„   „   „   ç = ch in English—as in church.
„   „   „   e = é in French as in été.
„   „   „   ë   is almost mute.
„   „   „   j   = y in English.
„   „   „   q = k-y in English—as in thank-you.
„   „   „   xh = j in English.

The Albanians decline all their nouns, both in definite and indefinite forms. This makes for confusion when it comes to names because they use either form as the mood takes them. Thus, Durrës or Durrësi, Shkodër or Shkodra. Nor does this confusion stop there, for Berati and Durrësi (definite) are seldom used—almost always Berat and Durrës (indefinite); whereas Tirana and Vlona (definite) are generally used, not Tiranë and Vlonë. I have employed that form commonly used in my hearing —for example, Iballja (definite) and Selcë (indefinite); and for the King's name I have written King Zog or Zogu—which happen to mean King Bird or The Bird.

Then there are foreign names for the chief towns— Argyrocastro (Greek) for Gjinokastra: Croia for Kruja: Durazzo (Italian) for Durrës: Koritza or Coritsa (Greek) for Korça: San Giovanna di Medua (Italian) for Shëngjin (meaning St. John): Santi Quaranta (Italian) for Saranda (meaning Forty Saints): Scutari for Shkodër: Valona for Vlona. Finally, the north and south Albanians do not always agree over a name—for example, the north prefers Vlona, the south Vlora.

AUTHOR'S NOTE

Notes upon certain ancient towns mentioned in this book will be found in the appendix.

The following Albanian words or terms have been used:

alla Franka	=	in the manner of the Franks, i.e. in western style. So *alla Turka*=in Turkish style.
baba	=	Bektash abbot.
bajraktar	=	hereditary standard bearer—or chief of a *bajrak* (a sub-division of a clan or tribe).
besa	=	inviolable oath of peace.
çafa (or qafa)	=	neck. i.e. pass or col.
çarapi	=	native coloured socks.
dervish	=	Bektash (or Moslem) priest.
dolama	=	native waistcoat.
fusha	=	field, i.e. a small plain.
fustanella	=	a short, heavily pleated, white kilt.
gjizë	=	native white cheese.
hamal	=	porter in a town.
han	=	rough inn—generally nothing but a barn.
hanxhi	=	keeper of the above.
kapedan	=	chieftain.
kos	=	yaghourt—i.e. milk thickened by bacteria.
kryeplak	=	chief elder—i.e. village head-man.
kula	=	house built for defence.
llumë (-i)	=	river.
lokoum	=	Turkish delight.
madh (-i)	=	great.
mal (-i)	=	mountain.
meze	=	kind of hors d'oeuvre—provided with raki.
opinga	=	moccasins.
qiraxhi	=	horse-boy.
raki	=	strong alcoholic drink.
shën	=	saint.
shkallë (-a)	=	stairway—i.e. steep pass, or precipitous track.
sofra	=	round table barely twelve inches high.
tekké	=	Bektash monastery, cell, or shrine.
urë (-a)	=	bridge.
vogël	=	little.
xhurdin	=	short native jacket.
zoti, zoja, zojusha	=	Mr., Mrs., Miss.

(Thus, *Malcija-e-madhe* means Great Mountain Land: *Ura Vezirit* means Bridge of the Vizir: *Fusha Arshit*, Field of Arshi—and so on.)

AUTHOR'S NOTE

A list of the main authorities consulted, and their works, will be found in the bibliographical note. Miss Durham is a widely known authority upon northern Albania. Byron, Dodwell, Hughes, Leake, Lear, Spencer, Hobhouse (who travelled with Byron), Holland (who doctored Ali Pasha—and Queen Victoria afterwards), and Pouqueville (French consul at Janina in Ali's day) have all left works upon southern Albania of which some are profusely annotated with references to the classics—and from these, and from Ugolini's books, I have drawn much material upon Albania's old places. Peacock provides much on the mediaeval history of north Albanian towns. My account of Caesar's campaign is borrowed from Meneghetti; and the quotations in my accounts of the siege of Shkodër and Skenderbeg's struggles are from Knolles who drew his account from *De Vita et Gestis Scanderbegi*, by Marinus Barletius, written in thirteen volumes between 1450 and 1467. There is a novel by Mor Jokai (The Lion of Janina: 1897) which weaves a romance round Ali Pasha: while the facts are well re-told in Mr. William Plomer's book: *Ali The Lion*, which was published after my pages were written. For information upon the Albanian language there exist *A Short Albanian Grammar* by S. E. Mann and an *Albanian-English Reader* by Margaret Hasluck.

My gratitude is due to the Albanian National Museum for much information upon the Bektashis and upon Albania's old places: and, among others, to Sir Robert Hodgson by whose intervention I was able to complete my travels in Albania.

J. SWIRE.

NOTE:—Since these pages went to press Mehdi Frashëri's cabinet has fallen and a government of the "old school" is again in office.

CONTENTS

CHAPTER		PAGE
	AUTHOR'S NOTE	vii
I.	MY INTRODUCTION TO ALBANIA	15
II.	SOME TOWNS AND THEIR HISTORY	28
III.	SKENDERBEG	61
IV.	CLANS AND CHIEFTAINS	86
V.	THE GREAT MOUNTAIN LAND	112
VI.	THE LOW COUNTRY	142
VII.	THE HIMARA AND THE LION	157
VIII.	KING ZOG AND HIS CAPITAL	193
IX.	WHERE ALI RULED	224
X.	IN THE SOUTHERN MOUNTAINS	250
	APPENDIX	283
	BIBLIOGRAPHY	285
	INDEX	287

LIST OF ILLUSTRATIONS

	FACING PAGE
ZOG I, KING OF THE ALBANIANS	*Frontispiece*
SKENDERBEG	44
SHKODËR CASTLE AND BOJANA RIVER	50
KRUJA: A GENERAL VIEW	64
SKENDERBEG'S CASTLE AT KRUJA	66
KING ZOG'S RUINED HOME IN MATI	90
MEN OF MATI WITH A STUDENT FROM TIRANA	95
GJON MARKA GJONI, HIS SONS, AND THE "MASTER OF CEREMONIES"	100
WOMEN OF MIRDITA	107
FORDING THE FÀNI GOJANIT RIVER	112
CROSSING THE DRIN NEAR FIERZA	116
PAL MIRASHI WITH HIS FATHER AND FRIENDS	124
"MALI" HERAPIT AND "ÇAFA" PES	127
ON THE WAY TO BOGË	129
ON THE WAY TO SELCË	137
GENERAL GHILARDI	158
EARLY MORNING AT ŽRIMADHËS	162
WOMAN FROM VUNA CARRYING HER CHILD IN A CRADLE	164
ALI PASHA, THE LION OF JANINA, AND ALI'S IRON CASTLE AND ROUND TOWER TO-DAY	188
A MARKET SCENE IN TIRANA, 1931. THE PARLIAMENT BUILDING IS SEEN BEYOND	193

LIST OF ILLUSTRATIONS

	FACING PAGE
IN THE GYPSY VILLAGE AT TIRANA	196
BOY OF THE LOWLANDS—NEAR TIRANA	198
BOY OF THE MOUNTAINS—NEAR TIRANA	200
PRINCE WILHELM	202
PETRELA CASTLE: LOOKING FROM THE ENTRANCE	212
GJINOKASTRA: LOOKING NORTHWARD TOWARDS TEPELENI	234
BERAT: THE LOWER TOWN	240
BERAT: THE OLD (OR UPPER) TOWN	245
"MALI" SKRAPARIT AND THE TOMORICA VALLEY	255
IN THE "TEKKÉ" AT PRISHTË	257
THE "BABA" OF PRISHTË	259
DINA JANO AND HIS FAMILY	261
FRESCOES AT VOSKOPOLI	266
MAP	282

KING ZOG'S ALBANIA

CHAPTER I

MY INTRODUCTION TO ALBANIA

TWELVE years ago Albania was almost untravelled ground, to most people an empty name, to our daily newspapers a strange land which was advertising for a king. My curiosity drove me there in March, 1924.

Albania was beset by enemies, racked by intrigue, paralysed by grinding poverty. Among her patriots many held that salvation lay in the choice of a king. They dared not ask their first king, the luckless Prince Wilhelm of Wied, to return, for the Allied Powers had been casting mud at all men and all things German for ten miserable years. So they looked round for another while the vacant throne was held by four Regents (representing Moslems, Bektashis, Roman Catholics and Orthodox Christians).

No Albanian had so risen above his compatriots that they would have accepted him as king, so the royalists looked abroad. Several European princes were approached, several men of title, and an English commoner whose tireless efforts for the Albanians' welfare had proved his love for them. Irresponsible individuals, caring more for dollars than decorum, went further, making overtures to millionaires and kings of industry; and some approached much humbler men who had happened to do minor services for Albania, among them a friend of mine. But in his case there was a condition—

he must marry an American girl whose work had also gained Albanian appreciation, so that the sum of their joint benefactions might make up for their want of money and royal blood. But the condition evidently proved beyond the bounds of their heroism. Our Popular Press broadcast these tales, so the Albanian authorities received letters from all kinds and conditions of people who thought they might shine as king—or queen—of Albania. Among them was an instructress of classical dancing who lived in Highgate—she claimed that she could soar like an eagle, a qualification she thought irresistible to the Albanians who call themselves " Sons of the Eagle." Another who wrote was a dentist —of him young Zogu, then Minister of the Interior, dryly remarked that " doubtless he considered himself a specialist in golden crowns."

It was from Corfu that I first sighted Albania—the rugged Acroceraunian mountains beyond the straits, their snowy summits pink in the last sun. Here I heard of Amet Zogu, then Prime Minister, who had narrowly escaped assassination a few days before. I heard too that a revolution was brewing: that there was a British Adviser to the Ministry of Interior—Lt.-Col. W. F. Stirling, Lawrence of Arabia's " skilled staff officer, tactful and wise ": and lastly, that the British Minister lived at Durrës.

The cliffs and scarps of the Himara coast were black under a pall of clouds which wrapped the heights from sight as the little Italian boat that bore me beat up the coast in a gale. Early next morning we anchored off Durrës, a sad place between grey sky and grey sea. I went ashore in a bobbing cockleshell rowed by two ruffians who would have drawn a crowd in the chamber of horrors at Madame Tussaud's; and the peasants in their shaggy black sheepskin cloaks and black brimless hats seemed to promise a wild hinterland. Durrës had no pretensions in those days. It was a jumble of squat stone or crazy mud-brick houses threaded by cobbled alleys. A companion led to a crowded restaurant furnished with rickety wooden tables and benches, the floor of it littered with sawdust and spittoons and the walls decorated with tawdry prints of Prince Wilhelm of Wied and Princess Sophie, a large Albanian flag (the black double-headed eagle on a red ground) and a bearskin. We breakfasted upon a meat stew and black coffee, then I made my way to the British Legation.

Sir Harry Eyres was surprised to see me, for the coming of an Englishman to Durrës in those days was uncommon. That afternoon we bumped over the low Rasbul hills and across the plain to Tirana. A final bump, over a derelict Austrian Decauville railway built during the War, which lay at the entrance to Tirana (now Tirana's centre), and we came into a town thoroughly Turkish with minarets and smells.

Tirana's streets were alleys mostly, cobbled and muddy, winding between single-storey open-fronted shops with no timber square, darkened by the wide eaves: or between high walls of mud-brick, the massive double doors in them sheltered by canopies of tiles in the style of lich-gates. Behind the doors were little gardens and mud-brick and plaster houses of two storeys, their windows heavily latticed to screen their women from the glances of others' men. The shops sold few imported goods except lamps and sugar, coffee and tawdry ware, but there was a profusion of tobacco and bread and eggs, skins and native clothing. In the silversmiths' shops, besides tobacco boxes of beaten silver and chains and rings of filigree work, were massive cigarette holders almost a foot long, with amber mouthpieces the size of hens' eggs and amber sockets for the cigarettes almost as large. The wood-workers had chip-carved holders of many lengths, richly coloured and decorated by wooden rings, some of them three feet long in sections.

Women were rarely seen. Those who appeared were swathed in black robes and veils from head to foot and clattered over the cobbles in wooden sandals. Their veils were plain, but their colourless hidden lives made plainer faces. The streets were filled with officers and men in untidy uniforms, laden donkeys and peasants in pierrot-like jackets and homespun trousers. There were never more than a dozen cars in the town, generally waiting to carry passengers to Durrës. There were no new buildings and Tirana seemed decrepit, muddy, grey for want of the sun which lagged behind heavy clouds. But there was charm in the weathered, mellowed place with its bright splashes of almond blossom here and there, its dark cypresses, its minarets standing beautifully against the snow-covered mountains, its slow cloud of blue smoke which hung like ground mist above the dull red roofs, and the sweet smell of burnt wood which saturated the air and part-drowned those other smells not so sweet.

Besides the Stirlings and the Legation people there were no British in the country; nor were there many non-Balkan people of any sort except the Italian, French and American diplomatic representatives. The Stirlings lived in the only baked-brick house in Tirana, a tiny place of British comfort in a comfortless town. They were learning, as I had to learn, that in the Balkans nothing comes to him who does not wait and very rarely anything to him who does. Nor did I know Balkan reasoning—that he who talks can be talking only politics: that he who talks to an opponent of the government can be no friend of the government: that he who talks to several people opposed to the government is

MY INTRODUCTION TO ALBANIA

plotting against the government. So I made friends indiscriminately and was soon suspected of sinister intentions. I had a plan to enter the Albanian Army as instructor, thus anticipating the Italians. With Stirling's backing I pressed this idea, but I had unwittingly chosen my first Albanian friend among the opposition so my plan was frowned upon and came to naught.

Among my first-made friends was Edhem Vlora, the portly indiscreet and extremely kind military commandant of Tirana. He spoke English and had a passion for Brighton pier; and he carried in his pocket book with pride some letters from General Gordon to his father, Ismail Kemal Vlora, who proclaimed Albanian independence in 1912.

Then Morton Eden arrived for relief work. Eden was with General Phillips in Albania after the Armistice as an "Observer" and had played a certain part in Albanian affairs. We planned to ride together into the wild north-east frontier area, and though assured that the passes would be blocked with snow we decided to make the attempt for the Albanians often exaggerate their mountains' difficulties.

We set forth with a gendarme as guide and escort, carrying little but some white bread in our make-shift saddlebags. Eden's pony was broken for riding; but mine, a scraggy beast, knew only packs and riders in peasant style. He preferred to move not at all. Urged, he would walk. Urged with violence he would break into a shambling run. For hours I strove to bring him into a level trot, but gave it up at last and adapted myself to his uncomfortable gait.

Beyond three flat miles our way led upward by some foothills, shrub-grown and sandy, till suddenly we turned a rock and saw before us the *Shkallë* Tunjanit. A great gorge cleaves the mountains, framing distant snow-capped peaks. The Tunjan stream crashes over a narrow rocky bed; and upward from it tower the mountain's scarps and cliffs, split by scree-choked gulleys and darkened by trees and bushes on the precarious ledges. Along one side of this great cleft lies a narrow track—the road to Dibra. At the end it climbs abruptly by zigzags, passes above a dizzy precipice, then drops by a steep stairway of mudholes to the gloomy depths of a valley. Here we came to a *han* where we thought to pass the night, but the *hanxhi* came out to us with a black scowl, so Eden told me to remain in the saddle—the *hanxhi* took us for Italians. But our gendarme's words dispelled his lowering clouds and we rode in.

The *han* was a barn, dark and cavernous. Our ponies were led to one end where they joined others round a pile of hay, exchanging kicks till each had a place. At the other end big logs blazed on a hooded hearth and several men made place for us on the rush mats within the circle of firelight. The *hanxhi* pulled off our boots, now doing the best he could to make up for his first hostility. He brewed coffee in a tiny pot upon the hot ashes while his companions rolled cigarettes, licking the paper to within an inch of the end and leaving the last lick for us. We ate our host's bread and eggs, then wrapped ourselves in our coats upon the draughty mud floor, rich new meat for bugs in their legions.

A rinse in the Tunjan, a cup of black coffee, then we went again in the grey dawn, splashing up the bed of a stream through a wood of plane trees then climbing stiffly to Çafa Muricës (4,117 feet) by a stony track. Beyond the *çafa* the snow lay deep among beech trees, but our downward path was hard-beaten and hard-frozen so soon we left the snow again and came to another *han*. Below was a windowless barn for wayfarers' beasts, but a crazy ladder gave into a small upper room warmed by a charcoal fire, the floor spread with rush mats. The aged *hanxhi* was warm as his fire as we ate his *kos* and eggs and listened to his slow talk. Going again we descended steeply to the Mati river which is spanned at the mouth of a wild ravine by an abrupt stone bridge —*Ura* Vashu—without a parapet in the usual Turkish style.

Rain and cold and wind painted this ride in my mind as a grey smudge with clear-drawn outlines here and there in the rack. The scenery was wild and bleak and lonely, swirling clouds among the dark pines high up. Each man we met carried a rifle. Clearest of all I remember the *kulas*, square and stone-built, of two storeys, with big stones on their rough tiles to weight them against the winds; and they had no windows but only loopholes and embrasures high under their eaves. Generally they stood apart on rising ground, each beyond range of its neighbours' muskets.

Rain fell for three days heavily and without slackening, turning the tracks into mud-slides. The water ran in streams from my oilskins into my boots and the wind stiffened my fingers on the reins. As this day closed we forded a swollen torrent precariously and sank thankfully into thick fug in a well-filled upper room in the *han* at Bulçizë. Big logs crackled under the hearth's hood and the loopholes were stopped with sacking. Rifles and cartridge belts hung from pegs all round the walls. Big men in black-braided white homespun trousers and *opinga*, lithe as panthers, sat on the floor cross-legged, placidly smoking and talking in slow deep tones of feuds and wolves and our coming. There was coffee, hot and comforting: eggs, maize bread and cheese like rubber. Then sleep, all together on the floor, while the wind howled down from the cloud-wrapped heights, driving pattering, splashing rain upon the tiles above the smoke-blackened rafters. The *hanxhi* woke me once by tucking a blanket round my feet.

Next day we rode into the Drin valley and crossed the river by a well-guarded bridge. Going on through a depressing district of burnt villages—prosperous till the Serbs laid it waste in 1920—we came to Peshkepijë, a little place of rough-hewn stone houses on a slight bluff, the outermost houses loopholed, the inner ones bold with windows. Below the houses was a flat space of mud which was the market place; and beyond it the bed of a mountain stream, a waste of stones, went down steeply towards the Drin a mile below in the wide valley. A sad place. We pushed into the *han*, this one having a room with a bar. It was filled with men in various degrees of dress from the local to the shoddy European, some of them sitting round a broken stove, others playing a game with dominoes and much clatter. We strangers excited curiosity; and one man was delighted at our coming, for he wished to reach a village where we were bound but dared not travel in this wild area alone.

The sub-Prefect (in national dress) put his office at our service—there was nowhere else for us to sleep, he said. There was a chair, table, stove and a cooking pot. At a rough cookhouse we bought some scarce eggs. One dropped. A boy and a dog rushed for the yellow debris in the mud. The dog was pleased. Food was very short. Some villages had no bread at all and people were dying of hunger.

Dawn, grey and dismal, called the neighbourhood to market. Chickens, onions, wooden cigarette holders and rough clasp knives in horn sheaths stand in a memory of rain and yellow mud. Riding not far up the stream's bed we came upon a tiny domed building in the mist, its eaves hung with icicles. Within, a large pool hewn in the rock held water from a hot spring and the bath-hot air was heavy with putrid fumes of sulphur. But the heat was comfortable and a wash overdue.

We left Peshkepijë with three gendarmes and three civilians armed with most antiquated rifles. Two of this escort went ahead carefully, almost stealthily, as vanguard. The spurs and bluffs to our right gave here and there, revealing the snow-capped heights of the Korab mountains rising nearly 7,000 feet from dark forests of fir and bare slopes of scree.

As the light began to fail we came to a large loopholed house with two storeys, surrounded by a high wall and alone on a bleak mountainside. A big rugged man in local dress came out to us, attended by another with a rifle at the ready. The first was Elez Yssuf, lord of the district. He was restless and sore against the government, so Eden had come to calm him if he could; but Eden failed, for Elez rose in support of Fan Noli three months afterwards and fell in December while fighting gallantly with his clansmen against Zogu's invading bands. He lived in a lawless district where raid and counter-raid over the border were life's interest; and he cared not at all for his neighbours the Serbs who had duped him more than once into trying to pull their chestnuts out of the fire. Serbian policy was to weaken Albania and embarrass the central government with the hope that at the last an Albania which appeared incapable of self-government would drop into Serbian possession or sphere of influence. The frontier which the Great Powers drew here in 1913 placed more than 500,000 Albanians under their hereditary enemies the Serbs who have dealt very harshly with them, expropriating many in favour of Montenegrin and Serb colonists; and it separated Albanian frontier villages from the pastures and market towns which had been theirs for generations.

Elez was glad we had come, for Eden was his friend. In a bare upper room warmed by a great fire we lay on the floor for talk and smoke and coffee, waiting for several hours, as Albanian custom decrees, while a meal fit to honour us was made ready. Elez declared he would not rebel unless others led. At last a man came with a basin and a jug and poured water over our hands; and another brought a *sofra* which he laid for five with a wooden spoon and a hunk of maize bread for each. Then we squatted at our places, the Albanians comfortably with crossed legs but Eden and I uncomfortably, without grace. A great metal dish like a round tray was set upon the *sofra*. In the dish stood a bowl of broth in the midst of boiled rice and we all fell to it, dipping our spoons in the broth and the rice alternately until the bowl was dry. Warned by Eden of more to come I held back from the rice. In another dish like the last came the fat lamb which had been killed for our honour, also surrounded by rice. Elez tore the carcase with his hands, giving a week's meat to each of us. Two more dishes were brought, one filled with sweetened rice and the other with a delicious pastry cooked with honey; but Eden and I were too full of meat to eat much of either, though the Albanians played their part noisily and afterwards expressed their satisfaction with customary but disagreeable emphasis.

Embroidered quilts were spread, and there we slept thankfully with the gendarmes of our escort. The Albanians lay each with his rifle close by his side, a precaution eloquent of the state of the district.

Here I left Eden and pushed northward for some miles into the Ljuma district, going sometimes high on the shrub-grown mountain-sides, sometimes close beside the Drin, till we came to a bridge. It had been a good bridge and the stone supports still stood; but between them was slung a precarious structure of boughs and planks and ropes which shivered and swayed above the torrent as we crossed. Then we turned south—myself and the gendarme from Tirana alone now as we were out of the danger zone, and as the day closed we came to Aras, a little village at the mouth of a side valley, where we ate and slept as the guests of Dervish At, the tall chieftain of the place.

Next morning Dervish came down to his yard in a nightshirt to wish us long life and a good road. The good road lay through fields of maize stubble and meadows and a squelching slobber of mud, and hundreds of magpies rose before us in flocks. My gendarme broke into song—a sad wail, high-pitched and nasal, which passes for singing in these parts. It is a melancholy sound which lies as heavy on the heart as the strange wild cry of plovers in spring over bare plough.

On a good track my pony stopped suddenly, looking at the ground. Seeing no obstacle I urged him violently till he leapt forward—into quicksand which came over my boots in the saddle. Happily it was narrow and he pulled us out with a convulsive effort. Topping a bluff we came upon a view of the Drin for many miles to the south. The river was spread in flood about the wide valley and leaden clouds flung about the sky shrouded the snow-capped tops of the ranges. It was a gloomy scene—beautiful yet inexpressibly sad, eloquent of the sufferings of this forgotten district.

In a muddy field the peasants of hereabouts had met to market their goods to one another, being cut off by the frontier from Dibra. While I watched, my gendarme bought some onions which he slung across his saddle. By carrying them to Tirana he would make a trifle and the speculation made him glad. That night we slept in the *han* at Bulçizë.

As the night fled before the cold grey dawn we were riding again, empty but for black coffee and a bite of dry maize bread. Going hard we came, about midday, to the snowy slopes of *Çafa* Muricës. A thaw had set in. We dismounted and led our ponies up through the trees. As we rose higher our progress became harder till at last we were floundering and slipping at every step. The track was frozen still, but the unbeaten snow beside it which was several feet in depth would bear no weight. Again and again I slipped from the track into snow to my waist, the pony almost on top of me; or the pony would slip, dragging me after him by his reins in a heap. So we struggled for two hours, gasping and sweating, till we covered this white half mile. When we gained the pass both ponies threw themselves down at full length and we collapsed beside them.

My feet were blistered and swollen so the unrideable *shkallë* of the Tunjan was passed painfully. As I walked there came a sudden call: " Hullo ! Where do you come from? Can you tell me the time?" Looking up in surprise I saw an Albanian in full local dress seated upon a rock with a rifle across his knee. His good English had been learnt in America. I sat to talk with him and eased my battered feet. Then we rode into Tirana as the shopkeepers were lighting their guttering candles and smoking lamps against the first dark. Our coming from Bulçizë in one day caused surprise.

In the hovel which passed as the old Hotel International my room-mate was Avni Rustem, who assassinated Essad Pasha in Paris in 1920. The French had convicted Rustem of political murder and fined him one franc, so he had returned to Albania where his grateful countrymen gave him a pension. I liked him—a little pale-faced man in threadbare tweeds. He expected assassination, for Essad's blood had to be avenged, and so it was, six weeks later, Rustem being shot down in Tirana by a hireling of Essad's family, a thick man with a red face whom I met several times in 1930 near my house with an innocent umbrella in his hand.

I stayed some days more in Tirana, making friends and drinking *raki* in sawdust-strewn cafés with a confusion of ministers, orderlies, deputies, peasants and regents who jostled and hailed and toasted one another with unrestrained democracy. Once I called upon a Moslem officer whose pretty wife received me in his absence and threw aside her veil to talk in fluent French. I was surprised by her western freedom with me till I learnt how lightly the veil was worn by educated Albanian Moslem women (and now most have cast it altogether). Once, too, I went to see the Minister for Foreign Affairs at his office. I found him before a table in a room bare of other furniture or archives; but behind his head, in an open cupboard, stood a loaf of bread and a bottle. And once I set out to visit Amet Zogu but he was recovering from his wounds and did not care to see me. Five years afterwards he apologised, saying this was an inadvertent breach of Albanian courtesy. Had we met then I might have had a part in his flight to Yugoslavia and his victorious return through the December snows.

At last I had to go. The British vice-consul in Bari asked me whether it was true that a revolution had broken out in Albania. His news was premature by two months.

When I reached London a friend, hearing where I had been, remarked: "Oh, that is where the Albinoes come from, isn't it?" And not many people were better informed.

It was exactly five years before I went to Albania again, and then her wild days were done.

CHAPTER II

SOME TOWNS AND THEIR HISTORY

For centuries Durrës has decayed untidily. The sea breezes, which should freshen the streets, shift the dust and sand from corner to chink, from chink to eye, then back to a corner again till the rain turns them into mud: then the fierce sun dries them and the wind shifts them round again. And as flies flock to decay so have come to Durrës the meanest and leanest in Albania, swarthy Turks, ragged gypsies, and Tirana's overflow of knaves. So an irresolute traveller to Albania might well feel discouraged here, nor would the new buildings or the ambitious harbour encourage him much.

Some years ago Tirana decided that something must be done about Durrës. So one morning several hundred people had notice that their houses would be pulled down next day, for Durrës was to have a boulevard. Now Durrës has a straight and wide main street between fair shops and not uncomfortable hotels; and upon the hill above perches the King's pink summer palace, precariously, because earthquakes thrice cracked it after local workmen had done their best. But the central Albanian does not shine as a builder. He will do everything the wrong way round if he can, and if he could build from the top downward he undoubtedly would.

Durrës has some 9,000 inhabitants and stands on a slight promontory at the southern end of a range of low hills, five miles in length, which rise steeply from the sea. Behind the range is a big marsh, divided at its northern and southern ends from the sea by strips of sand. In ancient times this marsh was joined to the sea by a channel at the northern end, making a perfect natural harbour when ships were of shallow draught. Where the channel used to be there are ruins of fortifications and harbour works known as the Porta Romana. The marsh now provides good duck and snipe shooting in winter and in summer an abundance of malarial mosquitoes.

The natural advantages of the place attracted seafarers in early times. Towards the end of the seventh century B.C. Corcyrean and Corinthian colonists established themselves there and soon the flourishing city of *Epidamnus* grew up under an oligarchical government. But a democratic opposition ultimately brought about the dissolution of this government and led Corcyra and Corinth into dispute. *Epidamnus* was vainly besieged by the Corinthians in 435, Athens supporting Corcyra. This dispute contributed to the outbreak of the Peloponnesian War (431–404 B.C.).

Involved in wars with the Illyrians, *Epidamnus* began to decline and in 312 B.C. it was seized by the Illyrian King Glaucias. It regained its independence but was so hard pressed by the Illyrians that in 229 it made a defensive alliance with Rome. After the Illyrian Wars it passed into Roman power as a free city, but the Romans preferred to call it *Dyrrhachium* (disliking the damnable implications of the other name). It became the starting point of the famous *Via Ægnatia*, the great military highway which led past Elbasan and Okhrida to Salonika and the East, and another highway led southward from it by *Apollonia* and *Buthrotum*.

Before Durrës Pompey made his last successful stand against Caesar. On November 28, 49 B.C., Caesar sailed from Brindisi with 15,000 infantry and 600 cavalry.

Early the following night news that he had landed at *Aspri Ruga* was brought to Bibulus, the choleric Admiral in command of Pompey's fleet at Corfu; and to Pompey (camped near Okhrida) by his friend Vibullius whom Caesar had taken prisoner in Spain and now sent with offers of peace. Pompey had more than 50,000 men— including 7,000 cavalry, 3,000 archers and 1,200 slingers, but they were vastly inferior to Caesar's troops both in morale and mobility. Caesar gave his men a day's rest, while his rival Bibulus had the satisfaction of burning the last of Caesar's transports on their way back to Brindisi and blockading the coast with his fleet of 144 warships.

Caesar climbed the Logara Pass and *Oricum* surrendered to him. On December 5 he entered *Apollonia* and in the evening crossed the Semeni. Pompey had advanced swiftly from Okhrida to Muriçiani (*Asparagium*): while Caesar tried to reach Durrës (where the fugitive senators and their friends had taken refuge) but only got as far as the Shkumbini, where he established a bridgehead on the right bank and camped on the left. Pompey had encamped at Kavaja at dawn on the 7th, and next day he drove in Caesar's bridgehead and camped on the right bank of the Shkumbini. There both armies stayed (in winter quarters) until February 19, 48 B.C.

Meantime Mark Antony, with about 17,000 infantry and 800 cavalry, had been waiting at Brindisi to join Caesar, but Bibulus's blockade prevented his crossing. Caesar grew impatient at his delay; and having sent over messengers to no purpose, hired a small boat and risked sailing himself for Brindisi to bring Antony. He had not sailed far when a storm arose. The skipper was for putting back to port, but here his hitherto unrecognised passenger revealed himself. "Fear not," he said, "for you carry Caesar and his fortunes." But at last the sea drove them back. On February 19, however Mark Antony disembarked at Shëngjin and Lesh fell to him two days afterwards.

Pompey, hearing of Antony's coming, led his army to *Mali* Lalës for an ambush. Caesar, learning this from spies, marched by a wide detour over the Krraba pass (2,100 feet) to meet Antony whom he found waiting for him north of the river Ishmi. So Pompey's plan failed. He fell back, pillaging the country on his way south, and camped at Muriçiani on the left bank of the Shkumbini. Caesar followed and challenged him; but Pompey, beyond the river, had no will to fight yet, so Caesar went on to Elbasan, crossed the Krraba pass and made for Durrës. Pompey hurried north. The two armies met close south of Durrës, camping respectively north and south of Sasso Bianco. Thus Caesar lay between Durrës and Pompey. Although outnumbered by two to one Caesar tried to invest Pompey whose men threw up defensive lines.

The first battle of Durrës occurred on May 5. Reinforcements from Africa under Afranius arrived at Durrës, and, in co-operation with part of Pompey's cavalry (which was transported across the bay), made a sortie from the city. After heavy fighting the original situation was more or less restored, but Caesar entrenched his right against further attacks from Durrës.

The second battle was fought on May 27. Pompey's archers and slingers were brought across the bay and flung against Caesar's right. After severe fighting and much manoeuvring Pompey's army broke through Caesar's to the north and their positions were reversed— Pompey to the north with Durrës close in rear and Caesar to the south.

On May 29 Caesar began a retreat towards Thessaly

by way of Muriçiani, Këlcyra and Melisopetra, sending his wounded and baggage down the coast road to *Apollonia*. Pompey pursued as far as Melisopetra, then marched away through the plain of Korça, and Kastoria, towards the valley of the Vistrica. Caesar, having picked up reinforcements, marched after him through Janina and Mecovo. On June 29 the two armies met at *Pharsalia* and Pompey was utterly routed.

Durrës was most prosperous at the end of fourth century when it became the capital of *Epirus Nova*. St. Paul is supposed to have preached here, and in A.D. 58 Durrës is said to have held seventy Christian families under a Bishop Apollonius. It became an Archbishopric in 449. In 481 the city was besieged by the Goths under Theodoric, and in the tenth and eleventh centuries it had to defend itself often against the Bulgarians.

In June, 1081, Robert Guiscard and his son Bohemund crossed with their Normans from Apulia and besieged Durrës. They defeated the Byzantine Emperor Alexius Komnenus who came to its relief and it fell in February, 1082. But soon after it was regained by the Byzantines through treachery within, then besieged again (unsuccessfully) by Bohemund in 1107. In 1185 it was taken by King William of Sicily, seized by crusaders and handed over to the Venetians in 1203, taken from the Venetians in 1205 by Theodorus, and in 1258 it passed (with Kruja) to King Manfred of Sicily. In 1272 Charles of Anjou, having overthrown Manfred, sent a Neapolitan army to occupy Manfred's Albanian possessions. The Neapolitans defeated Nicephorus and established a governor in Durrës; but next year the city was destroyed by an earthquake, so Charles abandoned it.

In 1274 Durrës became an independent duchy, at first under John (grandson of Charles of Anjou) and afterwards under Philip of Taranto until 1333. Then it was annexed to Achaea. In 1336 it was taken by the Serbs, but in 1358 it was in the hands of the Topias, an Albanian feudal family owing fealty to the Balshas. In 1392 the weakling George Topia ceded it to the Venetians who strengthened the fortifications, dredged the marsh which was re-opened to shipping, and restored much of its prosperity. It became the home of the chief Albanian families. It was vainly besieged by Mahomed in 1466; but on August 13, 1501, the marsh and dykes having dried up and left it defenceless, the Turks marched in, it "being before ruinous and almost quite abandoned by the inhabitants, as a place of danger, and not to be kept now that the Turke had got all the country round about it." Very little now remains of the old fortifications which originally resembled those of Salonika, but there are the ruins of three towers of the *enceinte* wall built during the reign of the Byzantine Emperor Anastasius (491-518), who was a native of Durrës.

On November 30, 1912, Durrës was occupied by the Serbs who rode their horses into the sea and claimed it as their own, but they had to withdraw on May 6, 1913. Prince Wilhelm of Wied, nominated Prince of Albania by the Great Powers, chose Durrës as his capital and arrived there, escorted by an international squadron, on March 7, 1914. From May 23 until his departure on September 3 the Prince was shut in Durrës by Turkophile central Albanian rebels while Great Powers and Balkan States intrigued against him. On October 2 Durrës was occupied by Essad Pasha who was also more or less besieged there until relieved by the Serbs in June, 1915. In December Italian troops were landed to cover the evacuation of the retreating Serbian Army. On February 28, 1916, the Austro-Hungarians came, making Durrës a naval base from whence their submarines harried allied shipping until October 3, 1918, when the port was bombarded by an Anglo-Italo-American squadron. From Christmas Day, 1918, to March 27, 1920, Durrës was the capital of the Albanian Provisional Government. Now it is being developed into a modern port and may in time regain some of its former greatness by providing a western outlet for Macedonian and Albanian trade.

Durrës seemed dusty and arid, notwithstanding its blossoming fruit trees, when I landed in March, 1929. It wallowed between the picturesque and the modern, having the advantages of neither. But there was a clean hotel—though not so "splendide" as its name—with whitewashed petrol tins planted with marigolds upon each of the steps to its door and cold beer in its restaurant. And in a corner of the hall there was a swallow's nest. Both the swallow and the electrician had thought of that hall, but being in Albania the swallow had got there first. So the electrician had passed the wires round the nest, leaving undisturbed the swallow's cheetering domesticity.

Tirana was awake to its responsibilities as a capital and had embarked upon a course of not altogether misguided self-improvement. But while the picturesqueness of the old town remained, that of its inhabitants had suffered. The poor seemed dirtier and more ragged, and many more men were dressed *alla Franka*. Sad that the pursuit of civilisation should mean a casting of national dress for shoddy ready-made western clothes!

My plans took me south—first to Kavaja, a pleasant little town with 8,000 inhabitants. It lies in the most fertile but least attractive part of Albania. The American Near East Foundation has at Kavaja an experimental farm and agricultural school (with about 100 pupils) and a fine domestic science boarding school for girls (where about sixty girls are freed from traditional

Turkish shackles). The agricultural school has done much to live down the wooden plough tradition. Most boys, when first they go there, will eat only their accustomed fare, maize bread and meat, and have to be taught to eat vegetables—which is, perhaps, a cause of the poor physique of the dwellers in the fever-ridden plains.

Beyond Kavaja the road goes to Elbasan by Pekinj (the Roman *Clodiana*), a rambling agricultural village. Elbasan is a huddled town of 14,000 inhabitants standing close beneath the mountains. In atmosphere it is medieval, in character Oriental, still unspoilt by the fanatics of progress. It is indeed a place of charm for all its lurking smells. Its streets are barely streets, cobbled and narrow, with open gutters at the sides and not much disturbed by wheels. (A car first came here in 1923, driven by an American from Durrës with pick and shovel and planks for bridging holes and streams.) Its shops and *alla Turka* eating houses (called restaurants) and bakeries are open-fronted, with wide eaves and weathered timbers, seeming as if they had been built first (long ago), then shaken to settle them. Its minarets and cypresses stand peacefully, softly, mellowed, and behind its walls there are little gardens and rambling houses pargeted and latticed. It stands upon the site of the ancient *Scampa* of which little is known except that it was the seat of a bishop in the fifth century and was destroyed by Bulgarians in the tenth century. The *Via Ægnatia* passed on the other side of the Shkumbini. The name *Scampa* is thought to be a corruption of Shkumbi, meaning foamy; and perhaps its medieval name *Valmes* came from *vale* (Albanian), meaning stormy.

The modern town was founded in 1467 by Sultan Mahomed. He built a strong quadrangular fortress surrounded by deep moats and having three entrance gates. Upon the south-eastern gate were inscribed the names of the Sultans and the date of the town's capture by the Turks; but the walls and gates are now either pulled down or smothered by houses. Elbasan had its part in Albania's feudal days, particularly in the time of Ali Pasha, but in 1832 the fortifications were dismantled by Reschid Pasha. An important nationalist Congress was held here in 1909, but its Moslems were foremost in the revolt against Prince Wilhelm. The Serbs came in June, 1915, the Bulgarians in January and the Austro-Hungarians in March, 1916, and the place was captured by the Italians in October, 1918.

The landlord of Elbasan's best "hotel" was sitting cross-legged, in peasant dress, upon a fleece on the cement floor of a dark café beneath his inn, but he stirred himself willingly and I slept unbitten. Washing was communal, upon the landing. A cracked enamel basin stood upon a packing case, below a petrol tin hanging upon the wall which gave grudgingly of its brackish contents through a microscopic tap. Mine host's son had learnt somehow to say "Good night," and he was so proud in his knowledge that he said it frequently that night, and again next morning, each time flinging wide my door suddenly and without preliminaries.

Wishing to visit a village a gendarme was sent as my guide and escort. He loaded his rifle as we crossed the Shkumbini. The old stone bridge built by Kurt Pasha over a century ago was partly destroyed by the retreating Austro-Hungarians in 1918, but it is now repaired and carries the road to the hot springs at Linxhë.

We waded for an hour through incredible mud and went to a farm among the olive trees on a little hill. An Albanian farm is generally as untidy as a rook's nest, a jumble of weathered beams and tiles and mud bricks, but it has a hint of snugness and peace, the air about it

SOME TOWNS AND THEIR HISTORY

heavy with the aroma of wood smoke from a hole in its roof. Rugged peasants, untainted by civilisation, squatted cross-legged on rush mats by their fire of charcoal at one end of a big room, bare and dark; they rolled cigarettes for us and made coffee, then led us to see their many womenfolk and infants—or perhaps to be seen by them, and I pressed some coins into an eager little hand, knowing our host would have them when we had gone. The head of the house walked a mile on our homeward track to mark respect for us and bade us long life with touching fervour. Then the gendarme would have me go to his neat little home in a neat little garden behind a high wall in the town. His wife left her weaving frame in the portico to make hospitable coffee while an elder—but not very old—son rocked his infant brother in a wooden cradle.

Eastward from Elbasan the motor road goes beside the Shkumbini for some miles through narrow gorges, having the habit of making hairpin bends a hundred feet sheer above the river. By Qykës (the Roman station *Tres Tabernae* on the *Via Ægnatia*) the valley widens and the road leads from it by a shallow ravine into Fusha' e Domusdovës, a grassy basin rimmed by hills. The inhabitants hereabouts used to have an evil reputation among travellers and the population is very mixed here and southward towards Korça. There are many Vlachs: and not a few Macedonian Slav villages where Macedonian is the language spoken. These Macedonians are recognised by the Albanians as a minority and have certain privileges. It was on their account that this part (including Korça and Lake Okhrida) were allotted to Bulgaria by the abortive Treaty of San Stefano.

From Fusha e Domusdovës the road took me up steeply by well-made zigzags to *Çafa* Thanës, and there, below, lay Lake Okhrida like a great carpet of bluebells, the water blending the green of the leaves with the blue of the flowers. Beyond, the Macedonian mountains, bare and snow-capped still, shrouded by a haze as by a curtain of powder-blue chiffon. Close at my feet, the little promontory upon which is Lin, and not far to the left the white Yugoslav frontier post. The ancient Greeks, who called the lake *Lychnis*, tell that in their day its shores were the abode of Pan and his shepherds. It abounds in immense trout which may be seen at a great depth in its crystal water and are exceptionally good eating. The water of this lake, which is more than 600 feet deep over half its area, filters through the adjoining mountains from the higher Lake Presba and flows into it by Shën Naoum monastery; and at Struga the Drin flows from it into a wild defile, the scene of more than one ambush and massacre of Turkish invaders by Skenderbeg's men.

The town of Okhrida (the ancient *Achris*) was, from Byzantine times onwards, a place of great military importance as it commands the lake and the defiles leading into the interior. The old fortress stands on a rocky peninsula, a strong place by the lake. It was occupied and repaired at different times by the Romans, Byzantines, Goths, Normans, Bulgarians, Serbs and by Skenderbeg's Albanian warriors; and at last it capitulated to the Turks who kept it as they found it. For many years it has been the seat of an Orthodox Archbishop.

The monastery of Shën Naoum or Sveti Naoum, which stands beautifully on the south-eastern edge of the lake, is one of the finest of its kind in the Balkans. It was founded by the Emperor Justinian, who endowed it very liberally with lands and privileges which the Turks allowed it to retain on condition that the monks would use part of the place as a hospital for sick soldiers and civilians of whatever faith. High Moslem dignitaries often stayed there. It was rebuilt in 1806. In 1925 Albania, to whom Sveti Naoum had been awarded by the Conference of Ambassadors, abandoned it to Yugoslavia.

We zigzagged down to the Lake and sped along a good road between the steep mountains and the water to Pogradec, a big village which borrows its charm from its lovely place mostly. Fishing boats with high prows and sterns reflected themselves in the still waters. There were many flocks of sheep and goats by the wayside; and immense black or white or tawny dogs rushed at our car, careering madly in its wake, barking and snarling. Every traveller who writes of Albania remarks about the ferocity of its dogs which are, perhaps, the greatest danger to be met with. They resemble wolves and are often bred from wolves. Against robbers or wild animals they are a sure protection to flocks and property, for none can ignore them. Their owners value them highly and in bygone days their fangs were less dangerous than the rage of their masters against anyone who harmed them in defending himself. Now the law permits a man to shoot a dog in self-defence if he can see a blade of grass between his feet—so the day is his with luck but the night is the dog's with certainty. By day dogs must be tied up or otherwise controlled, but at night you have no business to be abroad. Hughes suggests that these dogs are descended from the Molossian breed, celebrated in ancient times for their ferocity and fidelity. They were often used as letter-carriers; and he recalls that the dog of Pyrrhus always kept watch over his master while he slept, and, being inconsolable at his death, leapt upon the funeral pile and was consumed with his remains.

Beyond Pogradec the road sweeps over a low ridge to the marshy Lake Maliq, then across the wide plain to

Korça which lies at the foot of a high range beyond the treeless plain; but though its inhabitants maintain it is Albania's heaven the chief ambition of most of Korça's 23,000 citizens seems to be emigration to America. Those early emigrants who came back after the war to visit their relatives and were then cut off by the American Quota Law, will bewail their lot loudly and aggressively in debased American to every English-speaking stranger they meet. Korça is bleak for lack of trees, but it is cool, healthy, crisp in the cold, for it stands at 2,820 feet above the sea (yet tuberculosis is common). It cares for its streets, the main ones wide and metalled, the lesser ones cobbled, and all of them clean. But it is grey with stone, immature, and there is dust ever in its wind. Its richer people scorn their national dress as much as shaving, while the poor are particularly wretched in western rags. But Korça has a fair hotel, electric light and modern mills. There is talk of pushing the railway from Salonika across the frontier to Korça, which would have the advantage of making the place easy to get out of.

But Korça has given birth to many of Albania's foremost nationalists. Their nationalism grew upon Greek culture, which irked the Greeks who had taken much pains with their propaganda here. Greek troops occupied Korça on December 6, 1912, and set about painting it blue and white and locking up its nationalists against the coming of the International Boundary Commission —which was not, however, deceived, and the Greeks had to give the place up. But Greek bands took it again on July 10, 1914, after some street fighting, and Greek troops came again for official occupation in the autumn. They stayed until the arrival of French troops from Salonika. The French ordered the Greeks out to secure Albanian support, setting up an autonomous Albanian Province of Korça which issued its own stamps and paper money and carried on very efficiently until the politicians interfered again. There was some sharp fighting now and then between the French and the Austro-Hungarians and Bulgarians in the hills north and west of Korça before the end of the war. The French withdrew on June 21, 1920. In 1929 Korça, I learnt, cared little for King Zog's regime. Korça would have preferred Fan Noli, or perhaps Prince Wilhelm again—or his son; but Korça knew better than to say so openly. I found the Prefect—a loud nationalist in white spats—fresh from a ceremonious presentation of flags sent by an Italian institution to the Korça school-children who had massed in their red shirts and black shorts (or skirts) to hear fulsome words of allied fraternity; so now he was emphatic to me that never should Italy infringe Albanian sovereignty.

When Leake visited Korça early in the nineteenth century it had no more than 450 houses, more than half of them Christian. "The filthy streets and comfortless habitations proclaim the Albanian town," he remarked; but the place boasted a bishop—he was Metropolitan of Korça and *Selasforo*. The chief products in those days were snuff, local dress and furniture. On a bluff overlooking Korça are ruins of a castle which Leake ascribed to the Bulgarians; and there is a mosque founded in 1487. At Mborja a church first stood in 898, though it was rebuilt in 1391 under Slav direction.

North-east of Korça, in the mountain range which here bounds Albania ethnographically, is the Pass of Cangon, a natural gateway into Macedonia, and through it passes the road to Bitolje. This was Pompey's way to *Pharsalia*. *Selasforo*, now a small village (close to the pass) known as Zvezde, was once a place of some importance and was called *Deabolis* in the eleventh century. Alexius Komnenus came here often during his campaigns against the Normans, and a bishop of *Deabolis* first invited the Normans into the country. In those times *Açhris* (Okhrida) and *Deabolis* were the two chief places to the east of the *Candavian* range (the central Albanian mountains). The Korça plain provided abundance of forage for the Roman army under the Consul Sulpicius during a campaign in 200 B.C.

Returning to Tirana, I set out for Shkodër and Cetinje. From Vorra the Shkodër road lies always on the flat, sometimes passing through pretty woods, sometimes by swamps, sometimes by hayfields and pastures, little hills and cultivated places. And for most of the way, close on the right, rise the mountains (not so high but broken and scarped) which bar the low country from the highlands sharply. By Mamuras are valuable hot springs; and not far beyond, among the oak trees, two American travellers were shot dead in April, 1924, as they drove, by a band of men lining a wayside hollow. Their wounded chauffeur lay feigning death, so overheard the assassins' dismay when they found their victims were foreigners and not Albanian enemies. Fan Noli's political followers declared that some of themselves were the intended victims and the assassins government agents, so the affair was a pretext for revolt in June, 1924. Since then I believe the Italian Lieutenant Chesti has been the only foreigner murdered in Albania.

The Zogu bridge over the Mati river is unexpected in this poor land, for it is the biggest of its kind in existence. It was built by Italians in 1927 and before it there was no road to Shkodër during the winter floods. Not far on is another, spanning the Drin by Lesh. Here is a great swamp towards the sea, its rotten water breeding clouds of malarial mosquitoes in summer, but in winter it teems with wild duck, so a sportsman could be happy here if Lesh had a possible inn.

SOME TOWNS AND THEIR HISTORY

Lesh is a poor place of about 1,600 souls, strewn haphazard along the left bank of the Drin; but behind it rises an abrupt bare hill crowned by ruins of an immense fortress. Known in ancient times as *Lissus*, Lesh was founded and fortified in 385 B.C. by the Tyrant of Syracuse, Dionysius the Elder, and it was besieged in 213 B.C. by Philip V. It was repaired twice by the Romans— once by Caesar sometime after 59 B.C., and Cyriacus of Ancona (A.D. 1391-1449) described it as a very imposing castle. It was held for a time by the Serbs, but its native rulers were the Dukagjini who in 1393 made it over to the Venetians who had already developed important trade interests in these parts. The mouths of the rivers Drin, Mati, and Ishmi were important commercial ports for both Ragusa and Venice; and the Venetians built a castle at Ishmi (the Roman *Pistum*) which Prince Sturdza captured from rebels in June, 1914.

Some say Mount Shëlbuem (about 1,300 yards from the existing Venetian castle) was the site of the ancient fortress of *Lissus* because there are remains of fortifications still upon it. But it seems more probable that Shëlbuem was fortified only and that the Venetians rebuilt on the old site. The Venetian citadel and ·*enceinte* wall are well preserved, having been repaired by Sultan Selim I (1512-1520). On Mount Shëlbuem is the tomb of a Moslem saint, a butcher who slew all his goats, one by one, for a fastidious customer who swore the meat of each was bad. At last, in despair when he had no more, the patient man threw his knife into the air. It was caught by spirits who dropped it where his tomb now stands. Hard by, towards Shkodër, is the Franciscan Convent of St. Antoine which dates from 1240. It has a chapel built in 1562, but its church was destroyed by Austro-Hungarians in 1918.

In the church of Shënkolli (the Saint Nicholas) at

Lesh on March 1, 1444, Skenderbeg held a great council of Albanian and neighbouring Christian chieftains, abjured Islam for his father's faith, Roman Catholicism, and swore to free Albania from the Turks; and in that church the great hero was buried in January, 1468. When, in September, 1478, the Turks came to Lesh (which the garrison and inhabitants had evacuated) they burnt the town; but so great was Skenderbeg's fame that they reverently dug up his bones and strove, each one, to obtain a fragment to wear as a charm. And they called the place Lesh, which in Turkish signifies tomb, though in Albanian it means wool.

* * * * *

"The bloudie bane of faithlesse Turkes, and terrour of their name,
Epirus' strong defence and guard, lay buried there with fame:
Within that tombe wherein long since great Castriotus lay,
But now those limbs and tombe defac'd, are carried quite away;
The remnants of that worthie wight out of his grave were torne:
And being dead could find no rest, but were for jewels worne.
For after he farre spent with age, gave place to fatall doome,
And left his fathers kingdome got, and kept with great renowne:
Forthwith the cruel Turkes prevaild, and all things there possest.
Who worshipping his stately tombe, and place of quiet rest,
Dig'd up his bones, and brake the tombe wherein he did remaine:
And glad was he that could thereof, some little part obtaine.
As if in them some martiall force, or vertue great had beene:
Or fortune rare, such as before in him was living seene.
So vertue which to others gives a sepulture and grave,
Bereft it him, yet forst his foe in honour it to have."

Latin original by Gabriell Fairnus of Cremona.
Translated by Richard Knolles—*Generall Historie of the Turkes.* 1603.
Engraving from the same work.

* * * * *

SCANDERBEG.

Skenderbeg (Facing p. 44)

SOME TOWNS AND THEIR HISTORY

Northward from Lesh the mountains to the right withdraw, giving place to rich black tillage, tobacco and maize beside the Drin; but to the left there rise up little hills to break the level. At last the road passes over the joined Kiri and Drinasa rivers, rounds the foot of the castle rock narrowly, and opens into Old Shkodër. The newer part of Shkodër spreads northeastward, away from the cramped peninsula where the castle stands.

Shkodër is a place of charm, its mellowed walls steeped with history and the dignity of age about it. Prosperous for centuries it has now fallen upon hard times, its population dwindled to 29,000. Even nature turned against the old place, for in 1858 the Drin, in flood, carved a fresh channel, the Drinasa, which has silted up the Bojana and thus raised the level of the lake; so Shkodër's lower parts and bazaar are often flooded. But the lake (which is about forty by twelve kilometres in area) is set among mountains as beautifully as any in Europe. It is full of fish; and it is plied daily by small steamers linking Rijeka and Virpazar with Shkodër.

In the new town (so called) which is mostly residential, are good old stone-built houses with wide eaves; and quiet alleys, cobbled, leading nowhere in particular, given over to turkeys and sandalled feet, the walls grown with plants and the great dark doorways in them draped with wistaria or vines. There is a cathedral, a vast Turkish prefecture, barracks, cafés with tables under the acacia trees, and a broad main street. There are many strange costumes to be seen, particularly on market days when the mountain folk come to sell their simple goods, their embroideries and their çarapi. Then the bazaar below the castle hill springs to riot of life and colour. There are the married mountain women in dark bell-shaped skirts, homespun and heavy, topped by six-inch-wide metal-plated nail-studded belts: there are the women of the town in voluminous pantaloons fastened at ankles, the Moslems peeping from behind veils which envelop their heads: and men in close-fitting white black-braided trousers and gold-embroidered waistcoats. But the days of gorgeous national dresses are gone.

Formerly the *fustanella*—a white linen kilt—was worn by the Aghas (the Moslem aristocracy), but now they prefer baggy trousers *alla Franka;* so in these prosaic times the *fustanella* is rarely seen in any part of Albania, never in the north. The wearing of it was, in Shkodër at any rate, the privilege of the Aghas, who must have been gorgeous people in their flat crimson fezes with heavy blue silk tassels; jackets, gaiters and waistcoats of crimson cloth heavily embroidered in gold and black, and at least a brace of silver-embossed pistols in a sash at the waist. Now these gay plumes moulded in the family trunk—those which have not been bought up by curiosity hunters—or are to be found in antique shops which look as antique as the things they sell.

In bygone days Jack was as good as his master in Albania provided he had a gun and could use it; but now there are few weapons—even in the mountains they are scarce because the government have prudently collected all they can. So there are fewer manners. Now, the degenerate Albanian lowlander who is largely hybrid Turk jostles with impunity the dignified mountaineer whose proud forbears were the warriors of Skenderbeg, until the mountaineer slinks away with black looks and mutterings. Shkodër used to be notorious for feuds and a jostle in the bazaar or high words at cards were enough for a man to shoot his neighbour dead. It was no uncommon thing for a man to sit for days with his gun across his knee, waiting by his enemy's house for vengeance. The besieged man might not shoot first because he "owed blood"—that was a rule of the game; and had he broken it his foe's relations would have claimed two lives instead of one. But his servants and womenfolk could go about without fear.

Not so long ago the Shkodër authorities offered reward for the capture, dead or alive, of a notorious brigand. A man came to the prefecture. "By the Oath the reward is easily mine," he said; "so pay me now, that I may make merry with my friends, and by the Lord you shall have this bad man's head in two weeks." But the reward was retained until earned and the man went away boasting of what he would do. Some days later a sack was found upon the office table. From it rolled a head—the head of the boastful one, with the brigand's compliments.

Once an Albanian friend in Tirana who was going abroad asked me to take over his servant. "He will not go to his home in Shkodër," explained my thoughtful friend, "because yesterday his brother shot three men dead in a café there—one of them called him a weakling. So now, if my servant goes home, he will be shot by the dead men's relatives to pay his brother's blood debt—for his brother owes three lives. Of course they may come here for him."

The cathedral is new and bleak. It was built in 1858 and damaged by bombardment during the siege in 1912. Shkodër became an Archbishopric in 307 and had three Archbishops, then passed under the Metropolitan of Salonika in the fourth century and under Okhrida in the sixth century. In 877 the Bishoprics of *Svacia*, Shkodër, *Drivasto, Polat* and nine others outside the present Albania passed under the Archbishop of *Dioclea*, but in 927 *Dioclea* was utterly destroyed by Tsar Simeon and the Archbishop fled to Ragusa. In 1030, however, the Archbishopric of Antivari (including the dioceses of Shkodër, *Drivasto, Polat* and *Palachiensis*) was founded and has gradually come to be styled the Archbishopric of Shkodër.

After the Turkish occupation of Shkodër in 1479 the Archbishop had his seat at Budua until 1609, when the Sultan granted full freedom to the Roman Catholics and a salary for the Archbishop. This generosity was ill repaid. In 1645 the Archbishop conspired with his colleague of Durrës and the Bishops of Shkodër and Lesh to deliver Albania into Venetian hands. Their plotting was discovered, persecution followed, and many of the notables became Moslems or fled to Venetian territory. The cathedral church of St. Stephen Protomartyr was turned into a mosque and until 1858 the Catholics of Shkodër went for services to an open field. The Bishop lived in a village.

Shkodër claims it was the capital of the old Illyrian kings in about 1000 B.C., but Livy is the first Latin author who mentions it—in his account of the Illyrian Wars (229 and 219 B.C.). These wars were caused by the piracy of the Illyrians who rashly interfered with Roman trade and murdered the Roman envoy sent to protest. Their enterprising Queen, Teuta, King Agron's widow, stretched a chain across the Bojana and levied a toll on all shipping—a more lucrative scheme than may now appear, as there were some important towns on or near the lake in those days. Her avarice cost Teuta her throne, but her son was allowed to reign after giving up several islands, Durrës, and the towns of *Hecatompedon, Boea, Kodrion* and *Antipatria* in the country of the Attintanes near the Acroceraunian mountains. In A.D. 395, on the partition of the Roman Empire, Shkodër passed under Constantinople.

Shkodër was ravaged by the Barbarians who left few

traces of its earlier history. In the seventh century the Emperor Heraclius ceded it to the Serbs, from whom the Bulgarians wrested it; but at the end of the eleventh century the Serbs made it their capital for a number of years. Thereafter Serbian power decayed and the Byzantines and Bulgarians in turn had a second spell of ascendency. But after the defeat of the Bulgarians at *Velbuzhd* in 1330 Stefan Dushan re-established Serbian power in Albania, so the Venetians, who had previously taken Shkodër from the Serbs, gave it back to them —probably because the benevolence of the ruler of Albania was more advantage to their trade than the precarious occupation of the city in face of his ill-will. Shkodër became the centre of the government of north Albania and Montenegro—a government which ruthlessly persecuted the Roman Catholics.

After Dushan's death in 1355 his Empire broke up and several of the local governors proclaimed independence. Among them was George Balsha, of Norman descent, who in 1366 established himself as ruler of Herzegovina, Montenegro and northern Albania with Shkodër as his capital. By conquest and marriage he and his son (who succeeded him) extended their dominions to Vlona, Gjinokastra and Berat. His son was killed in 1383 while fighting the Turks near Berat; and Balsha III, who is said to have fought with an Albanian contingent against the Turks at Kosova (1389), was made prisoner by the Turks and forced to cede Shkodër and *Drivasto* as the price of liberty; but he soon recovered these towns in exchange for a daughter whom the Sultan desired. In 1396, however, seeing that it would be difficult to hold Shkodër and *Drivasto* against renewed Turkish aggression, he followed the example of the lord of Durrës and sold them to the Venetians. Then he retired into Montenegro.

Venetian interest in Shkodër, *Drivasto*, Lesh and Durrës was commercial and their fortresses were held only for protecting their trade from the pirates and bandits who preyed upon it. There were important towns up the Drin; and the trade route which led from the upper valleys (Dibra and Prizren), the old Roman route, remained important until the building of a railway through Macedonia diverted trade to Salonika and ruined Shkodër.

The fortress of Shkodër is a grim place, vast and well-preserved. It crowns a steep rocky hill 435 feet in height, isolated on three sides by the Kiri and Bojana rivers. On the fourth it is separated by a col from another hill. The *enceinte* wall forms a rough oval measuring 311 yards by 231 yards, with a perimeter of 656 yards. Formerly it held the town but now there are no habitations within its lonely walls. It was built in the fourteenth century by the Venetians upon the site of the earlier walled town and is known as Rosafa. The origin of this name is variously explained. Some think the place was named so after the Syrian city Rosafa, centre of the cult of Saints Sergius and Bacchus, there being near Shkodër an ancient monastery dedicated to them, but others hold that the name originated from the Albanian *Rojs e fatit*, meaning Guardian of Destinies. There is a pathetic legend about the building of it. The work was entrusted to three brothers, but however hard they and their men laboured during the day all they did was undone during the night. So they consulted a wise man who decreed that one of them must sacrifice his wife. She must be built into the wall alive. They cast lots. The sacrifice fell to the youngest brother whose wife was nursing an infant boy; and her last expressed wish was that her child might one day become lord of the fortress. A hole was left in the wall through which

Shkodër Castle and Bojana River

(See p. 50)

she might suckle him until she died. Among Shkodrani women it is still a popular belief that once a mother with dry breasts drinks water running from the clefts of the rock on which the fortress is built, her milk comes again.

Livy mentions the earlier fortress, which he describes as a very strong place difficult to approach. It was built or repaired by the Romans, Byzantines and Slavs, and the Venetian fortress was repaired by the Turks.

After Skenderbeg's death the Turks gradually conquered his domains until only the Venetian towns were closed to them. These they attacked.

On May 25, 1473, Solyman Pasha arrived with 80,000 men before Shkodër, "a city of great strength," wrote Knolles, "as well for the naturell situation thereof as for the strong fortifications therein made by the hand of man." He had brought cannon with him, and he bombarded the place repeatedly and furiously. But under its gallant governor, Antonio Laurettano, Shkodër defied the Turks who suffered terrible losses. The Venetians sent galleys by the Bojana into sight of the defenders and encouraged them with hopes of relief by lighting bonfires. The Turks tried unsuccessfully to trap the galleys by throwing chains across the river. Equally in vain the Venetian Admirals Mocenicus and Grittus tried to throw fresh supplies into the city. Meantime Mathias Corvenus, King of Hungary, the ally of Venice, hearing that Shkodër was besieged, made such desperate incursions into Turkish territory that the siege was raised and Solyman sent to oppose him. The Turks had lost 14,000 men, "whereof the greatest part died of sicknesse taken by long lying in the rotten moorish ground neere unto the river."

"With this dishonour taken at Scodra Mahomed was so discontented that he appointed a yearely fee unto one, to put him in mind dayly of the siege."

This poor wretch evidently earned his fee, because in 1478 the Sultan again invested Shkodër with an immense army.

The governor, Antonio da Lecci, had sent away all the old people and infirm and had filled the town with able-bodied men from the surrounding countryside,

"manie marriners taken out of the gallies, and other men of like qualitie, which got their living upon the river and lake of Scodra, lustie bodies enured to hardnesse."

The Turkish vanguard of 80,000 white-capped irregular horse arrived before the walls in May, leaving a wasted countryside behind them. Next came Taut Gaiola (an Albanian by birth), the great Pasha of Constantinople, with 25,000 men and 12,000 camels "laden with metall in mass, for to make great ordinance of, and other necessaries for the campe." The Pasha's great purple tent was pitched on a hill. A timber bridge was thrown over the Bojana so as to command both sides and small galleys were built to deal with the lakeside fishermen who harried the Turks by night from the water. Then the Beglerbeg of Asia arrived with 30,000 Asiatics and pitched his green pavilion on the other side of the town. Four cannon were now mounted on "the Pasha's hill," firing stone balls of 300, 400, 400, and 650 pounds weight respectively.

On July 2 came Mahomed himself, in the cool before sunrise, with another large army. "Divers rich pavilions" were set up for him and a great Council tent. Round these the white-capped Janissaries camped, and about them the rest of this host.

"All the countrey, as farre as a man could see, was covered and white with tents, much like as when the ground in winter is covered over with a deepe snow: . . . so that it was deemed by men of great experience that Mahomed had then in his armie of all sort of people about 350,000 men, all gaping to devour that poore citie: a sight of it selfe sufficient to have daunted the courage of right valiant men."

But the defenders were exhorted and encouraged by Bartholomeus, a priest, formerly one of Skenderbeg's soldiers.

The Turks mounted three more cannon, the seventh being

"of an incredible greatnesse, discharging a shot of twelve hundred pound weight . . . they battered the citie, with the aforesaid seven great peeces: and ceased not oftentimes by night out of their great mortar peeces to cast great bals of wild fire. . . . At the same time also the Turkes out of their short mortar peeces cast huge great stones of incredible weight. . . . In few days after, the enemie mounted three other great peeces. . . ."

Breaches were made, but the defenders repaired them with earth between planks. These the Turks assaulted repeatedly and furiously, hoping either to carry or burn them, but were always repulsed with heavy losses. Every day the cannon fired 160 to 190 shots until the total fired was 2,539. The walls had been sadly battered, worst round the great gate, when a general assault was delivered from all sides on July 22. The Turks attempted to rush the breaches before daybreak and a desperate struggle ensued. They set their banners on the walls but reserves were called from the market place and the standards of St. Mark soon took their place. At last the Turks fled, leaving 12,000 dead. The defenders lost 400 killed and many wounded.

"Now as soone as the new moone began to show her selfe, the Mahometane priests going about the armie gave the souldiours knowledge thereof (as their manner is) by singing of a song, in the manner of a procession; whereunto the whole armie answered with a short responde, but with such a terrible noise as was wonderfull to heare: and at the same time lowring themselves to the ground, saluted the moone with great superstition."

Then the Turks made another assault, before dawn. Again and again they planted their banners on the walls. Again and again they were hurled back. Again and again the Turkish cannon were discharged into the weltering mass of men in the breaches, destroying Turk and Christian alike; while Mahomed threatened his commanders with horrible death if they failed to take the place. The Turks swarmed over the bodies of their dead, which they used as stepping stones; and

"the great ordinance also sore annoied the defendants, so that with one shot (whereby the greatnesse of the harmes done at other times may be gathered) eighteene of the Christian defendants were slaine. As for arrowes, they flew as thicke as haile into the citie: so that they obscured the light of the day and lay in most places of the street a span thicke: so that for the space of a moneth after, the inhabitants used no other fuel to burne but Turkish arrowes. It was a ruthfull sight to have seene the bodies of the valiant Christians rent in sunder with the great shot, and peeces of them cleaving upon everie wall thereabout, everie street was stained with their bloud, the great ordinance continually thundred, churches and houses came rattling downe, yea the heavie countenance of the ayre seemed to bewaile the miserie of the poore Christians: besides the noise of the trumpets, drums, and other instruments of warre, with the horrible crie of the hellish Turkes, was so great and hideous that it seemed as if heaven and earth should have gone togither: nothing was to be heard but the very terrour of the eare, nothing to be seene but death and the very instruments of death."

The Turks, terrified of the Sultan, fought with the courage of desperation. But in vain. At last Mahomed ordered a withdrawal, having lost 30,000 men. He now gave up all thoughts of assaulting Shkodër and decided to reduce it by blockade. He himself took *Zabiache*, *Drivasto* and Lesh: then in September he marched away to Constantinople in a towering rage, cursing the land and everything in it "but above all other things the citie of Scodra, with all that therein was, for that he had never received greater dishonour or losse than there."

SOME TOWNS AND THEIR HISTORY 55

The Pashas of Constantinople and Asia built a great bridge over the Bojana with a castle at either end, so that no relief could reach the beleaguered town: then they too retired to Constantinople, leaving Achmet Pasha to continue the siege with 40,000 men. With so much care did Achmet blockade the place that the garrison were soon reduced to sorry straits and

"the poore Christians were fain to eat all manner of uncleane and loathsome things; horses were daintie meat, yea they were glad to eat dogs, cats, rats, and the skins of beasts sold: it exceedeth all credit to tell at what exceeding great price a little mouse was sold, or puddings made of dogs' guts. All these bare shifts and extremities the poore Christians were content to endure even unto the last gaspe, rather than to yeeld themselves into the hands of their mercilesse enemies."

But at last there was a mutiny. It was quelled, however, by the gallant governor who, standing before his men, smote his breast and cried: "Here is flesh! Let him who is hungry eat it."

Meantime Venice, finding the war with the Turks too costly, opened negotiations which led to peace. The Venetians agreed to surrender Shkodër and other possessions and to pay 8,000 *duckats* annually, receiving in return freedom to trade in all parts of the Turkish dominions. The citizens of Shkodër preferred exile to Turkish rule, so in January, 1479, they were carried, with their belongings, to Italy.

Thereafter, Shkodër was ruled by a Turkish governor; but in the middle of the eighteenth century Mehmed, the bey of Bushati, quietly usurped power. The Sultan sent an emissary to suppress him; but the astute Mehmed gained by bluff the title of Hereditary Pasha of Shkodër and in this guise managed to unite most of Albania north of the Shkumbini under his leadership. He captured Ulcinj—a pirate stronghold—and burnt the pirate fleet. Then he negotiated with the Austrians for arms and money to throw off Turkish suzerainty; but he was assassinated before anything came of this intrigue.

His son Mahmoud the Black (Kara Mahmoud) defeated Kurt Pasha of Berat; and following a plan to seize Kurt's domains he concentrated an army at Okhrida. Kurt appealed to the Porte. Meantime Mahmoud beat the Montenegrins (in 1785) and invaded Venetian territory. Venice likewise appealed to the Porte, so Ali Pasha was ordered to occupy Okhrida. Ali did so. Whereupon Mahmoud marched into the Kosovopolje, routed a Turkish army, and annexed that region. Meantime Austria began to play a hand, offering to support Mahmoud as Prince of Albania if he would embrace Roman Catholicism. He agreed. By conversion he won great popularity among the Catholic north Albanians. Joseph II of Austria sent a legion of priests to Shkodër and five hundred veteran troops, promising that more aid would follow.

But a Turkish fleet blockaded the coast, and Ali Pasha, with his customary energy, led an army northward, its ranks being swelled by Moslems who were incensed by Mahmoud's proselytism. Mahmoud, thoroughly alarmed by this vigour, shut himself in Shkodër with his Austrians and opened negotiations. But the Mirditi utterly routed a second Turkish army which was advancing upon Shkodër from Okhrida, whereupon part of Ali's army deserted to Mahmoud with all the artillery. Mahmoud was saved. The Porte, embarrassed by war with Russia and Austria, thereafter let him be.

The fanatical Roman Catholic priests played upon Albanian racial hatred for the Orthodox Slavs. So Mahmoud, in agreement with the Porte and with the connivance of Austria (which was seeking to limit Russian influence in the Balkans) invaded Montenegro in 1785. But the Montenegrins knew their rubbish heap of rocks and boulders better than the Albanians and defeated Mahmoud. Next year he tried again, but at Cetinje he was routed and slain. The Montenegrins annexed the tribal districts of Piperi and Bijelopavliç.

Mahmoud's successors, Mustafa and Ibrahim, were more wary and less ready to do any Austrian or Russian chestnut-picking. In 1822 another Mustafa Bushati skilfully commanded Turkish forces operating against insurgents in western Greece; but in 1829 he fought against the Turks during the Russo-Turkish war, occupying Nish with 35,000 men. At the close of this war Mustafa made peace with the Porte, but other Albanian chieftains rose in revolt against projected reforms which threatened their liberties. The Grand Vizir, Mehmet Reschid Pasha, marched against them, easily securing the support of the *rayahs* (the Christian tenants or serfs). At Bitolje he camped and opened negotiations with the rebels. He told them the Sultan wished to meet their wishes, would pardon them and honour them. Eventually he induced about 400 of the noblest chieftains to come for discussion of terms, and the splendour of that cavalcade which rode into Reschid's camp may well be imagined; but at a given signal the Turks closed round and massacred them to a man. At a blow Albania, which had hitherto preserved local independence almost unimpaired, was decapitated; and with this massacre began the establishment of direct and effective Turkish authority in the less inaccessible parts of Albania.

Mustafa, now without a rival, led the indignant northern Albanians, Moslems and Christians, who clamoured for vengeance. At the head of 30,000 men he carried all before him. But his infuriated men pillaged, looted, and massacred every Turk and every Christian *rayah* bearing arms. The Vizir appealed to the Osmanli (telling them the north Albanians had sworn to massacre every Turk in European Turkey) and to the Orthodox Christians (to whom he exaggerated the northerners' excesses). Both rallied to him, the Orthodox subscribing 500,000 *piastres*. Thus strengthened the Vizir marched upon Prilep where Mustafa was giving elaborate feasts to his men in an ill-defended camp. Zinai od Bosna was marching with 20,000 men to join Mustafa for a projected march upon Constantinople, but Reschid reached Prilep first and utterly routed Mustafa who fled to Shkodër. But the Mirditi fought desperately before being overcome.

After four months' siege Shkodër surrendered upon condition that Mustafa received free pardon and a guarantee for the security of his private fortune. He retired to Constantinople and a Turkish governor was appointed in his stead. He had to hand over all his archives, which revealed that both he and his father had received regular allowances from Austria; also that he had made a treaty with Mehemet Ali of Egypt for the dethronement of the Sultan. Mehemet was to have Constantinople, Greece and Asiatic Turkey, and the rest of European Turkey was to be split between Mustafa and Milosh of Serbia!

Bushati, once rich Shkodër's summer resort, is now merely a humble village.

Although the Turks had to contend with many local revolts, the downfall of the Bushatis marks the end of the old feudal order in Albania and the inauguration— except among the northern clans—of modern government with an Oriental interpretation. The lowlands of Albania became Orientalised. Shkodër was made the capital of a vilayet.

From October 25, 1912, to April 23, 1913, Shkodër was besieged by Montenegrins, reinforced during the later stages by Serbs. The perimeter of its very inadequate field works measured some 28 miles, the average distance of the lines from the town being about two. They were defended by 14,000 men under Hussein Riza Bey, reinforced at the last by a reserve division of 10,000 men from Elbasan under Essad Pasha. The fiercest fighting took place at Bardanjolt and on Mount Tarabosh. Essad Pasha, who had treacherously contrived the assassination of the gallant Hussein Riza on January 30, surrendered the town upon terms very favourable to himself just as an international force was preparing to relieve it (though he may not have known that). The siege led to a serious international crisis and the surrender almost precipitated a European war. On May 14 the Montenegrins handed over Shkodër to an international Naval Brigade under Vice-Admiral Sir Cecil Burney, having burnt half the bazaar. Foreign troops remained in occupation of the town until July, 1914. The Montenegrins reoccupied it on June 27, 1915. It was entered by the Austro-Hungarians on January 23, 1916. On November 5, 1918, French and Italian troops entered it and the Serbs, who had got there on October 30, withdrew. A British detachment also came and inter-Allied occupation continued until March 11, 1920. Thereafter, an Italian detachment represented the allies in Shkodër until March, 1922.

Shkodër was keen to be Albania's capital and had most to offer for the honour of any Albanian town, but it lies too near the frontier and Yugoslav guns. Moreover the south would have been sore had the north been given such favour. So Tirana was chosen for its central position and Shkodër is bitter with disappointment, for a capital's business would have revived its trade.

In Shkodër this time I stayed at the "Grand Hotel," which looked well enough from without, standing in a garden with big trees. Within, it was a poor place, though rich in smells. Two British officers had lately arrived to take over locally as inspectors of gendarmerie. Destined to live here they found little good in old things, and Shkodër had given them no delights but the sticky Turkish one. A British Inspectorate of Gendarmerie was established first in 1925 by Stirling at Zogu's behest, the British Government having no part in it though not unwilling to see Italian influence counteracted. In 1926 Stirling resigned and Major-General Sir Jocelyn Percy took over from him; and in April, 1927, Percy also took command, for a year, of the Albanian troops in Shkodër and the north, to quiet Yugoslav fears of Italo-Albanian aggressive intentions. Percy has under him eight British officers who are paid by Albania. Their gendarmerie numbers about 3,000 men scattered in posts about the country, fine fellows who do admirably when decently led.

The way to the frontier by the north-eastern side of the lake is without interest, for the peaks of Malcija e madhe (the Great Mountain Land) are hidden by the bold bare shoulders they turn towards the lake and the road lies always over shadeless flats. (The way to Cetinje by the western side has better views.) The Albanian and Yugoslav posts stood unfraternising, a mile apart; and beyond them a wooden bridge (over a creek of the lake) was too broken to bear a car. Our chauffeur had lied that he had telephoned for another car to meet us from Podgorica, so there were three hours to wait in the sweet clover meadows by the lake until at last a Ford arrived in a hurry, clattering and hooting and flapping and done up with string, pullulating passengers for Shkodër who had overflowed and festooned its flanks. We piled in, then rattled away through Tuzi to Podgorica and gaily coloured Orthodox Easter eggs.

CHAPTER III

SKENDERBEG

>"Then onward he rode and afar,
>With scarce three hundred men,
>Through river and forest and fen,
>O'er the mountains of Argentar;
>And his heart was merry within
>When he crossed the river Drin,
>And saw in the gleam of the morn
>The White Castle Ak-Hissar,
>The City Croia called,
>The city moated and walled,
>The city where he was born,—
>And above it the morning star."
>
>   (*Scanderbeg*: Longfellow.)

A BROWN sunbaked track wanders between the maize and tobacco fields in the plain, passing now and then by trees which splash it with black shade giving a moment's relief from the tyrannous sun. Our feet lag in the shadow, then we cross its sharp-cut edge into the glare again, a sensation like sinking from steam-heavy air into the over-hot water of a bath. Movement is mechanical, the sweat of it on our exposed parts condensed into gritty salt grains; and the dust, which we stir about us in a dense white cloud, clogs our lungs and turns to a brown cream in the creases of our moist flesh. The heat has struck us speechless. There is no sound but the incessant " tzig, tzig " of a myriad crickets (a fit accompaniment to the dizzy shimmering of the air), the muffled plodding of our pack ponies through the dust, and an occasional " drrrtch, drrrtch " of exhortation or a hard word from our *qiraxhi* Abdulla to his five charges. Heat and crickets together fill me with a sense of unreality as my sore eyes look from beneath my topee at this scorched world.

Far to the right, flickering in yellowish haze like a picture upon a vast cinematograph screen, tower from the plain the strangely regular blocks, massive and abrupt, which bar the low country of central Albania from the wild highlands—a chain of gigantic rocky sentinels in a uniform of woods and scrub. At their feet are sandstone foothills grown with bright green shrubs or grey-green olives which throw into relief rare orange scars where the sandstone is bare. They hold a hint of romance, those warm hills, with their narrow sandy tracks leading to sudden little villages—and beyond, into the unknown mountain land whence came raiding bands (until not long ago) to harry the plain-dwellers and drive off their flocks, and they hold wild pig too, of which there are still enough for the sportsman's joy and the lowland farmer's exasperation. Away to the left there are more low hills holding tiny villages of wood and mud-brick among their olive trees and sandy paths and woods and aromatic shrubs. But Albania is a place of charm in all its corners. Even after summer drought it stays green (unlike Greece and Dalmatia) and thus makes it up for the lowlands' unremitting winter rains or the highlands' snows.

It is the beginning of September, 1930. I am setting out with friends for a "trek" through the northern mountains, and the fertile but steaming plain between Tirana and Kruja must be crossed.

The hire of each pony (and its food) was about 4s. 3d. a day and my contract with the owners (who "signed" with finger-prints) cleared me of all responsibility for the beasts' safety and welfare. Our *qiraxhi's* hire and food were paid in the price of the animals, for he was the owners' chosen representative and came as such to load, unload and care for their ponies. These ponies were skin and bone without animation, but they filled us with wonder when they set to work. Two of them, described as riding ponies (which I seldom rode, preferring to bring up the rear of my train on foot), were fitted with bits and saddles which might have excited an antiquarian. The pack ponies had common native saddles which are massive wooden frames, like trestles, padded more or less to fit and secured by a single loose girth. They stay on by balance—and some luck. So the load slung from either side of this precarious saddle must not project to catch obstacles and must balance with the other. One pony carried tinned foods to help down the mountaineers' maize bread, tea and dry foods, also a spirit lamp and can of paraffin as firewood is sometimes scarce. Another bore bedding and clothes in stout saddlebags to protect them from dust and rain and all those things which conspire to rip anything tearable. Our third pack pony carried camp equipment and light tent, for *hans* are rare in the mountains and not often fit even for a well-bred pig; nor are villagers' houses much improvement upon them for they are seldom free from bugs and dirt, never from stinks.

Now, as we go in the heat, Abdulla is perched with a nice balance upon the leading pony's load, swaying gently and idly smoking between his urging words. He pretends alternately, as excuse for his sloth, that he is lame or that the leader of our train needs him upon it or it will not budge; but he is a good-natured fellow, a grin confirmed upon his tanned unshaven face. He wears (nor ever takes off) a *xhurdin*—that short black homespun jacket, too small nor meant to fasten, decorated at shoulders and elbows with black rosettes and a fringe of long black wool at the back—which all the central Albanian peasants (though Moslems) wear in mourning for Christian Skenderbeg. Beneath that is a dark blue homespun waistcoat (*dolama*) thick as the *xhurdin*, fastened high and square below his throat; and beneath that again a shirt of a colour it would be hard to tell. His trousers are of the plains too, homespun and thick, baggy in Turkish style and dark brown. Wound at his waist is a woven sash of several colours and several yards in length, which holds his tobacco box. His trousers are gathered at the ankles over thick socks of bright colours and on his feet are soft *opinga*. On his head is a tall cap, like a fez but white and with no tassel, which holds beneath it for protection of his neck a dark red cloth.

We meet a string of ponies bearing firewood to Tirana where there is no fuel but wood or charcoal. Neither party's ponies will give way on the narrow beaten track though there is space enough on either side. Nor do the wood-merchants nor Abdulla take any care till opposing flanks of loads are in collision. Then, amid shouts and abuse, the ponies are dragged aside and we go on with slackened loads.

Peaceful wood-sellers, these men, who have hewn their wood honestly—or their wives have hewn it for them—from communal land. In earlier days they might have been less peaceful, for when no man stirred unarmed there was a strong temptation to lawlessness. Now the country lies disarmed, and though there may be weapons in the rafters no man may bear arms without a licence. King Zog's authority may not lightly be defied, in the lowlands anyway, so peaceful trade may prosper if the Albanian can throw off his Oriental lethargy and develop it.

The wood-sellers have empty petrol tins for water-carrying, tobacco, rice, coffee or sugar to buy with their takings for the wood—easy trade done between slow

Kruja: A General View   (*See p.* 66)

talks over cups of syrupy coffee with town-dwelling friends in the deep hot shadows of the bazaar. If their talk is of personal matters it is as like as not about money—the price of wood and skins and oil: but if or national matters the chances are that the latest rumours of Italian iniquity are being reviewed. Talk and business done, there is an unhurried return to the village in the hills as the crimson sun sinks into a purple sea and the night damp revives the herb smells. Then, while the women make ready the evening meal, the men squat cross-legged to retail the bazaar's news and gossip to eager friends.

There is a tinkling of goats' bells in the scrub ahead. By a stream a goatherd reclines in the deep shade of a great plane-tree. An immense dog springs from his side with a snarl, but his master sharply orders him back. We exchange the invariable preliminary to talk. "To you long life!" I cry; and he replies likewise: "*T'ungjat-jeta*"—an appropriate wish till not so long ago! Inevitably he then asks where we are going and from whence we come. He takes my cigarette with courtly gesture, then I bid him long life once more and we go on.

At last we are upon the road and wind upward 1,800 feet until we come to the olive groves of Kruja as the sea, far beyond and below, deepens from powder blue to a more sombre shade and the sun sinks in an orange glow, suffusing the shadows with a mysterious purple flush and the crags above with pink.

Kruja combines antiquity with beauty to a perfection hard to match. It has scarcely 5,000 inhabitants and they so scattered that their number seems less than half. It is a haphazard place, with only two sizable buildings in it—the castle and the bazaar. The rest, strewn about among the silvery olive trees, are square stone houses with dull red roofs and wide eaves and rows of latticed windows, or little white cottages with flower-decked window-boxes, overhung by fruit trees. Here and there a sombre cypress stands out, in sharp relief against the silver-green background which is misty with lazy wood smoke. Behind tower 2,000 feet of rocky buttresses and frowning precipices; and before, the ground falls away, gently at first—forming the sloping shelf on which Kruja lies—then more abruptly till the olives of the upper slopes give way to rich green scrub. Below is the plain, flat and wide, with an edge of low hills which part it from the Arzen and Shkumbini valleys. Far to the south is the massive Tomori, towering over 8,000 feet: to the east the Bay of Durrës: and to the north, far across the Gulf of Medua, faint in its distance, looms Mt. Lovçen.

Kruja is divided by a spur crowned by a long sloping slab of rock. The edges of the slab—which is well away from the great buttresses behind—are broken away sharply above a hundred-foot precipice; and along those edges stand the crumbling walls of the mediæval Kruja, the stronghold of that immortal Albanian, Skenderbeg, whose fame once rang throughout all Christendom.

Close beside the castle's northern side is the bazaar, a matchless antique. Two parallel lines of adjoining shops, their rough-hewn timbers mellowed with age and worn with use, gape at each other for over 300 yards, a cobbled street barely nine feet broad between them. The wide irregular eaves almost meet close overhead, deepening the gloom in the shops and sheltering them against the sun or rain. When it rains the water pours from the eaves and falls into a shallow ditch in the middle of the street. The bazaar was built in those days (not long over) when a raid by predatory neighbours was no uncommon event, so its outer walls have no light-admitting windows in them but only narrow loopholes, one or two to each shop, close under the eaves. Its gloom is furtive, its noises restrained.

Skenderbeg's Castle at Kruja

(See p. 66)

The front of each shop, where westerners would put windows, is open. And here, on the worm-eaten counters, are spread all the goods to sell, the owner among them as often as not, cross-legged and at ease. There are vegetables and fruit in one—onions, purple figs, melons and other kinds according to the time of year: in another, circular white caps of local shape and local make— here the trader is busy replenishing his stock with wool and soap and a mould. Other shops sell tin vessels of all shapes and sizes, made from empty petrol tins: *opinga* and brightly trimmed shoes, all serviceable and many soled with rubber from old motor tyres: gaily coloured cloths and waistbands, cheap goods from Italy or Czechoslovakia: earthenware pots and jugs: tobacco and cigarettes, in heaps and piles: brightly coloured *çarapi* in many designs and all the other sartorial needs of men in these parts. But here is only a glow of charcoal embers in cavernous depths and a rich smell of coffee. Best of all, a baker's shop, the circular loaves stacked in the shop front, the baker at work in his shop's depths by the flickering light of a great wood fire.

A new road from Kruja into Mati has opened magnificent scenery to the motorist. It swings up the mountain side beneath the wall of crags, then turns abruptly into a wild ravine and clings fearfully above its great precipices, bringing into sight a valley with tiny white specks in its rough pastures far below and the tinkle of sheep-bells in the clear air. The mountaineers come down this road to Kruja market from villages seven or eight hours' tramp away. More women come than men— for the women bear the burdens, staggering under great bundles of wood to sell and marching home again with the loads they have bought in exchange strapped to their backs, yet often spinning as they go along. The men scorn to be burdened, unless with a rifle. Many of the women wear white robes like nightgowns, girdled at their waists: and over these, little bodices which seem several sizes too small, and woollen aprons—dark and heavy. Often one of them carries a massive wooden cradle, covered by a thick blanket to shelter the infant in it from the dreaded Evil Eye; but it shelters the infant equally from all light and air, so it is small wonder only the strongest children born in the Albanian mountains survive their mothers' ignorance.

The mountaineer trusts his own impressions of his guests more than official letters, even if he can read them—and few Albanians over thirty years old can read or write, so strong was Turkish objection to educating people who might learn to think of nationalism. But here a state policeman, a municipal policeman and a gendarme spelt out the words of my official pass with care, impressed to that trouble by the seal upon it; and either seal or words took slow effect till all this authority became almost brisk. Leave to bivouac within the castle walls was soon obtained, a cask of drinking water sent up to us, and the commandant came to pay his respects—a swarthy sergeant who was said to have the death of eighty-seven people to his credit. A gendarme, he said, would be at our service in the morning as guide and escort, and from here we should be passed from post to post—the usual routine with foreign travellers in the northern mountains.

Kruja, that night, was a place of wonder and dreams. We strolled through the bazaar, which was deserted, eerie. The shop-fronts were shuttered. A full moon cast its brilliant light between the eaves, laying a sharp-cut white belt at our feet and blackening the shadows by contrast. A cat on the roof was serenading a preoccupied colleague which optimistically pursued a rat across the cobbles. At our bivouac my companions threw them-

selves down at once to sleep. Abdulla was already
snoring hideously, his head upon my unwanted tent.
I wrote my diary by the light of the moon, unrolled my
blankets, then stood awhile to gaze at one of the most
entrancing sights I have ever seen. The moon, now
almost directly above the great mountain wall, had
transformed the ravines and cavities into patches and
streaks of the profoundest blackness and struck wet
rock into molten silver. The minaret and the houses at
my feet were of a whiteness unrevealed at full day.
The bazaar's long outer wall lay black in its shadow.
There was a velvety silver-green sheen over the olives.
Far down in the plain the lights of Tirana twinkled
through the haze like a thousand fairy lanterns. In the
distance was the sea, a mystery of black and silver.
A dog's barking stabbed the stillness. The ponies munched
in idle content. There was no other sound—even Abdulla
stopped his snoring. I rolled into my blankets, lit a
cigarette, and lay back to dream of the sounds those
crags have re-echoed and the strife these walls have
seen.

While the Turkish tide was flowing into the Balkan
Peninsula, while the Balsha Princes (1366-1421) were
striving to preserve from the invading hordes the Albanian
state they had established, and while the Venetians—
taking advantage of the anxiety of the Balshas and their
Albanian chieftains—were extending their possessions
along the coast and developing their trade with the
interior, the family of Kastriot, hitherto obscure, was
working to set itself within the ranks of Albanian feudal
families. Pal Kastriota held only two villages in the
Mati valley. But Gjon, his son, a warrior leader and
diplomat of consequence, extended his authority from
Cape Rodoni to the neighbourhood of Dibra, building
castles to meet his needs—among them one at Jubani,

on a hill by where the Drinasa leaves the Drin. The Venetians recognised his qualities. Moreover, a well-disposed chieftain capable of setting and holding his authority in the interior was worth supporting as a means of advancing and protecting their trade. So in 1415 they made over to him their fortress at Kruja.

Little is known of Kruja's earlier history, though it is thought to have been the ancient *Albanopolis*. The large number of Illyrian graves found and the natural strength of its position point to a very early importance. Probably it was one of thirty castles about Durrës captured by the Bulgarian Tsar Simeon in 896. Its existence is mentioned in 1250 by the Byzantine historian and statesman Acropolita; and it was part of the dowry of Michael Angelus's daughter who married King Manfred of Sicily in 1258. In 1272 it passed under the rule of Charles of Anjou, but was retaken for Byzantium by the Emperor Michael and in 1343 it was occupied by the Serbs. In 1358 it fell to the Topias, a powerful Albanian feudal family who rebuilt the fortress in 1366. In 1393, their power weakening, the Topias ceded it to the Venetians, though a Topia stayed to govern it under the standard of St. Mark; but he died in 1415, so Gjon Kastriota came to it.

In 1423 came the Turks. The Venetians had no mind to defend Kruja, so Gjon, not strong enough to stand alone, submitted to the invaders and (so goes the popular tale) had to yield as hostages his four sons who nominally adopted the Moslem faith. When Gjon died some years later one of the Sultan's chief commanders seized all his domains, Kruja among them, and his three elder sons were poisoned. But George (born in 1403), who had won the Sultan's favour, was spared. In time he rose to high military rank; and he so distinguished himself that he was compared with the Great Alexander and therefore named Iskender (or Alexander) Bey—in Albanian, Skenderbeg.

But his native mountains were dearer to Skenderbeg than the Sultan's favours. There stirred in him too that will for independence which has been ever strong in the Albanian mountaineer. But above all, his brothers' blood cried for vengeance—and blood must be avenged by blood in the Albanian mountains. At last his mind was made up. His chance came when in 1443 he shared, as a subordinate commander, the Turks' defeat at Nish by Huniades. It is said that he played a hand for the enemy. However that may be, with a handful of trusted followers he fled from the battlefield. He caught up with the Commander-in-Chief's principal secretary whom he forced to write an order to Sabel Pasha, the governor of Kruja, ordering him, in the name of Murad (called Amurath) II, to give up the fortress. The hapless scribe was then slain by Skenderbeg, who afterwards made his way with all speed by Dibra to Kruja. Sabel at once handed over the fortress and departed for Adrianople, leaving the garrison under Skenderbeg's command. In the dead of the next night a party led by Skenderbeg overpowered the watchman on the castle walls and 600 men from Dibra were brought softly into the town. Then every Turk who would not embrace Christianity was slain.

News of the happenings at Kruja were cried from crag to crag and hill to hill, just as news is passed through the mountains to-day. Everywhere the Albanians rose, massacring every Turk outside the castles' walls (even Sabel Pasha); and in few days 12,000 men were gathered at Kruja. With this army Skenderbeg went first to Petrela which surrendered without resisting. Next he marched through the snow to *Petra Alba* "in such hast," writes Knolles, "as if the citie had been running away from him," and this strong place also surrendered immediately. Eager to liberate Mati, his father's domain, he then moved upon *Stellusa*,

"a strong citie of *Æmathia* . . . upon the top of an high hil, standing in the middest of a pleasant and fruitfull vallie, with great plaines round about it."

The governor refused to surrender, but the garrison mutinied and handed over the fortress to Skenderbeg.

Hearing that the "strongest cities" had surrendered and that their garrisons had been spared, all the other fortresses in the country followed their example except *Sfetigrad* in upper Dibra, "upon a high steep hil as if it were an eagle's nest." Notwithstanding Skenderbeg's threat to hang the góvernor of *Stellusa* and his "willful partakers" before the eyes of the defenders, the governor and garrison of *Sfetigrad* agreed upon resistance; so Skenderbeg carried out his threat. Then, leaving a force under his chief lieutenant, Moses Golemus, to take the place, he returned to Kruja; and shortly after, he made a predatory raid into Macedonia to reward his soldiers whose only pay was plunder. A Turkish army was routed in lower Dibra; and then the Albanian footmen, mounting the horses of the fallen Turks, made another raid into Macedonia.

On March 1, 1444, there met in the Cathedral Church at Lesh an assembly of Albanian chieftains, Prince Ivan Crnoievic of Montenegro, and delegates of the Venetian Republic. Skenderbeg was proclaimed "Chief of the League of the Albanian People" and the chieftains agreed to unite under him against the common foe.

Skenderbeg's fame had reached the ears of Vladislaus, King of Hungary and Poland, who wrote a flattering letter asking his aid against the Turks, observing that "wee Christians have been too too slacke and backeward in helping one-another," and concluding: "Fare you well from our regall citie of Buda, the fourth of July,

1444." Skenderbeg replied on August 3, agreeing to go to his assistance. But his way through Serbia was barred by the Despot George, "a man adorned with all the graces of nature, but otherwise a verie wicked damned Atheist and a Christian but in name only." So Huniades and Vladislaus were defeated at Varna on November 10, 1444, Vladislaus being slain. Had the Serb Despot acted otherwise, probably the Christians would have triumphed and the Balkans might never have passed under the Turkish heel. Skenderbeg carried fire and sword through Serbia in revenge before going back to Kruja.

A messenger came soon afterwards to Kruja with a letter from the Sultan. "Amurath Ottoman, King of the Turkes and Emperor of the East, to the most ungratefull Skenderbeg, wisheth neither health nor welfare," it began. Skenderbeg was reproached, threatened, and described as a "very serpent in mine owne bosome." But if he would now behave himself he would be pardoned; and he might have what his father held if he would give up all else that he had seized. Skenderbeg suspected treachery. He showed the messenger the strength of his forces, gave him a piece of his mind about his royal master, then sent him off with a reply which read:

"The souldiour of Christ Jesu, George Kastriot surnamed Skenderbeg, prince of Epirus, to Amurath Ottoman, King of the Turkes, sendeth greeting. . . . We have with patience received and seene both thy letters and messenger; and to confesse a truth, they have ministred unto me greater occasion of smile than choller: whilest at the first thou shamest not to accuse me of much ingratitude and treson: and presently following a milder passion seemest carefull of my soules health, being ignorant of thine own miserable estate, as a studious defender of a most damnable errour."

Ferises Pasha was sent against Skenderbeg and marched south through the Albanian mountains from Mokra Gora; but he was ambushed by Skenderbeg's footmen in the forests and rocky fastnesses "where the Turkes, having no use of their horses but rather by them encombered, were slaine as Deere enclosed in a toyle." Another army under Mustafa Pasha, was surprised in camp and almost annihilated.

Meantime, Skenderbeg had quarrelled with his Venetian friends whose claim to the property of one Lek Zakari—who had been "shamefully murthered by his unnaturall kinsman Lek Dukagjin"—he disputed. The Venetians seized *Dayna*, a small town about ten miles east of Shkodër, so Skenderbeg invested it. Hearing this news Mustafa Pasha again advanced; so Skenderbeg leaving his nephew Amesa in charge of the siege, marched to meet him. The Turks were utterly routed near *Oronychium* and Mustafa captured—he was afterwards ransomed for 25,000 *duckats*. Skenderbeg again plundered Macedonia, then made peace with the Venetians.

The enraged Sultan now gathered a mighty host against Skenderbeg who, having warned neighbouring princes to prepare, mobilised his forces, victualled his fortresses, bared the countryside of supplies, and ordered the peasants to retire either to his own or to the Venetian walled cities. He garrisoned Kruja with 1,300 men under one Vranacontes; and he ordered all women, children, aged and infirm to leave the town and go with their flocks, herds and valuables to safety.

The Sultan, with 150,000 men (among them many "pioners, and men appointed for other base services necessarie at the siege of townes") advanced upon *Sfetigrad*, second in importance only to Kruja among Skenderbeg's fortresses. *Sfetigrad* was held by Peter Perlat, with a garrison of Dibrani who "were alwaies accounted the best men of warre in all Epirus." After three days' continuous bombardment the Turks delivered a series of desperate assaults, but they were overwhelmed by the shot, stones, timber, lime, wildfire and other missiles poured upon them from above while Skenderbeg constantly harassed their rear. At length Amurath, despairing of storming the town, sent envoys offering enormous rewards to the garrison if they would surrender. These offers were scorned by all but one man who found a means of communicating secretly with the envoys. This traitor devised a scheme

"which of all others a man would have thought to have been of least moment"; as the Dibrani "were men of great courage, so were they exceeding superstitious both in their religion and manner of living, putting nice difference betwixt one kind of lawfull meat and other: accounting some cleane, some uncleane." The town had water enough, but from only one well sunk deep into the rock. "Into this common well the malicious traitour in the night time cast the foule stinking carion carkas of a dead dog, knowing that the conceited garrison souldiours of Dybra would rather indure the paines of death, and starve, or els yeeld up the citie upon any condition, than to drinke of that polluted water."

When the discovery was made it was in vain that Peter Perlat explained the well would soon purify itself and drank from it before his men. So, "full sore against his will," he had to surrender and the garrison were allowed to go free. *Sfetigrad* was occupied by 1,200 Janissaries, and the Sultan then returned to Adrianople. Skenderbeg's efforts to retake the fortress were fruitless.

In the following year Amurath came before Kruja on May 14, 1450, with 160,000 men "wherewith hee filled all the countrey round about." It being too difficult to drag artillery over the roadless passes, the Turks had brought metal from which sixteen great cannon were cast. In fifteen days they were ready mounted upon carriages, six facing Kruja from the side towards the plain and ten others opposite the gate, the fortress being at all other points "naturally defended with impregnable rocks, upon the tops whereof were built faire battlements more for beautie than needfull defence." Constantly bombarded for four days, the walls at these two points were beaten down or seriously battered and the Turks much encouraged. But the garrison were undaunted, realising "that the eies of most part of Christendome were as it were fixed upon them," and they were exhorted by Vranacontes in these heroic terms:

"Things readie to fall need shoaring, and thether hasteth honour, and there (worthie souldiours) appeareth courage and valour. Wherefore let our valiant right hands defend those broken breaches and in stead of these dead wals couragiously oppose our lustie and lively armed bodies against the force of our enemies. . . . This rising of the hill . . . the steepness whereof, as it will be troublesome unto them, so will it keep us most fresh in strength: and make our shot more forcible."

Amurath ordered the assault

"and first with the multitude of his archers and small shot laboured to drive the defendants from the wals . . . at the same time other common souldiours of baser account brought scaling ladders and other things needfull for the scaling of wals. After whom also followed the Ianizaries and other chosen souldiours, readie to mount the ladders as soon as they should be set to the wals. But whilest they climbe up the high hils in this order, the garrison souldiours made such slaughter of them with shot from the wals and out of the citie, that they would have presently retired, had they not been forced forward by their captaines, who spared neither stripes nor wounds when words would not serve. By this tyrannicall meanes, the scaling ladders were with great slaughter of the common souldiours set up against the wals, and the Turkes climing up, came to handie blowes with the defendants at the breaches; nothing was to be heard but the crying of people, the clattering of armor, and the instruments of warre, which was terribly redoubled with the ecchoes from the mountaines round about."

The Turks were repulsed and Prince Mahomed, a ruthless man, caused those "common souldiours" who retired to be slain; but two further assaults with better troops were not more successful.

In that hot season the Turkish encampments had to be widely dispersed (for obvious reasons); so Skenderbeg marching "by certaine secret by-waies" from his entrenched camp on *Mount Tumenist* (Mali Skenderbeut), fell upon one side of their encampments while Moses Golemus made a diversion by advancing against the other "with much noise and tumult." The Turks suffered heavily before the Albanians withdrew.

Amurath now "sent his purveyors for corne to *Lissa*, a citie of the Venetians," but Skenderbeg destroyed the convoy. Thereafter, however, the Albanians did not intercept the corn, oil, honey and other supplies with which the Venetians provided the Turks because these supplies could have been drawn from Macedonia without overmuch trouble, and Skenderbeg did not wish to offend the Venetians by spoiling this ready Turkish market. Doubtless the doughty warrior and his men shared with them a very handsome profit on those supplies!

Another night attack upon the Turkish camp from three sides caused much havoc therein, and a Turkish attack upon Mt. Tumenist was defeated. Meantime, attempts to undermine Kruja proved too tedious, nor possible once the garrison discovered them. Then an envoy was sent with offer of enormous rewards to the governor and garrison if they would surrender; but his eloquence was lost upon the governor who

"commaunded him to depart: straightly charging him that neither hee nor any other should after that time presume to come from his master to the citie to speak with him about such dishonourable matter; for if hee did, he would in detestation thereof cause their hands, their noses and their eares to be cut off, and so returne them dismembred instead of answere. And so the Bassa was with his presents againe turned out of the citie and no man suffered to receive anything of him in reward, although the soldiours could have been well content to have eased him and his servants of that carriage, if the governour would but have winked thereat."

Yet another furious assault failed. Thereupon Amurath, overcome with rage,

"sat downe in his tent, all that day full of melancholic passions, sometimes violently pulling his hoarie beard and white locks, complaining of his hard and disaster fortune, that hee had lived so long to see those daies of disgrace, wherein all his former glorie and triumphant victories were obscured by one base towne of Epirus."

As a last resort he offered peace to Skenderbeg upon condition that the latter would pay an annual tribute of 10,000 *duckats* (£4,700); but the proposal was scorned and Skenderbeg redoubled his harassing tactics. At length, "sicke for griefe," Amurath raised the siege on October 26 and returned to Adrianople. Three months later he died.

Mahomed II (The Conqueror—1451-1481), at the beginning of his reign, renewed his father's proposals for peace. Skenderbeg answered by a raid into Macedonia, routing armies sent against him at *Modrissa* and *Pologus*. So Mahomed ordered the governor of *Sfetigrad* to spare no pains or gold to seduce Moses Golemus, commander of Skenderbeg's forces about Dibra. The "faire glozing words" of the governor's envoy, who offered Moses the Kingdom of Epirus, took effect, and the faithless commander assured the Turks they would not in future find him "any great enemy." He advised Skenderbeg to besiege Berat, saying he himself would stay to defend the Dibra region.

So Skenderbeg wrote to his old friend Alphonso (The Magnanimous), King of Naples, who had previously lent him

"civile pollicie and warlike strength: all sort of people, of what condition soever," asking him to send "such souldiours as know how to fight a farre off, I mean harquebusiers and canoniers, for of others we have store plenty." Alphonso sent "such aid as Skenderbeg had before requested, and a

great deale more: for Alphonsus, fearing the greatnesse of
the Turkish Emperour, in what he could furthered Skenderbeg
his actions, reckoning Epirus not above sixty miles distant
from his dominions, to be the strongest wals of his Kingdome
in Apulia (as not many years after, it by proofe appeared,
when as the Turks having taken Otranto, put all Italy in
no small feare)"; and he humourously remarked in his letter
to Skenderbeg "that he had sent him Italian souldiours which
could according to his desire fight well both with men and
wals: but better with women."

so that his Albanians had better have a care for their
wives when the Italians were about!

Skenderbeg besieged Berat with 14,000 men and soon
so distressed the city that its garrison concluded an
armistice whereby they would surrender if not relieved
within sixteen days. So Skenderbeg encamped with
4,000 men on a hill nearby, sending the rest a short
way northward "into a large plaine, where they might
encampe themselves in a more wholsome and fresh ayre,
in that hoat season of the year." But Sebalias Pasha,
marching swiftly to the relief of Berat with 40,000 men,
surprised and almost annihilated them, slaying their
commander Myzeki. Skenderbeg fell upon the Turks
with some effect as they were looting, then retired northward, leaving strong garrisons upon the passes. He lost
5,000 men—among them most of the Italians—his tents
and "great artillerie." Sebalias reinforced the Berat
garrison, then went back in triumph to Constantinople
(which had been captured by Mahomed on May 29, 1453).

Meantime Moses Golemus, having failed to induce his
subordinates to join his treachery, fled to Constantinople.
The next spring he led 15,000 Turks into the Dibra
district where he was completely routed. Soon afterwards he returned to Skenderbeg, who pardoned and
reinstated him!

Then Skenderbeg's own trusted nephew Amesa went
over to the enemy, his tale being that Skenderbeg had

not restored his father's property to him and on false charges had dispossessed another relative.

Isaacke Pasha, with 50,000 men, now marched against Skenderbeg who decided to resort to strategem. The country was bared of supplies, the inhabitants sent into the fortresses, and Skenderbeg withdrew towards Lesh that Isaacke might think he would show no fight. Whereupon Amesa was proclaimed King of Epirus, that the people should know the Turks marched only against their ruler and had no quarrel with them. But in the plain near Kruja Isaacke allowed his troops to scatter for pillage. Skenderbeg widely distributed his men, and in the midday heat of a July day they suddenly advanced upon the scattered Turks "with such horrible shouts and noise of instruments of warre, as if heaven and earth should have presently gone togither; the hils and vallies with their hollow ecchoes, increasing the terror of the alarum." The Turks, thinking an overwhelming host upon them, fled and were routed with the loss of over 20,000 men. Skenderbeg had the bodies of the slain men and horses buried, so "that their loathsome carkases should not infect the countrey"; then he returned to Kruja. Amesa, who had been taken, was sent prisoner to Naples, but a year later—on King Alphonso's death—he was incarcerated at Kruja. At last he was pardoned by Skenderbeg who let him appear to escape so that he might return to Constantinople to bring back his wife and children; but in Constantinople he died.

For two years Skenderbeg was unmolested, then Mahomed concluded a truce for a year more. On its expiry, Skenderbeg successively routed four large Turkish armies which invaded his principality; whereupon, on May 10, 1461, Mahomed sought peace with him upon condition that Turkish armies might pass through Albania to attack the Venetian possessions: that Turkish merchants might trade freely in Albania: that Skenderbeg's son Gjon should be given as hostage: and that Skenderbeg himself should visit Constantinople! Skenderbeg answered that he could not betray his Venetian friends, that Gjon required a father's care at home, that he desired the merchants of both countries to have all possible facilities, and that he himself could not yet leave his country, being too busy governing his subjects who "love alwayes to have something to doe; being by nature a fierce and ruthless nation whom I my selfe have much adoe to rule and governe." In June Mahomed replied agreeing to peace on the sole condition that the merchants of either country should have free access to the other; and he recognised Skenderbeg as "Prince of Albania and Epirus." There was much rejoicing in both kingdoms; and Mahomed loyally maintained peace, suppressing the raiding into Albania in which his troops on the frontier began to indulge.

Skenderbeg, secure at home, now crossed to Apulia, chivalrously leading an expedition to support King Ferdinand—the son of his old friend Alphonso—against the French invaders under John of Anjou. But two years later he let himself be persuaded by Paulus Angelus, Archbishop of Durrës, to take up arms again; so he led a sudden raid into Turkish territory, causing great harm and taking much booty. Mahomed wrote, in May, 1463, reproving him for his breach of faith and for "stealing our cattell, more like a theefe and robber than an open enemie," urging him to renew peace on oath. Skenderbeg replied in an insulting letter, explaining that he had made the raid because Mahomed had failed to punish certain freebooters or restore what they had taken. "I have your faith in such distrust and your friendship in detestation," he added, and concluded by urging Mahomed to embrace Christianity and abandon "all that filthie superstition which the most filthie false Prophet Mahomet hath left amongst you." Urged by Pope Pius II who was raising a crusading army, Skenderbeg declared war, made another big raid into Macedonia, and almost annihilated a Turkish army near Okhrida. But in August, 1464, Pope Pius died and the Crusaders dispersed, so Skenderbeg was left to his own resources.

Mahomed, sore at defeat which "stucke in his stomacke," sent 18,000 men against Skenderbeg under Balabanus Badera, "an Epirot borne, a chorles sonne of that countrey." Skenderbeg sent Balàbanus a spade and other farm implements, bidding him take to those and leave the conduct of armies to others. The Turks, attacking in the valley of *Valçal* near Okhrida, were repulsed; but Moses Golemus and seven others of Skenderbeg's best commanders, pursuing too impetuously, were ambushed, captured, and barbarously executed in Constantinople. Skenderbeg avenged them by another raid into Macedonia. Meantime, Balabanus reorganised his army at Okhrida, then tried to surprise Skenderbeg by night at *Oronychium;* but the Albanian leader, who often kept watch himself, "in the silence of the night a farre off perceived the comming of the enemie by the noise of his horses," and the Turks were defeated after a desperate fight. Three months later Balabanus met with another disaster near *Sfetigrad*.

Mahomed now sent two armies against Skenderbeg simultaneously. One, of 24,000 men, was commanded by Balabanus to whom Mahomed promised Skenderbeg's crown should he be victorious: and the other, of 16,000 men, by Iacup Arnauth (James the Albanian). But Balabanus was routed yet again in the valley of *Valçal*. Skenderbeg then heard from his sister Mamic at Petrela that Iacup had advanced from Berat, laying waste the country, and lay encamped "in the plaines of Tiranna the lesse." He hastened thither, dismayed the Turks by exhibiting the heads of Balabanus's men, then utterly routed them. Those who escaped, "stragling through the countrey by thicke woods and blind waies," were caught or slain by the countryfolk.

There followed another raid into Turkish territory, then the timely discovery of a plot by two men, masquerading as deserters, to murder Skenderbeg.

In 1466 Mahomed himself led 200,000 men into Albania. Arriving before Kruja, the Turkish heralds called upon the governor, Balthasar Perduci, to surrender; but he replied by "continuall thundring shot" into the Turkish camp. So Mahomed bombarded the place, though with little hope of taking it, "knowing by his owne experience that it was a place almost impregnable." Skenderbeg constantly harassed the Turks till at length Mahomed, fearing to lose prestige by failing before Kruja, left Balabanus with 79,000 men to continue the siege and returned to Constantinople. On the way he laid waste the country, massacred men, women and children, and took several small fortresses; and he put to the sword 8,000 inhabitants of *Cidna* whom he had promised to spare if they surrendered.

Skenderbeg's army lay exhausted, unable to relieve Kruja. So Skenderbeg appealed for aid to the Venetians and to the confederate princes of Albania, Illyria and Dalmatia. He was assured by them that he should have it. Then he went to Rome "disguised in simple attire" and was well received by Pope Paul II who could not, however, raise help for him. Returning to Albania he found the promised reinforcements waiting for him, among them strong contingents from the Venetian garrisons of Shkodër, *Drivasto*, Lesh and Durrës, in all 13,400 troops trained and disciplined as the Turks never were. With this army he intercepted and routed Turkish reinforcements marching to Kruja, capturing their commander Jonuz and his nephew. Next he carried by assault the main Turkish position before Kruja, *Mt. Kranje*, and from the summit displayed to the infuriated Balabanus his brother Jonuz and nephew in chains. Then Balabanus himself was killed during a sortie by the garrison. The Turks, dismayed, withdrew to the plain, abandoning their tents and supplies, whereupon Skenderbeg sent forces to block the passes on their line of retreat. Hearing that they were cut off the Turks offered to surrender their horses and arms if they might go with their lives; but Skenderbeg replied "that as they came into his countrey without his commandement, so should they not by his leave depart thence." But, fighting desperately, they managed to escape by night over *Çafa* Krraba, "for whose escape the common souldiors murmured greevously against Skenderbeg and were not without much ado appeased."

In the spring of 1467 Mahomed led yet another great army against Skenderbeg. First he rebuilt with much labour the ruined fortress of Elbasan which he garrisoned strongly, then marched upon Durrës but found it held by Venetians and Albanians in force. In his vain effort to take it he lost many men. Then, suddenly, he marched to Kruja, hoping to surprise the place. But Kruja was well prepared; so he offered the garrison and citizens great rewards and privileges if they would surrender, offers to which the garrison answered "out of the mouth of the cannon or by many most brave sallies." Harassed by Skenderbeg he withdrew to Cape Rodoni where he razed to the ground a new castle which Skenderbeg had begun to build; and he undertook various other minor operations to vent his fury, but suffered so heavily from his invincible opponent's tactics that at length he returned in despair to Constantinople.

After the Turks' withdrawal Skenderbeg made a tour of his kingdom, then repaired to Lesh to discuss with the Venetians a plan for taking the new fortress at Elbasan. But at Lesh he fell sick of fever. He commended his wife, his son and his kingdom to Venetian care; and on January 17, 1468, he died. When the Sultan heard the news he is said to have exclaimed: "Asia and Europe are mine at last. Woe to Christendom! She has lost her sword and shield."

In May, 1477, Kruja was again besieged. The Venetians sent an army under Franciscus Contarenus to relieve it and the Turks were defeated after fierce fighting in the plain of Tirana. But the Venetians, instead of following up their success, stayed to loot the Turkish camp and baggage and while they were thus engaged the Turks rallied, routing them with heavy loss. Contarenus was slain.

On June 14, 1478, after a whole year of siege, Kruja

"for lacke of victuals was yeelded up unto the Turke, upon condition that the hunger-starved defendants (who then seemed rather ghosts than men) might at their pleasure in safetie depart."

But the Turks put them all to the sword.

Late in eighteenth century and until 1832 Kruja was within the Hereditary Pashalik of the Bushatis; and in 1820 it was occupied for a short time by Ali Pasha's son Mukhtar who was fighting the Pasha of Shkodër. After the surrender of Mustafa Bushati to Reschid Pasha the castle was dismantled.

Crumbling walls, the stronghold of lizards, are all that remain of Skenderbeg's great fortress.

CHAPTER IV

CLANS AND CHIEFTAINS

KRUJA is night's last refuge from an invincible sun. The black shades beneath the scarps and buttresses grow pallid grey and violet as dawn's first sunshafts reach from the hidden east into the western sky. Of a sudden the distant hills which hem the sleeping plain bear crests of molten gold; and the gold flows slowly down their flanks to the plain, then across the plain with an edge cut sharp by Kruja's sheltering crags, the air split into full day's sunlight above and dawn's still grey about. At last, in a moment, the fierce sun is blazing over the crags, stirring the sluggard and saturating the night-cooled air with heat.

Our way from Kruja lay south-eastward for an hour below the mountain wall, then through a great ravine choked with trees, a glass-clear stream cut deep into the limestone bed of it. A fit gateway to a wild mountain land. It opens into the softer valley behind the mountain wall, and here our escorting gendarme passed over his responsibilities to a commune guard who waited by a shaded spring.

Albania is divided into 189 communes, each with a president, secretary, and a council elected by the people: and the council appoints local police or guards to co-operate with the gendarmerie. Formerly the clan or *bajrak* (a sub-division of the clan) was the political unit in the mountains, governed by a Council of Elders who appointed executives. So the new system is not much changed except that the boundaries of the communes do not always correspond with those of the clans and *bajraks*. In war and affairs of blood each *bajrak* followed its hereditary *bajraktar* who still has responsibilities where danger threatens from neighbouring clans.

As night fell we came upon a gendarmerie post, a wooden shack in a clearing high up among pine trees; and here we stayed. The post commander, bewhiskered and hoary, brought forth his supper, a pot of beans, to flavour our macaroni—a mess he relished too; and when we had all eaten his comrade brought coffee to prepare at our fire. Then we talked beneath the cloak of stars, the fire red between us against the cool.

The hoary one was proud of the revolver at his belt which Zogu had given him for good work against bandits: but there had been no trouble hereabouts for five years. The commune guard spoke of feuds. There were not many in these parts now, but not long ago a man had found his wife with a lover—an offence the mountaineer will never pardon. So he killed the lover and his wife too, then gave himself up to the authorities. After a few weeks he was released, for the authorities see that the traditional laws of centuries cannot be swept away in a day. The new Penal and Civil codes are applied gently in the mountains; and though Tirana will tell the stranger they are everywhere fully applied, Lek Dukagjin's unwritten law still holds in some parts.

Lek Dukagjin was a contemporary (and no great friend) of Skenderbeg's; but while Skenderbeg found a proud place in history, Lek's fame survives him only in his hills. In Skenderbeg's time the Dukagjini (meaning the Dukes John) ruled Mirdita, the Zadrima plain (by Lesh) and most of Albania north of the Drin (though to-day only this last part of their domains bears their name). It is said they had a fortress near Perlat; and the last lord of Zadrima and *Dayna* was ousted by the Turks in 1479. A "Luca Ducagini, Duca di Pulato e dell stato Ducagino" appears in Venetian records of 1506, which suggests that some of the family fled to Venice. The head of a house which sheltered us in Shala said certainly that he was a twenty-first descendant of Lek's, and probably he spoke a truth, for the Albanian mountain folk often know their genealogies better than most of us know ours for all our written records. The hereditary chieftains of Mirdita also claim descent from Lek.

In those parts which were Lek's domains his fame far exceeds Skenderbeg's. To his word are attributed innumerable customs but the truth of his deeds is lost in a fog of mythology. It seems that after the fall of the Balsha princes Lek set himself to better his clansmen's lot, so laid down certain (unwritten) laws which have guided the mountain men until to-day, for the Turks' commands were generally ignored. Christ, that other legislator, lived afar and was no Albanian so could not understand the Albanians. Perhaps he could cast spells against the Evil Eye and other inconveniences and on that account was worth obeying when his laws happened to be Lek's; but Lek's had the benefit of the doubt every time. The custom of blood vengeance has come to be attributed to Lek's decree, whereas in actual fact it seems he did all he could to stop it. He laid down only two punishments for crime—fines and the burning of property (imposed by the Councils of Elders)—and avoided the death penalty which would start a new feud. But seemingly it was beyond even Lek to make laws for his wild subjects which fitted the doctrines of Christianity, because Pope Paul excommunicated him for his barbarous code.

The blood feud was governed by firm rules. Blood was the price for any deed which stained a man's or a family's honour and honour lay blackened till blood washed out the stain. So much blood flowed, for a mountaineer's honour was a tender plant. Even an accidental blow might start a feud. But if not convenient a feud might be suspended with common agreement by inviolable Oath of Peace (called *Besa*) for a fixed time—perhaps for a feast or market day or when foreign danger threatened. And a man's blood was safe when with a guest or a woman. The blood of women is of no account so women are always safe.

Women had no choice of husbands. They were betrothed by their fathers in infancy and sometimes before birth, their price often a heavy one for they were the drudges, the breeding stock, the beasts of burden. Their lot was, and is, the household toil—and not only that but any work whatsoever, as distinct from the manly tasks of war and feud. Nevertheless they were held in much respect, their advice often sought and followed. If widowed they were taken by their brothers-in-law as concubines, for it was held cruel to make them live alone.

A stranger had no part in feuds and went freely. A guest was sacred, his host in honour answerable for his safety till he became another's guest. So a shamelessly vindictive Lord of Blood (him to whom blood was due) might doubly blacken his enemy's honour by killing his enemy's guest; but that was indeed bad form, so rarely happened.

Such, in brief, was the law of the mountains.

Going down through oak scrub and beech woods we reached the wide Mati valley which has good fields of maize and tobacco, and *kulas* scattered about it. Burelë is a poor, parched, shadeless place where Prince Xhelal Zogu, the King's step-brother, has a white villa in Italian style, blatant with red tiles and green shutters. It was unenclosed, very simply furnished. The Prince received us readily. He is of middle height, past his prime and somewhat corpulent, his clothes entirely *alla Franka* but uncared for. He has none of the King's graces. But he was kind enough, keen to be informative. A gendarme brought coffee and royal cigarettes while we talked of Mati and its 40,000 clansmen. There were almost no feuds now—the effect, he thought, of education. The valley's full development depended on roads to bear away surplus produce; and two were then being built— one from Kruja and one from Miloti (for Burelë is important in the Italians' scheme of military defence).

Fording the Mati river precariously upon swaying packs and pushing through lush meadows dotted with fruit trees and bushes overgrown with blackberries, we reached Burgejet's few *kulas* at red sunset; but it cost many words to gain from a house lord the favour of lying for the night beneath a mulberry tree in his meadow near Burgejet's spring, for he feared our ponies' greed with his hay. He was a tall man, in a long white shirt girdled at the waist and baggy white trousers gathered at the ankles. In the fitful firelight he looked an Arab, or an athlete in a nightshirt. There was no firewood to gather, so we bought a bundle from some women, also a large basket of purple figs, grapes and a chicken to carry with us. But the chicken decamped in the night, probably not without aid. The benightshirted one was sociable to the point of staring and smoking, but not chatty. But he did tell that Burgejet was proud of King Zog, that every able Mati man had joined him against Fan Noli in 1924, and he warned us against Mati's thievishness, hoping perhaps that after such show of anxiety for our welfare we should not suspect him of conspiring with the captive chicken.

We lay upon the flank of an isolated hill with a wide view of the valley. It is a soft hill, well grown with

King Zog's Ruined Home in Mati

(See p. 90)

CLANS AND CHIEFTAINS

mulberry, walnut, cherry, and chestnut trees apart or in clumps. Upon its crest stands the ancient home of the Zogus, a gaunt ruin smothered with shrubs and thistles, a mournful sight. Though small, it must have been a fine house, stone-built with two storeys, an Elizabethan touch about it. It was rectangular, with two small wings, facing into a walled courtyard. Bourcart, who was the guest of the Zogus in 1919, was surprised to find it well furnished in European style, and he noticed it was the only house about which had true windows and open doors. It was put to flames in the summer of 1920 by Serbian bands. King Zog told me that when this happened he was away, and most of his clansmen fighting the Italians at Vlona. But his mother and sisters called every remaining man to arms and resisted the invaders until aid came. He added that Burgejet means "Prison of Life," for in a deep ravine hard by Skenderbeg incarcerated many Turks.

The Zogus' origin is somewhat obscure. Legend and the Albanian official story (which in these matters are often much the same) have it that the founder of the family came to Mati from the north towards the end of the fifteenth century and married Mamic, Skenderbeg's daughter. (Knolles mentions Skenderbeg's *sister* Mamic). The newcomer stirred the Mati people against their Turkish governor whom they slew, then usurped power and induced the Turks to recognise his position by becoming a Moslem. The governorship was made hereditary.

The fourth hereditary governor was Abdulla Zogu, whose tombstone at Burgejet bears the date 1621. There followed him in direct line of descent Amet, Mahmoud and Xhelal, and in the middle of the nineteenth century a Xhelal Zogu visited Russia where he was encouraged to liberate his country from the Turks; but he was arrested, tried, and interned at Constantinople. He was succeeded by his son Xhemal who married, as his second wife, Sadié, of the powerful Toptani family of Tirana (who formerly lived at Kruja, in a house within the castle now given over to local officialdom). The Toptanis are descended from the Topias of Venetian times. On October 8, 1895, Sadié bore a son, Amet, the King. So King Zog comes of a line of hereditary chieftains who governed a virtually independent principality somewhat in the style of our medieval barons; for Mati was never more than nominally under the Turks and bowed only to the laws of Lek.

Xhemal pasha Zogu died in 1905. Thereafter Sadié ruled Mati and held it from Turkish interference till Amet should grow up. Her stepson, Xhelal, never seems to have played much part. Amet went first to school at Galata Serai, then attended military schools at Constantinople and Bitolje. He went back to Mati shortly before the outbreak of the Balkan War in 1912. Stormy days followed. Gathering his clansmen he set upon Montenegrin and Serbian invaders but lost above 200 men in a sharp fight so had to withdraw. Then he was called to Vlona for the proclamation of Albanian independence on November 28, 1912; but he was soon back in Mati harrying the Serbs on his borders.

In 1914 he stood loyally for Prince Wilhelm, going to Durrës to talk with the Prince who thought much of him; but Essad Pasha, War Minister and Amet's uncle, who himself secretly aspired to the throne of Albania and thought his nephew dangerous to his schemes, planned his arrest. Here Prince Wilhelm intervened, so Amet went free to Mati again. Xhelal, his step-brother, stood for Essad whom he defended to me in our talk at Burelë.

Then Amet led his men against the central Albanian

rebels, the fanatics. He took Kruja; but his force was too weak to do more so he withdrew again. The borders of Mati were manned and none might come or go without the young chieftain's permit. After Prince Wilhelm went from Albania many leading nationalists fled here from Turkophile rebels or Slav invaders, so there were many intrigues, many negotiations. Indeed Amet's fame spread so wide that both Bulgaria and Austria-Hungary played for his support, and in 1915 Prince Ludwig Windischgraetz was sent to him at Burgejet by the Austro-Hungarian General Staff.

Encouraged by disaster to the Serbs and Essad Pasha's flight with them from Durrës, Amet led the nationalists from Burgejet to Elbasan which they reached on January 31, 1916, two days after a company of Bulgarian infantry. The Serbs, when supporting Essad, had crushed the Turkophile rebels, so Amet was easily able to raise again Prince Wilhelm's flag over the palace at Durrës, reform the Prince's government *ad interim*, prepare for a national congress, and organise demonstrations of loyalty to the absent Prince, all with Bulgarian sympathy. But early in March came the Austro-Hungarians who prohibited political asemblies while military operations continued. The Albanians had to bow to this decree which was made partly by Turkish wish (for the Turks hoped to get Albania again) and partly because Austria planned to annex Albania.

Austria had always posed as the Albanians' friend and paid well, so Amet led Albanian irregulars against the Italians. But soon he was caught conspiring with the Bulgarians for administrative independence and was suspected of negotiating with the enemy too, so he was invited to Vienna and interned there.

The Armistice signed, Amet set out from Vienna for Albania; but his only way lay through Italy and the

Italians kept him, for his nationalism did not then fit their game. Nor did the cautious Albanian Provisional Government at Durrës wish for his return. When at last he did reach Albania he drafted his clansmen secretly into Shkodër to resist the Serbs who were planning (with French connivance) to seize the town when the inter-Allied force withdrew in March, 1920. But fighting would have painted Albania's national claims in bloody letters which the Powers could not ignore, so Amet's action upset the Serbs' plan.

The Provisional Government appointed Amet governor of Shkodër, but he had other aims. On January 28, 1920, at his instigation, a national congress had met at Lushnja, proclaimed *Besa* throughout the land, and decreed elections for a national assembly at Tirana. The assembly set up a fresh, nationalist government on March 27, and Amet became Minister of the Interior.

Thereafter, Amet's tale is the tale of his country. Secretly he was behind the uprising which pushed the Italians from Vlona. On November 28 he resigned (with the cabinet) and took command of Albanian forces resisting invading Yugoslavs. On Christmas Day of 1921 he became again Minister of the Interior and in March he bravely defended Tirana against rebels from the mountains, finally settling their dispute. On December 2, 1922, he became Prime Minister (at the age of twenty-seven). But there were many who held that Albania lagged on the way to progress and believed that Amet played for the rich beys. On February 21, 1924, he was fired at and wounded. A few days later he resigned but his resignation did not satisfy the Opposition who wished to be rid of his influence. So there took place in June a revolt under Bishop Fan Noli's political leadership. Amet retired across the border and went to Belgrade.

Men of Mati with a Student from Tirana

(See p. 95)

The Yugoslavs thought this was their chance to establish their influence in Albania. So they helped Amet. With their aid he recrossed the frontier and after some sharp skirmishing regained Tirana on Christmas Eve, 1924. He took power as Dictator and Commander-in-Chief and on January 31, 1925, was proclaimed President of the Albanian Republic by the rump of the Chamber. He found the aid which Italy now proffered—to further her strategic interests—safer and more profitable than Yugoslav good wishes for a price. Italy provided a loan, capital for a National Bank and, as time went on, many military and civil organisers and advisers. There followed the Pact of Tirana with Italy on November 27, 1926 (which has since lapsed), and the Treaty of Defensive Alliance with Italy on November 22, 1927. On September 1, 1928, Amet was proclaimed King of the Albanians.

King Zog is a slight man of middle height, his hair, moustache and complexion fair, his eyes keen and alert. He dresses well but simply and wears no unnecessary baubles. When President he sometimes wore a white uniform, designed in Prince Wilhelm's time, which in those days seemed incongruous; but he wore it for effect upon his impressionable subjects and not for choice. He is courteous, with an easy grace, though somewhat nervous. His courage is proved, so, too, his wit and foresight, and his diplomatic skill is matched by his suave evasive words when dealing with the thorny problems and tortuous minds everywhere about him.

We passed through an intricate country of ravines, gullies, and woods of scrub oak, orchards, and open meadows where the new hay was stacked upon the lower branches of trees (from which the upper branches had been cut) beyond the reach of wandering flocks. In a part-tilled hollow with grim *kulas* about it a crystal-clear torrent flowed from a precipitous gorge and tumbled past the maize fields; and here peasants came to discover, in a polite unobtrusive way, what we were about, selling milk from a copper can and a great disc (two feet across) of maize bread. If well-made of fine-ground corn this bread is not so bad, though it is always unleavened, leaden, and very filling; but if badly made it is a yellow abomination at the very bottom of the food scale.

Through a forest of gnarled oaks we climbed gently, a range of big mountains thrusting their bald heads above a clear-cut tree line far to our right, and at evening we reached Perlat. There is a cluster of rickety houses crowning a flat-topped hill, its flanks steep and shaded by oaks. A narrow path near the top girdles the hill to a trickle from a mossy bank; and in the glory of twilight the women of the village trip down softly to fill their jugs of beaten copper or the wooden casks they carry on their backs with woollen cords.

A chicken for our supper heralded her unwilling coming from far below by squawks of protest. Later, we sat about our fire to talk with our new gendarme from the local post. There were not a few bandits and outlaws in the forests, he said, but in two months there had been only two fights with them. But there were feuds, and three days before a man was gravely wounded. The blood-taker was under arrest at the post and would go to Burelë next day for trial. Next morning the arrested man was walking about the post freely, smoking and joking, on the best terms with everybody. He had done no wrong.

As we rolled in our blankets in a meadow near the spring a great lazy moon like a Chinese lantern crept from behind a distant crag. The slow grey smoke from the red embers between us curled upward to a ceiling of solid ink hung thick with stars. Below and beyond us lay a mysterious world of forest, pasture and rock—and there are vampires and devils, witches and feuds and brigands down in that silent primeval land, a land where men live as they did in the Dawn of Time, striving to propitiate a relentless God and frustrate the Powers of Evil. True they had no guns or tobacco in that dim past. They fought their feuds with *yataghans* and clubs or bows and arrows, and they wore skins instead of cloth. But what else has changed? Fires twinkled through the night just as that one down there beyond the gaunt dead oak. The cries of a night-bird, weird and ghostly, and the barking of a dog disturbed by a sound in the shadows—these were the same. Women came down to the spring through all the centuries, then hurried home again before the devils began to flash among the trees. The Vampire Spirit went forth at night from the wizened witch and sucked the infant's blood till it died because its mother forgot to hang a charm round its tiny unwashed neck; but the crop was saved by the horse's skull on the mulberry tree at the end of the plot. A twisted petrol tin will do as well this year if one can be got in the bazaar to-morrow. Abdulla swears by the blue beads on his ponies' halters—*Syni keç* (the Evil Eye) cannot face them. But the gendarme says that in his village they use two pieces of wood crossed—the priest told them about it—and it is a very good charm to have on a house.

Going through the oak scrub next day we met two men in dirty white smocks with a tiny cart. Drawn by two oxen scarcely bigger than St. Bernard dogs, it had solid wheels of stone and sides of laced twigs. But it was a sign of progress, for I saw no other thing on wheels in all the mountains. Water was scarce. After three hours going we were told at a *kula* that there were no more springs for several hours. As the Albanian mountaineer always knows every spring in his neighbourhood and the quality of each this lie must have had a purpose —probably the sale of the *kula's* milk and fruit.

Then we entered a forest of splendid pines. From a post at its edge our gendarme-escort was reinforced against possible "bad men" by a commune guard; but I suspected the dangers were exaggerated and, as we were now seven and one of us complaining of sickness, resolved we should bivouac by a spring among the trees. My decision caused a clamour of protest from the Albanians who swore "by the Lord" and "by the Oath" that there were bandits, bears and wolves to be feared, no fodder for the ponies and no food for themselves. But these objections were overruled by mocking their fears and by a show of essential firmness. Soon two pillars of blue smoke, heavy with the incense of pine resin, rose through the last sunshafts. There was wood in abundance, bracken for luxurious beds, and hay and milk, bread and cheese, from a house not far away.

We lay close to the brow of *Mali* Gjana. Deep below was the Orosh valley, a strange place of dark green pines and purple shadows from which the sunlight had fled to the hilltops; and the pines swelled up from the depths by the steep mountain-side till they were all about us, tall and straight, silent and majestic, the angels' ladders from among their branches putting a stipple of gold upon the soft brown carpet of pine needles at our feet. Here and there the gossamer of spiders' webs caught the glow from the last sun. To the right, across the valley, rose the serrated crags of *Mali* Shenjt, a rich pink against an azure sky, and to the left towered the dark green dome of *Mali* Mnela, the sky behind it golden. Far beyond, we could see great white cliffs like distant snow-caps—the Accursed Mountains, so called because it is said the Turks first came by them.

As we ate—our guard and gendarme (mountain men) with us for they despised the urban Abdulla who stayed by his picketed ponies—the peasant who had brought our supplies and gone again stole suddenly into the firelight with trouble on his face. He told that while on his way home he had been stopped by some men who had enquired about us, then warned him not to return to us. So now he had come, to stay with us until morning.

Though I thought his tale strange our gendarme whispered that his house was a pledge for his honesty so precautions might be well. He and the peasant and guard would keep watch—and they kept awake by throwing blazing embers at each other. We passed a cord through all stealable things and threaded pots upon it to rattle at a touch, they lay around on the edge of the firelight with axe and sticks to hand.

The wind soughed gently in the tall straight pines and the full moon crept above their gaunt black tops. Then we slept.

I woke with a start, conscious of an anguished sobbing and wailing. "A pony is hurt," said somebody. "It fell across a stump and disembowelled itself. Abdulla is sitting by streaming tears—he wants to know if you can push the guts back and sew the pony up again."

But it was a hopeless case. So I asked the gendarme and guard to shoot the poor beast with their rifles.

"By the Lord, we cannot," they said. "We have not the heart to kill in cold blood, by the Oath."

Nor would words, nor promise of a tip equal to a week's pay change the minds of these men bred to the hunting of men. Meantime the poor creature settled matters for itself. It walked off into the night and vanished. At dawn we found it in a ravine, stone dead.

Down through the pines we went to the valley where an old woman ran from a house with a gift of cucumbers and words of welcome. Then, by a steep hot climb, we reached the house of *Kapedan* Gjon Marka Gjoni, Hereditary Chieftain of Mirdita and paramount chief of all the Catholic clans of northern Albania. Gjon met us with solemn greetings as we scrambled over the last few yards of rough track. Like his house he is square-built and sturdy. Beneath a white skull cap his hair was close-cropped, his face bronzed. His dress was a collarless shirt, tweed coat and waistcoat and breeches, stockings, elastic-sided boots, and at his waist a dark red sash holding a tobacco box and a silver-mounted pistol from the King.

The house is of stone, whitewashed, with narrow iron-barred windows, standing enclosed by rough wooden palings 2,000 feet above the valley of the Fani-i-vogël river. It was built in 1925, much in the style of a Scottish highland farm. By it are plots of maize and scrub but no big trees. Before it, beyond the valley, lie tumbled hills of light brown loam mottled with scrub and smudged, here and there, with sombre pine forests. Behind it the mountain goes up yet more steeply to the crags of *Mali* Shenjt (the Holy Mountain), so called because the famous Abbot of the Mirditi, Primo Doçi, built on its summit a small wooden house and chapel for his use in summer. Behind those crags lies a wide grassy plateau, rich pasture, hemmed by great fir trees; and on the mountain's eastern side are the tall forests and fertile plain of Lurja.

We sat under an arbour of oak branches for coffee while Gjon talked of himself, his land and his clansmen. He is *Kapedan* of nearly 20,000 Mirditi. He could raise 5,000 fighting men from his own clan in three days and as many more from neighbouring clans within a week if the cause was popular.

Two legends tell the origin of the name Mirditë. Some say that once there lived three brothers whose

Gjon Marka Gjoni, his Sons, and the "Master of Ceremonies"

(See p. 100)

father left nothing when he died but a saddle and a winnowing sieve. The eldest son took the saddle (*shalë*), the next the sieve (*shoshë*), and the youngest went his way empty-handed, wishing his more fortunate brothers *mir ditë* (good day). This legend gives the three clans —Shala, Shoshi and Mirdita—a common ancestor, and they still consider themselves all one family so do not intermarry. In Shala and Shoshi the *Kapedan* of Mirdita is looked upon as a kind of "head of the family" and is widely respected. The other legend is that the Mirditi fought for the Turks at the Battle of Kosova and after the victory the Sultan exclaimed to their chief: "*mir ditë!*"

The Mirditi are divided into the *bajraks* of Oroshi, Spaçi, Kushneni, Fani and Dibrri. The three first say they fled from the Turks early in the fifteenth century, coming here from the Pestriku mountains in Hashi (near Djakova) which points to Serb origin. (The present inhabitants of Hashi, Moslems, are not related to them.) In Mirdita they found and adopted the *bajraks* of Fani and Dibrri who differ in type, being darker and smaller. The neighbouring Kthela clan (divided into the *bajraks* of Kthela, Perlati and Selati) afterwards joined their group. When the Turks took Shkodër and threatened the Mirditi from the west they fled back again, they say to the Pestriku mountains and only established themselves finally in Mirdita in the middle of the seventeenth century. They claim Lek Dukagjin as an ancestor and because Lek and Skenderbeg were related the Mirditë women wear the *xhurdin* as well as their men. Lek was succeeded by his nephew Pal-i-bardh from whom the Montenegrin clan of Bijelopavliç (Sons of White Paul) claim descent.

The Mirditi were constantly at war, either against the Turks or with them against the Montenegrins. Though nominally under Turkey they paid no taxes and were independent in all but name. The founder of the present line of chieftains was one Marka Gjon, who assumed the title and position of *Kapedan* in 1700.

Hughes, describing a review by Ali Pasha of his army at Janina, wrote:

"The troops which struck us most in this assemblage were the Miriditi or Mirditës, the bravest of all the tribes settled in Albania, who wear the red shawl and the vest à la Tancrede . . . and can arm 10,000 men against an invading enemy. . . . They acknowledge the nominal authority of the pasha of Scutari and send him a small annual tribute, but they never admit his troops within their territories. The predecessor of their present chief was treacherously assassinated in the very palace of Scutari: this one never enters the pasha's dominions without an escort of 300 men, 50 of whom attend him in the audience chamber with their hands upon the triggers of their muskets, ready to fire upon the first appearance of treason. . . . Ali recruited his Mirditë detachments by distributing presents to their leaders and by offering double pay."

The present *Kapedan* Gjon's great-grandfather, Kol Prenka, who greatly distinguished himself against the Russians in 1829, was killed by his cousin Skender in a feud. But Skender had not taken account of Kol's wife, which was his mistake. This lady shot Skender and both his sons, then retired to a cave to escape death at the hands of Skender's relations. Her son, Bib Doda, succeeded to the *Kapedancy*, but his wife neglected to bear him an heir—and, being Catholics, there could be no divorce; so his mother came forth from her cave and shot the barren girl! No wonder the son of this she-devil was strong enough to violate the Mirditë tradition that any man of the clan who married a Moslem must leave Mirdita! He carried off from Lurja a beautiful Moslem, had her baptised Maria Angela, and had by her a son, Prenk (Peter), and a daughter who became a nun at Shkodër.

Towards the Turks Bib Doda was equally daring. He defied them openly, planning independence. The Porte tried to buy his obedience with the title of Pasha, but his price was higher. So in 1868 he was induced to go for negotiations to Shkodër and there assassinated. The Turks would not let Prenk, who was being educated at Constantinople, return to Mirdita; but the Mirditi became so threatening that at length they had to let him go.

In the war between Turkey and Montenegro in 1876 the Mirditi played no part but the Turks learnt that they were again planning independence (in agreement with the Serbs and Montenegrins). So when an armistice released the Turkish forces on the frontier eight battalions marched into Mirdita, supported by Moslems of Djakova Ljuma and Mati, devastated the district, and burnt Prenk's house. Orosh, a flourishing village of a hundred houses, was ruined; and now there is no village, though houses are dotted about the mountain-sides. Prenk escaped and took a lead in the Albanian League which strove to resist the provisions of the Treaty of Berlin and establish Albanian autonomy. In 1881, however, the Turks thought Prenk was growing too powerful. So one day at Shkodër he was invited by Dervish Pasha to inspect a Turkish warship off Shëngjin. Against the advice of friends he accepted, and once he was aboard the warship carried him into exile. For twenty-eight years he was held in Turkey, at the last in Constantinople as A.D.C. to the Sultan with the title of Pasha; but Austria-Hungary and France prevailed upon the Porte to leave Mirdita free and the clan was held together by its Abbot, Primo Doçi.

Doçi, a Mirditë, exiled by the Turks, spent some years in Newfoundland as a priest, then at Bombay where he used to hear confessions in English. In 1886 he came back and planted at Orosh an oasis of culture. Though the old Benedictine Abbey of St. Alexander—patron Saint of Mirdita—had long disappeared, he succeeded to the title *Abbatë*. He built a big house and a church—the largest in the mountains. The labour of such building in this roadless land must have been enormous! He died during the World War.

When the Midhat Constitution was restored in July, 1908, the Mirditi would not accept it until Prenk was sent back to them; but he was no success, for in twenty-eight years a wide gap had opened between him and his clansmen. In June, 1911, the Mirditi rose in spite of Prenk, proclaimed autonomy, attacked Lesh, and defeated a Turkish force sent against them. In May, 1912, they again beat the Turks who thereafter left them alone. They took no part in the Balkan War. Prenk planned a Mirditë principality—of Mirdita, Lesh, and the Zadrima—under Serbian protection, and the Serbs gave him money to bribe his clansmen on the understanding that they should have a way to the sea through Mirdita. The formation of an Albanian principality under Prince Wilhelm frustrated this plan; and under Prenk the Mirditi made some show of supporting the prince against Greeks and rebels, though Prenk and his family were very half-hearted about it. In October, 1914, Mirdita repulsed Essad Pasha's troops and stayed autonomous under Prenk who presided over the governing committee of Shkodër and negotiated with both Slavs and Italians. When the Austro-Hungarians occupied Shkodër in January, 1916, Prenk retired to Mirdita; and in December, 1918, he became vice-Premier of the Albanian Provisional Government. In 1920, while travelling with Eden and several Mirditi through Bregumatit (round the mouth of the Mati river), the party was ambushed by the brothers Soko to whom Prenk owed blood. Prenk had incurred this inconvenient debt eight years before by bringing

CLANS AND CHIEFTAINS

about the murder of Djeto Soko. He had resented the growing power of the Sokos, who were Selcë (Klementi) clansmen, and in about Lesh which Prenk's family had ruled for generations, although the Klementi clansmen had winter pasturage rights there. Crying out: "Where is Prenk?" the assailants opened fire. The old *Kapedan* and his men were killed but Eden escaped with a wound in the arm.

Prenk's heir was Marka Gjoni, his first cousin and father of the present *Kapedan*; but Prenk, knowing his cousin to be unpopular and believing the days of chieftains were gone, had disinherited him and left the property to the clan. But Marka would not abandon his rights and was encouraged by the French. He refused an administrative post offered by the Albanian government, and in April, 1921, went to Prizren for Yugoslav aid. This aid was readily given because the Yugoslavs planned an autonomous Mirdita under their suzerainty. Furnished with money Marka returned to Mirdita. He tried to stir the clansmen against the government, and his plans were made easier by the government's threat to tax the whole country equally—whereas the Mirditi had never paid taxes—and to interfere with liberties they had always enjoyed. Nevertheless, Marka won over only the *bajrak* of Orosh. The others stayed quiet, their *bajraktars* and priests reaffirming their loyalty to the Tirana government. But from Prizren the Yugoslavs proclaimed a Mirditë republic in Marka's name, and supplied him with arms and irregular reinforcements until he had with him 1,300 men. In July he routed some government troops, but reinforcements were sent, Marka driven over the border, his house and some sixty others at Orosh burnt. In October the Yugoslavs invaded most of northern Albania, but through British intervention they were forced to withdraw again. Marka, with his son (the present *Kapedan*) and about fifty adherents, fled with the retiring Yugoslavs and remained in exile until December, 1924.

When Zogu was in Yugoslavia in 1924 he asked Marka Gjoni's co-operation against Fan Noli's government, promising he would recognise Marka as hereditary *Kapedan* of Mirdita. Marka gave his support. But Zogu, once in power, said he would make him a colonel or a prefect but could not recognise him as *Kapedan* because that would set awry his uniform administration. But Marka would have nothing else. He died in 1925. His son, Gjon (born in 1886), is *Kapedan de facto*, and is recognised as such by the Mirditi and other Catholic clansmen but not by the central government who have, nevertheless, compromised in practice. Invited by Zogu, Gjon went to Tirana for the proclamation of the kingdom; and he has sworn to support the government in war, so young Mirditi are sent for military service. But no more would the Mirditi do. Mirdita remains a last stronghold of feudalism in Europe.

"We pay no taxes," Gjon told me. "We never have, nor do we see why we should until the government are of use to us. We have supported ourselves for generations and can still do so. Nor will our men work on the roads. When the government builds roads in Mirdita we will labour on them, but we will not build other people's roads for them." No order by the Prefect could take effect without Gjon's consent, and commune officials were chosen by the people and approved by Gjon. As there were no roads, only enough corn and other produce was grown for the clan's needs and a margin for exports against very modest imports. In winter the flocks must go to the lowlands by Tirana and Lesh since Mirdita is under deep snow. There are many wolves, a few bears, ibex, chamois and wild goats.

WOMEN OF MIRDITA

(*See p.* 107)

CLANS AND CHIEFTAINS

Mirdita still abides by Lek Dukagjin's laws which are modified at need by the official codes. "But the new laws only confuse us," said Gjon. Of feuds there are almost none and they caused only four deaths in Mirdita in 1929. But only six weeks before our arrival Gjon had been nearly killed for blood himself. The cause of the trouble was the commonest one—an infant betrothal. When the time came for the couple to marry, the girl would not have her man—from whose parents hers had doubtless taken her price long since; nor would she swear perpetual virginity which alone would free her. So she fled to Gjon, whose mother sheltered her until he could send her safely to Shkodër. The outraged bridegroom and his father scrambled down the mountain-side behind Gjon's house and fired at Gjon through a window. But they missed and were chased away. A few days later they cut off Gjon's water, then lay in ambush, but they were outwitted and overpowered. Such cases were difficult, because if a girl refused the man her parents had chosen and eloped with another, the man she went off with was held guilty of abduction; and for abduction a man was liable to imprisonment by the authorities and owed blood under the laws of the mountains too. Now the government is trying to stop infant betrothals.

Mirdita had its own laws for regulating blood vengeance within the clan. Vengeance cost the avenger a fee for his privilege of five Turkish pounds and an ox, payable to the *Kapedan* immediately the blood debtor was killed. Then a council was called to settle what further fee should be paid—it ranged from ten to twenty sheep or goats. But the blood-taker's house was not burnt, as was the custom in other clans. Then, to compound the feud, a further sum was paid to the house of the dead man. So the whole affair cost about sixty pounds—a very considerable sum in the mountains and a strong deterrent from quarrels over trifles but no big price for unblemished honour. A rule peculiar to Mirdita was that except within twenty-four hours of a feud's starting (when the wronged man's blood would be hot) the life of the actual offender only might be taken and not that of any relative. Of course these restrictions did not apply to blood-taking outside the clan.

Both Mirdita and Kthela used to be notorious for cattle-lifting, a hundred head being no uncommon haul from the plains in a successful raid. Yet the old trade route from Prizren to Shkodër was protected by Mirditë gendarmerie who did their job well enough when paid—and they were said to be the only gendarmerie whom the Turks paid regularly, because if their money was ever much in arrears they held up all traffic until they had it.

Our room in Gjon's house was comfortable with tables, wooden chairs, one iron bedstead, carpets, a gramophone (from the Italian Minister) and a big metal lamp hanging from a ceiling of stained boards. On the whitewashed walls were crude photographs of Gjon's father and mother and other family groups, much like those in any English cottage. A big table was spread with a cloth and there were even table napkins! Gjon's chief man attended us—a delightful character, a fair-haired highland Scot in type, who seemed to combine the functions of personal servant, Master of Ceremonies, and Privy Councillor. Over a collarless shirt he wore a coat and waistcoat *à la Franka*; but his baggy white linen trousers were like pyjamas and his shirt tails hung from beneath a red sash at his waist. In the sash were a revolver and a silver tobacco box. He never stirred from the house without his rifle.

Gjon's sons, lithe silent youths, waited upon us in true medieval fashion, directed by the Master of Ceremonies. The eldest, Mark, had married here only six weeks before with all the pageantry which has always characterised the wedding of the *Kapedan* of Mirdita's heir. Stirling wrote in *The Times* this account of the event:

"It was a wonderful sight to see the escort of tall, gaunt mountaineers crossing single file, with the bride in the midst of them, riding a white horse and enveloped in a scarlet silk veil. Two days she had had to ride blindfolded, for none may see her face until she arrives. Nearing the house the escort fired again and again, and the noise, as the 900 or 1,000 guests replied with their rifles, was deafening.

"On the following day the bride is unveiled and she receives the salutations of the guests, but she must remain as motionless as a stone statue and never raise her eyes from the ground. This custom is rigidly enforced, even in the presence of her husband's family, and continues until either she has a child or another bride is brought to the house. Immediately after the unveiling she is taken in procession to a spring, where she fills a pitcher of water, returns to the house, and pours water for each and every member of the family as a symbol of her obedience and duty to her husband's kin. . . .

"The festivities lasted for six days and guests arrived all day long, each and all, rich and poor, bringing gifts, generally cattle ranging from six to eight bullocks down to one small lamb. However, all were welcomed alike. After a salute of rapid fire from all the men guests the women came out, in their multi-coloured embroidered robes, to form a lane through which the new arrivals passed while the women sang the song of welcome. There were over a thousand guests; and 700 people sat down to dinner nightly; 5,000 cups of Turkish coffee were served one morning before luncheon, and the consumption of raki, the potent spirit of the country, ran to 400 or 500 quarts a day. The religious ceremony, on the third day after the bride's arrival, was very simple, only near relatives being present. Bride and bridegroom, dressed in gorgeous tribal costume, made an impressive pair."

The Italians, being keen to win Gjon's friendship (since the passes of Mirdita are strategically important) and to be sure of his support for the present regime in Albania, invited him to Italy soon after my visit. He went, and was received by Mussolini. He is not rich, so he gladly accepted the Italian Government's offer to send Mark to Mondragone College.

We slept comfortably, upon mattresses on the floor; and next morning there was an excellent breakfast of coffee and cakes. Then the Master of Ceremonies led us, by the precarious track which is the only way to and from Gjon's house, to the old home of the Bib Dodas and Marka Gjonis not far away. Destroyed in 1921, part still lay in ruins; but Gjon had rebuilt the less ruinous part, a solid building of grey stone, and let it to the government as a boarding school. Then he asked the government to enlarge it; but the government, who never did more for the mountaineers than they were obliged, pleaded poverty. "Unless they do enlarge it," said Gjon, "I will enlarge it myself and put up the rent." He equipped the school but the government paid the teachers. There were forty-three boarders and twenty-five day boys in five classes. A blackboard, a neat time-table and a row of cots seemed anomalies in this wild land!

Gjon's was the only boarding school in all the northern mountains; and though education is nominally compulsory, not half the children go to school. Boarding schools in the mountains are urgently needed, but the mountaineers have been sadly neglected in favour of the influential lowlanders and townsmen. When the mountains lie in the iron grip of winter, covered deep by trackless snows and roamed by ravening wolves, children cannot tramp miles each day to school. Nor can they go readily in summer, for communities are too widely scattered and distances too great.

Next day my three friends left me, returning to the capital under Abdulla's guidance; and their places were taken by Major Oakley Hill (of the gendarmerie) who joined me here with his wife, his gendarme-orderly Ahmed, and a little *qiraxhi* (dubbed *Tirana*) who bounced and rebounded after his ponies like a piece of india-rubber and spoke in the sonorous nasal tones of the central Albanian lowlander.

CHAPTER V

THE GREAT MOUNTAIN LAND

"May you burst! May the dead eat you, miserable wretch!" quoth Tirana, kicking the hindquarters of the rearmost pony as it grabbed a last mouthful of hay from a pile near the gate of Gjon's enclosure.

"Long life to you! May you go with health! May your way be smooth!" said our hospitable host—the last wish with unintended irony.

We went down steeply past the Abbot's house and the church to the bare valley of the Fani-i-vogël and came to Shëpal (St. Paul), three whitewashed houses together and others casually thrown about within a mile or two in the manner of these mountain places. The local store might have been a remote English village shop, selling candles and tobacco, soap and rice, coffee and *opinga* and other simple needs.

The sub-Prefect welcomed us in his office, which was decorated by an Albanian flag and a tawdry coloured print of King Zog (like an old-fashioned illustration from a child's first picture book) which must hang in every official place. He seemed anxious that the gendarmerie should guard us well, for some Tirana authorities imagined an attack upon an Englishman might serve the political ends of the country's foreign enemies by bringing discredit upon Albania. But the chance of any such incident befalling a traveller is very remote, except possibly in the wild frontier districts

Fording the Fani Gojanit River (See p. 112)

where outlaws, who in Turkish times dared hunt richer grounds, still find refuge.

Climbing next day to Spaç gendarmerie post (1,500 feet), we went on by friable scratches on a crumbling mountain-side then down a narrow valley through woods and meadows to Khalivare's little church in a clump of trees. At the priest's house there were two priests, one an Italian Jesuit—though most of them are Albanians trained at Shkodër and Rome. Khalivare, said the Jesuit, wanted a new church, for which the Italians had given a bell. His colleague said he would ride with us, so forth he came in his black cassock and "yachting cap" with half a loaf of brown bread under his arm and mounted a sturdy pony.

Now we came into the valley of the Fani Gojanit and splashed through its shallow river. A string of crimped basins holding meadows and maize fields are linked by defiles and bounded by abrupt mountain-sides of friable red earth from which the rain has swept or sun scorched all but the hardiest shrubs and a few stunted oaks. At the head of this valley is *Çafa* Malit (the Pass of the Mountain) leading over to great beech forests. This way struggled in tragic retreat a great part of the shattered Serbian Army in December, 1915. The clansmen let them pass unopposed, though a cruel winter took a heavy toll of them.

Next morning, by a track high up and often less than eighteen inches wide we reached Shëmija (a scattered place like Shëpal), and found the land about us, on other days so empty, alive with mountain folk gathering for a religious festival. They trickled down the mountain-sides like strings of tiny white beads and grouped in two masses, several hundreds of them, before the little stone church which could never hold them all. The women were in their best white robes; over those they wore long white coats, coarse and sleeveless, open in front and embroidered at edges with red: black bodices: fringes of red wool at their waists: coloured cloths on their heads: chains of gold and silver coins about their necks. They faced my camera with shy giggles. The men were all unarmed, some in *alla Franka* jackets, or military tunics which were booty of the war.

An Italian company prospecting for copper had driven shafts into the hillside and rich copper deposits are being worked hereabouts. There is asbestos too.

At Fusha Arshit, a place of fruit trees and corn between bare mountains on the old trade route to Prizren, the gendarmerie post commander warned us gravely that the forest of Iballja was dangerous, so we must take four of his men—making our armed strength seven. An obtuse schoolteacher, a townsman full of fears, urged a detour through Puka, a long and dreary route we would not take—though Puka is historic, the Roman *Epicaria*, and at Komani many Illyrian remains have come to light. But the whole land is strewn thick with antique ruins. At Puka the Turks kept a military post and a a *kaimakam* who collected such taxes as the clansmen ever thought fit to pay.

At Kryezezë that night heavy rain drove us to seek shelter in the church-house, which stood by a graveyard of rough crosses with birds rudely carved upon them. The priest was away; but his aged sister put a room and her kitchen at our disposal and brewed sickly herb tea to drink with evil-smelling native cheese. There was a pile of begrimed mattresses to sleep on and strings of tobacco leaves upon the walls. Chickens had used the room before us, so there were fleas in serried ranks, all happy at our coming, and many of them travelled several days with us. Ali Pasha's physician once said truly that the Albanian flea is the fattest and largest in the world. We took half a dozen different opinions on the state and distance of our way to Iballja and slept on them in spite of the fleas.

In a drizzle of rain we trekked on next day through a great silent forest—giant pines mostly, but sometimes firs or beeches or oaks. All about was rotting timber, and in parts fires had cleared the undergrowth and sadly charred the gaunt trunks, for the people take no care of their trees, letting fires burn and felling without thought. First we went up steeply, then down as steeply over slippery pine needles and herbs, each of us hanging to a pony by its tail to brake it. Then up again, the ponies climbing like cats. Our escorting gendarmes begged us to keep together. Two of them went always ahead, two brought up the rear with me; and if I delayed, one of them stayed by me. Two ponies caught their loads against a tree, an uncommon accident which they walk always on the outermost edge of a track to avoid. Both went down into a shallow ravine in a heap but neither was hurt. At last we emerged into a wide glen, Iballja's little white houses set about it among maize fields, its hilltops cut to a plane by sullen clouds. A cairn topped by a cross marked the death-scene of some feud's victim.

This cold wet night we wanted a roof and warmth, so we sought out the *kryeplak* (Chief Elder) of the place who sent us to a house where rude wooden steps outside led up to a gloomy room with light from four loopholes. Its floor was of mud but there was place for a good fire. The beams of its roof had been daubed by a hand dipped in white paint and laid flat along them in regular pattern. The chamber beneath, meant for animals, had no loopholes even, yet it sheltered a family with many chickens, goats and children and an outsize in smells. The hand pattern had significance, for Iballja is part of Berisha where there is magic in the imprint of a man's hand. Long ago, goes the legend, a man buried vast treasure, then left his hand's imprint in a soft rock near the spot. The rock hardened. So the imaginative still find that imprint sometimes, but the treasure never.

While we were washing at a stream close to our door an old man approached. "You should go inside now," he warned, "because it is getting dark and brigands may come down from the mountains." The commune secretary said the same, begging that we would not stir from the house before daybreak. In Iballja the rule still held that none should go out until there is light enough to see a man's head among the bushes. There had been eight murders hereabouts in three months, and five napoleons (£4) would buy any man's blood.

Hill, meantime, inspected the gendarmerie post. His uniform and nationality drew to him everyone with a woe wherever we stayed. A youth came to play wild tunes on a native banjo, an elaborately chip-carved and painted affair with three strings; and we bought *çarapi*, the native socks, which are beautiful with bright intricate patterns, those for men with pointed tops stiff with black braid and shaped like the soft leather shoes worn in medieval times. Ahmed slept across the door to guard us that night.

Going down next day through a fine forest of beech and oak, groves of big chestnut trees and gullies grown over with brambles, we came to the post at Fierza. Below was the Drin, which here starts into narrow ravines and precipitous clefts through which it flows until near Shkodër, but eastward to Kukës its course lies through gentler country thick with forests. Opposite us, the great mountains were flaked with patches of maize and dotted with rare *kulas*.

We crossed the river by a ferry. Ferries are few, and between the antique five-arched *Ura* Vezirit and Shkodër

Crossing the Drin Near Fierza

(See p. 116)

there is no bridge. The ferry boat was made of two hollowed tree trunks with pointed prows of planks, fastened together with a gap between them which was boarded over for a seat. The two ferrymen steered with big paddles across the swift current diagonally. Our ponies swam across.

We were now in the lands of Merturi. Merturi and Berisha claim to be the oldest clans in the mountains. Tall, fair, blue-eyed men, a common type here, came, they say, from Bosnia in the fifteenth century, fleeing before the Turks, and either drove out or intermarried with the short dark people here before them.

In a wide stony river-bed, beside a dashing stream of crystal water which contrasted strikingly with the muddy Drin it joined, we decided to bivouac, for the way ahead was hard. Walled by wooded heights this was a glorious though somewhat mysterious place, filled with the noise of tumbling water. Our two gendarmes from Fierza had been strongly opposed to our staying here, saying the people of Raja were robbers and savages—probably because they had friends in Raja but could not go to them without us. The commander of Raja post, on the mountain above, sent two of his men to reinforce them for the night. Some women tripped down through the shadows with a cask of spring water, bread, eggs and milk, and were hardly persuaded to take a few coins for them. "You are guests in our land," they protested. But alas! Their milk was goats'. Possibly Albanian goats give peculiar cause for the filthy taste of their milk.

An hour through hay in the valley brought us to the foot of *Çafa* Kolshit as the river mist which had enveloped and saturated us melted before the sun, unveiling a towering peak cut sharp against blue sky and a daunting climb to 5,000 feet. It was hard labour at first, but there were springs enough, and clumps of big chestnut trees to shade us when we rested. The air lay peacefully, heavy with the hum of bees. Tirana sat on a bank, cross-legged, pushed his white fez to the back of his head, and rolled a cigarette.

"Oh how far I am from my home," he moaned.

Tirana cared for the mountains not at all; and he was ragged unmercifully by the gendarmes who found fun in his dress, his accent and his little size. The gendarmes were mountain men, and the mountaineer has ever despised the lowlander—not without cause, for the lowlander is often far less a man. But Tirana took all their chaffing in good part and got along well with them in spite of it.

Major Muharem (*Bajraktari*), Commandant-General of the Gendarmerie, had passed this way a few days earlier, sent to pacify chieftains who were sore because the government, who up till now had paid them as reserve officers, had decided to pay this premium for their loyalty no longer. Muharem is a chieftain (or *bajraktar*) of Kosova. He had called the other chiefs to the prefecture at Kukës but they cared nothing for his official cloak and sent their horses instead, as a sign of contempt. (In 1935 Muharem himself became rebellious and was chased over the frontier.)

At last we were upon *Çafa* Kolshit and had before us a view of the mountains in all their grandeur. Deep between fearful precipices lay the narrow Nikaj valley, ending in the frontier wall—the Accursed Mountains—a range of great irregular fangs gleaming white in the sun and towering into the hollow silence of their height above a sharp-drawn tree line. The tinkling of sheep bells came from far below. Here lived that famous old chieftain Bajram Curi, who made his last stand at his water mill in the valley with his two sons in 1925 and went down gallantly before Zogu's men. One of our

THE GREAT MOUNTAIN LAND

gendarmes had served with government troops who held Çafa Kolshit for five days against the Dukagjin insurgents during the rebellion of 1926.

Going down through a beech forest we came to a grassy slope by the dark valley's stream. As we off-loaded, the commune president, in rough tweeds, came by with two armed guards in local rags. He complained that he had been two years in Nikaj and thought that two years too long. From his pocket he pulled a rough bomb, bought in Shkodër for twopence, lit the fuse, then flung it into a pool. The guards plunged after it. Up floated about twenty fish, among them some good trout—a welcome change for our supper.

Breakfast was a meal which always puzzled Ahmed and our notable one next morning staggered him. Told to bring a cup of water he exclaimed: "You have eaten fish, bread, pig, eggs and honey; and now you are thirsty, by the Lord! Drink—and eat less!" Of his meagre pay Ahmed had saved enough to buy a little farm near Korça, and he meant to marry and settle down—he was preparing by buying women's clothing whenever he could acquire it cheaply! Naturally, his wife had to fit the clothes. He found one such and all was going well; but at the last her parents' price for her was more than Ahmed would pay.

Generally the Albanian is honest so long as he dwells far enough from civilisation and when the clans ruled themselves the Elders imposed heavy punishments for thefts. Cattle and girl lifting from neighbouring clans were not theft but good business—and good amusement too. The mountaineers had no other amusements save feuds, for they do not dance and they sing no songs but those of strife. But the Nikaj post commander set a guard of six men over us, for the Nikaj people, about 1,600 souls, have long been notorious for lawlessness. Miss

Durham found them not even obedient to their own Elders, wretchedly poor, knowing no law but that of their own most primitive instincts, crying for a government with power to save them from themselves. Nominally they are Christians, believing in the cross as a charm against the abundant devils of the place. They tell that long ago a shepherd called Nikol came over *Çafa* Kolshit from Krasniç and settled in Nikaj (Krasniç was Christian then and claims to have fled from Bosnia, but is now a Moslem clan having a long record of feuds with Nikaj). None would marry Nikol's ugly daughter; but at last she bore a son by a gypsy whom Nikol accepted as her husband, and from them are descended the *bajrak* of Curi at the head of the valley. Another part of Nikaj traces origin from Klementi.

There is a direct way to Shala from Nikaj, over *Çafa* Nermandjesh, but we preferred to go by *Çafa* Agrit. Upward steadily we went through maize plots, chestnut groves and oak scrub until high above the Drin's clefts. Men were cutting and stacking oak leafage for fodder; one of them, almost naked, had his head all shaven save a patch of long hair on the crown. There are several hair styles among the clansmen; and among the Christians the first shaving is a more important rite than baptism. Girls are shaved too, except always a fringe over the forehead. This hair-dressing probably caused Von Hahn to write of the Albanians: "There are two kinds of them, those with goats' tails and those with little horses' tails."

The track now became all that was bad and much that was dangerous. In parts it was but a foot wide above a precipice, and in such places ponies generally elect to scratch their ears with their hind legs. There was a long toil upward through the grateful shade of a beech forest, our six escorting gendarmes ever watchful and suspicious

THE GREAT MOUNTAIN LAND

of every bush; and as we came near the pass a fresh escort from the other side rushed to meet us, embracing and rubbing cheeks with the men from Nikaj post.

Çafa Agrit is a narrow grassy saddle breaking forth from a ragged forest of wind-blown beeches which crawls up to it on either side. It is somewhat like a South Down but it is the roof of Albania, its view incomparable. Before us towered the fantastic peaks of the Great Mountain Land, mysteriously blue black as a thunder-cloud, brooding over the ills of this forgotten land unknown to wheels or progress. Defiant they stand, those peaks, in a long serried rank, and defiant they will stand till the end of time. Nearer to us, jostling one another, rose lesser gentler peaks, hemming in and darkening the Shala valley, bearing on their knotty flanks the silent forests and pastures from which primitive men wrest bare existence. Behind us too the ground rolled away sharply beneath turf and trees to the brink of an unseen precipice above the Drin, and beyond the river the cleft face of the Berisha mountain rose sheer from scree and forest. In the dim distance, through a dancing haze, we could see the wide valley eastward, and beyond, the peaks of Yugoslav Kosova. From somewhere the sound of cowbells rose from the still green valley's depths, reassuring dazed senses that this scene was real.

In the evening, when the sun went down, blue-black gave way to pink, and the crags and pinnacles and gulleys betrayed themselves by purple shadows; and the lesser peaks, and the valley, changed chameleon-like from deep green through indigo to velvet-black. Then, here and there, a watch-fire like a low-hung star came out and twinkled through the night.

In a glade of the smoothest turf on a shoulder below the col we pitched our camp; and we agreed to spend a day here, for we wished to watch this scene in all its moods. There were butterflies of many kinds, dragon-flies, scarlet-winged grasshoppers, and pale mauve crocuses set about the mossy carpet where we lay. It was cold, at nearly 5,000 feet, but there was wood for a hundred fires, and water trickled among the trees. Our new escort—four fine cheerful fellows—readily fell in with our plan, though we had expected protests in the usual vein.

In the morning, from where I lay in my sleeping-bag, I watched the peaks above the dawn's grey mists flush pink, then glow like burnished copper in the sun's first warmth. After a chill wash and breakfast and a spreading out of bedding to air, we climbed again to the col for photographs; but the scene was too vast for mere man-made things. Peasants trickled by—in parties, none alone—delaying for a word with us, all of them desperately poor but all mannerly. Some were on their way to Shkodër, a two-days' journey, with cattle to sell—their bitter complaint was that they had no road. Others were going to the church at Theth to burn candles in memory of the dead. One party asked if we were doctors. There was no doctor nearer than Shkodër, they said.

Talk turned on the revolt of November, 1926. A gendarme said it was stirred up from across the border, easily, for the clansmen were poor and ill-content, many wishing for a Christian President instead of Moslem Zogu. A clansman by us took up the tale. "The cause was simple," said he. "We were sore with grievances then, just as we are now. The government did nothing for us and the officials they sent among us were bad. —they did not understand us. It is the same now. And when a man is so discontented he listens to all who give him counsel. In all Dukagjin there were only 500 licensed rifles but we had others hidden, and many more, and ammunition, were sent over the frontier to us. Three Albanian officers came from the south and told us to rise. We marched upon Shkodër but we were beaten when we were nearly there. Then the soldiers came and burnt our houses, so now we are poorer than before. Some of our leaders were caught—others fled across the frontier."

I was told that there were 8,000 insurgents but this I doubt. Mirdita and Klementi had planned to rise with the other Catholic clans but the others rose a day earlier than agreed, so Mirdita and Klementi stayed quiet. The Yugoslav Press declared that Italy had organised the revolt to stampede Zogu into signing the Pact of Tirana and the clansmen had Italian rifles; but in Tirana the general conviction was that it was organised by certain Yugoslav authorities with the aid of Albanian enemies of the present regime but without King Alexander's knowledge.

Several who talked to us complained bitterly of their poverty and the government's neglect. "True," said one, "we have not yet paid taxes—King Zog knows we are poor and has let us off. He is a good man trying to do good for our country; but we feel, sometimes, that he has forgotten us. Yes, tell the King we feel he has forgotten us and does not trust us." When, afterwards, I gave this message to the King he admitted the government had neglected the mountain people. "I feel very ashamed of it sometimes," he added frankly. "Our only excuse is that we cannot do everything at once."

Big black clouds were rushing up from the west and thunder muttered moodily behind the heights. So we set up our tents and cut trenches to carry off the water. The storm came on in the evening, putting out the last light. It was fantastic, like a nightmare. Vivid flashes rent the blackness. The thunder rolled heavily round the peaks, thrown back and forth by the echoes till its crashing was a continuous roar; and the rain battered on the canvas of the tents furiously, as if mad at being baulked of us. Wrapped in their British khaki greatcoats beneath dripping trees our gendarmes lay before a great fire and laughed.

The lord of the pasture, Pal Mirashi (he who had the grazing rights), came up in the rain next day and asked us to his house an hour away. "We are only poor mountain men but what we have we will give you—bread, salt, and our hearts." We accepted gladly because we could not feel easy while our uncomplaining gendarmes lay unsheltered. It was a typical *kula*, high on the mountainside among big trees. Beneath were the animals' winter quarters, and a ladder led above to a smoke-blackened chamber with big rafters, rude stone walls, loopholes and rough-hewn floor-planks. A fire on a big hearth lit the gloom. Of furniture there was none but a *sofra*.

This place was Vuksanaj, three *kulas* together, and most of Vuksanaj crowded upstairs with us. The head of the house was a proud old man, gnarled and ragged, with an eagle eye and a white moustache, who claimed to be a twenty-first descendant of Lek Dukagjin whose laws he still obeyed. His daughter, who sat smoking on a wooden stool, was crippled physically and mentally. The old man lit her cigarettes. We had a string of questions fired at us as we sat on the floor for coffee. How much money did we make? Why had we no children? Had we any brothers? Were our sisters married? How many children had they? What did our parents do? What were their names? And so on. But they readily answered the questions we asked.

They hated the Serbs. When they came in 1915 they looted and burnt, so there were many skirmishes. But the Austro-Hungarians were almost as bad—they

PAL MIRASHI (CENTRE) WITH HIS FATHER AND FRIENDS
(*See p.* 124)

took cattle and sheep at their own poor price and they made the people work. So when they were retreating in 1918 the mountaineers rose and entered Shkodër with the French.

Pal Mirashi visited me in Tirana that winter, bringing with him a friend—a stalwart merry fellow with an unruly top-knot of hair in the middle of his shaven poll. Both were in mountain dress and drew exclamations of admiration from an Italian officer who had little but amused contempt for the Tirana Albanians. They behaved with a quiet dignity and ate with a natural ease, though sitting at table must have seemed as strange to them as crouching by a *sofra* was to me. They showed a childlike interest in everything—books, clock, gramophone—but in no way were they clumsy. They were pathetically grateful for the shelter of my sitting-room where they slept on rugs before the fire and took a touching farewell—Pal giving me a sudden and resounding kiss upon my neck. They were looking for work and were offered it upon the roads—but that was more than their pride could bear. They would be foremen—but labourers under some lowlander? No, they could never do that!

That night at Vuksanaj they did us well. There was *raki*, a pile of excellent hot dough cakes and a bowl of honey, fried rice and a chicken. The old man tore the chicken for us with his fingers. Suspecting that the cracks in the floor and crannies in the walls might harbour scorpions we asked, before spreading our bedding, if there were any. Our hosts were as shocked as a suburban housewife would be if asked whether she had cockroaches in her kitchen. "No, none," said they emphatically. But there was one, which Pal picked from the wall with chips of wood. "That is the first we have ever seen in this house," he lied, for we killed another before we slept.

Next morning Vuksanaj escorted us to the spring to wash. Then a pretty girl in full Shala dress shyly stood for my camera. She wore a brown and orange shawl over her head: a heavy woollen skirt, black, bell-shaped: a black apron heavily fringed with wool and richly embroidered with gold thread, and another (half length) behind even more richly embroidered: a black blouse with wide sleeves: heavy fringes of wool on her shoulders: and at her waist a thick leather belt with silver studs. From her neck hung a chain of gold and silver coins and her fingers bore several large barbaric rings.

We went down steeply through oak trees and scrub to *Llumi* Shalës, a shallow river among tumbled boulders which we followed up-stream to Abatë post. The valley is rocky, with scrub and fir trees, but we had lost the high peaks behind the enclosing spurs. A precipitous though well-worn *shkallë* brought us to a higher level by the old abandoned church at Theth.

It was bitterly cold and blowing a gale down the valley. We went to the post, a snug clean place with ten gendarmes: its commander, in British khaki, smart as a good British N.C.O. One of the men brought coffee while Hill looked into pay, communications, water supply, clothing and all the kindred administrative details of a post.

Not so long ago Shala was renowned for blood-taking and proud of it (though Mati and Toplana held the record). Twelve men once died at Abatë because of one's loss of a cartridge which he accused another of taking, and seventeen were shot at Okol in dispute over the size of a star. Disease, as everywhere in the mountains, added heavily to these casualties and the infant death-rate was frightful, so it is astonishing the race survives. Shala had a weakness for raiding too and used to carry off many

"Mali" Herapit (left) and "Cafa" Pes

(See p. 127)

girls, cattle, or sheep from its neighbours. But now Shala was peaceful and the local brigands had all been driven out. Murders or crimes of any sort were rare. And there were very few rifles in the valley—too few for safety from wolves and brigands, said the people.

We went to the church-house to call on the Franciscan, Father Sajakaj, a kind old man in a brown cassock who gave us *raki* in his comfortable little room and asked us to stay. Unfortunately the gendarmes had already arranged that we should sleep in a house at Okol. There are ninety-six Franciscans in Albania. This one's house and church, which are all one building, high and wide-eaved in a style somewhat like Swiss chalets, had been burnt down the year before and King Zog had subscribed towards rebuilding it.

As we left the house a massive rocky peak glowed in the sun's last rays like a molten mass from a giant's furnace. Then the clouds shut down over the valley like a lid, and before we reached Okol driving rain on the wings of a gale was lashing the trees and swelling the stream to a riot of tumbling water. We rounded a spur, and it seemed that we had come to the end of the world for we looked into a *cul-de-sac* of stark grim precipices rising from black smudges of pine forest. A perfect natural frontier to a wild land. On the right was the Jesera group's mass of rocky buttresses: on the left a great wall curiously lined with almost horizontal strata, crowned by a cone-shaped peak, *Mali* Herapit of the Radohina group, towering to almost 9,000 feet; and between these a precipitous track to Gusinje in Yugoslavia crosses Çafa Pes. Thirty years ago Gusinje was a most dangerous district, its inhabitants Moslems who resented any foreign intrusion, and constant were the frays between these fanatics and their Christian neighbours of Shala.

By some wooden steps and through a smoke-blackened unlighted chamber—where a woman was baking bread in wood ashes on the hearth—we reached a clean room with wooden ceiling and two small windows. Our host, a tall man in native dress, seemed displeased that we had been foisted upon him by the gendarmerie, but he had to put up with us all next day for it poured with rain. Our house was one of several, all of them well built of stone with steep roofs of wooden tiles; they were dotted about not far apart upon a sloping space covered by terraced maize fields. On one side of this space were steep-rising screes below great precipices, and on the other side the wide rocky bed of the valley's stream.

The Frontier Guard detachment commander here, a lieutenant from Dibra, was glad to see someone from the outer world. He told us mournfully how he was laying in six months' stores because, for most of the winter, the rough house which sheltered him and his detachment was cut off by twelve feet of snow. There was no telephone. He had a gramophone and a few books to pass the time. In summer the detachment mans a frontier post on *Çafa* Pes but in winter snow guards the pass more surely than man. There are only two ways over the frontier between *Çafa* Pes and Vermosh, neither of them passable by mountain artillery or heavy packs; and between Vermosh and *Han* Grabom there are at most two ways across, equally difficult. A month earlier some Austrian mountaineers had been to Theth which delighted them as a climbing centre—and they wrote of it in the *Swiss Alpine Club Journal* (May, 1932).

Towards the next midday the lagging clouds, which had rolled and broken in the eddies as they smudged and swathed the upper precipices, suddenly withdrew and the straggling wisps thinned and melted as the sun broke through the greyness. So we set out to cross *Çafa*

On the Way to Bogë

(See p. 129)

e Shtegut të Dhenvet (the Pass of the Sheep Path). Soon we had passed through a beech forest and came upon a vast scree sweeping down between the bases of the immense rock peaks on either hand, and our track climbed over the scree in an agony of zigzags. The ponies panted and stumbled and stopped, then struggled on again, kicking loose stones into space. We laboured upward in an atmosphere of dust and sweating horse flesh and endeavour, each of us behind a pack pony, pushing on the loads to help them and prevent both load and saddle from backsliding to the ground. At last we passed through the great rocks by a cleft which echoed our clattering feet and looked down upon the head of the Bogë valley. Then down we went again, through a forest of great gnarled beeches, stumbling over slippery rocks under the leaves. On our left were imposing crags, a chaos of unexplored pillars and pinnacles and buttresses, and by the wayside a cross stood to the memory of two travellers murdered here by brigands in 1928. In four waterless hours from Okol we reached Bogë and bivouacked near the village spring. Beyond the spring, in a fertile basin deep in the valley, were twenty or thirty little square white houses scattered like thrown dice.

Bogë is a *bajrak* of the Klementi clan which numbers about 6,000 souls divided between the *bajraks* of Selcë, Vuklë, Niksh and Bogë, its lands extending from *Han Grabom* to Vermosh. In 1623 it practically annihilated a Turkish army retreating from Montenegro, but a punitive expedition drove it from its fastnesses. However, it soon came back and attacked the Turks again in 1683. A body of Klementi men shared defeat with the Austrians at Valjevo and fled from Turkish vengeance into Hungary where their descendants still preserve various Klementi customs. The number of the clan's border frays with Montenegrins only its rocks could tell.

Here Hill and I decided we would take two men to carry coats and rucksacks and cross the mountains on foot to Vermosh, the northernmost village of Albania. The remainder of our party would go with the ponies down the valley to Shkrelë, then round to Rapsh where we would rejoin them, because there is no way from Bogë direct to Vermosh for ponies which must go there either from Okol or Rapsh.

But this plan was strongly opposed. First, the post commander said the route from Bogë to Vermosh lay through a very dangerous forest which was unpatrolled and open to the frontier, a haunt of brigands and outlaws. These brigands are mostly fugitives from justice, or injustice, on one side or other of the border. There is water for them, and maize from the valley plots, and a sheep from a flock when chance offers. Their other needs are few, though these may inspire violence when violence might be well repaid. But we over-ruled objections, arguing that as we should have escorting gendarmes and no pack animals an attack upon us would not be worth the candle. Then the *bajraktar*, an old man bent with age, protested that he would not let any of his men go with us because the only rifles in the place could not be spared, and without rifles his men could not go; they would be safe with our escort, but on their way back there was every possibility they would be shot. Bogë was "in blood" with Niksh and Selcë and only a few days before a Selcë man had been shot by a Bogë man (who had got clear away across the frontier). Now, of course, Selcë was all agog to shed Bogë blood and the *bajraktar* saw no point in letting it be shed just because we would not carry our own packs. We agreed —and got over the difficulty by promising his men should come back under escort.

Bogë was short of bread, for the harvest had not been

gathered. But at last some was brought to us at the post by an old man who not only demanded payment—hitherto our difficulty had been to get the people to take money—but asked threepence too much. The post commander and *bajraktar* were indignant with him and would let him have only the regular price. He went his way muttering and as we ate his bread we felt sorry for him. But next day he was arrested and sent to Shkrelë for trial for defying the Elders by trying to overcharge. Fortunately we heard of this and Hill secured his release.

It was September 26. As sultry dawn came the women of the village gathered at the spring to wash clothes and the sheep, cattle and pigs came down to drink. From a house close at hand a man tried repeatedly to establish communication with someone far away. With hands to mouth and head thrown back he cried for his friend into the still air in a long-drawn-out high-pitched wail, a sound which carries for miles (and thus news is passed). At length he gave up that one and called another from whom came a faint reply out of the distance.

Hill and I set out with two civilian porters and four gendarmes. Our way lay over Çafa Megzes to Kozhni and thence to Vuklë. On the map there was a blank and there was no track to be seen.

We scrambled over steep scree to a beech forest high up; and as we went through it one of our escort, stopping suddenly, pointed to the ground. There was a strip of torn clothing and a crimson stain—the blood the Selcë man shed for Bogë's honour. His murderer had lurked in the shadows and shot him twice at close quarters.

Crossing the brow of the *çafa* we emerged upon a plateau of limestone rocks and holes like a huge sponge, covered by a forest of great beeches and rotting timber. Pushing on, we reached the edge of this deserted wilderness and began to descend through the trees. Then, crossing a pine-clad shoulder, we came clear of the forest and gazed down upon a giant's maze. Below us lay an immense amphitheatre, silent as a cathedral, walled by stark precipices towering from their bases three thousand feet and more. From where we stood a steep bush-grown scree gulley gave access to the depths where, in a strip of green by a spring, sleep three tiny houses which are Kozhni; and from the depths there is but one passage—a narrow ravine. It leads into a great canyon walled by yet higher precipices; and this one joins another, like it, at Tamarë.

We slithered and scrambled down to Kozhni and sat under a tree which rained ripe red fruit upon the soft turf. The sun had gone, long since, from Kozhni's cold depths, though the cliffs high above glared harsh and white in its rays. It was childhood's dream-land—an unwritten place where men play the games of children and dragons lurk in caves. Here the gods of early man reign on, defying civilisation, rewarding tenfold the allegiance of those who pay them homage.

An old man came forth from one of the little houses. "*O civilë*," called a gendarme, "bring us water to drink." So he came, bearing an earthen pitcher, and a handful of tobacco in leaf which the gendarmes cut up on a stone—furtively, asking that we would forget it, because they were not supposed to cut their own tobacco and so escape payment of duty.

Following the stream from the spring we passed the cleft ravine which links Kozhni with the world and came into the sunlight. It was four o'clock. The pools of the stream were so clear that the great fish in them seemed suspended in air between the boulders.

We turned up the hollow canyon by a stony track and soon reached Vuklë post. A shepherd lad was fishing with a willow rod and home-made hook and had a dozen small trout by his side. Up here the people often poison fish with a herb which is put into a bag and beaten, then thrown into a pool. The fish like the milky sap which kills them instantly they take it.

At Vuklë the valley softens and widens. High mountains shut it in and its few houses are scattered unobtrusively on a sloping shelf above the stream. We found it a place of strange characters. The post commander was a decrepit old man whose well-intended incompetence seemed to creak when he moved. Nor could he read or write—but that was neither here nor there because he was a cousin of the commandant-general. The scowling commune guard, scarcely younger, wore native cap, trousers and *opinga*, but his coat was an *alla Franka* antique. His waist was martial with belt of cartridges over a red sash and across his shoulder hung a rifle; but in his hand he carried an umbrella. The president and secretary of the commune shared a kitchen and tiny living room in a rough stone house. The secretary was shabby but alive. The president was a caricature of a man, long and lean, with large flat wandering feet and trousers ending half way up his spindly legs. They took us to their home and fed us and insisted upon turning out of their plank beds for us. They give you their all, these people in the wilderness, and are hurt if you do not accept. They said proudly that there had been only one robbery in Vuklë in eighteen months—not like the prefectures of Kosova and Dibra which were very bad.

We set off in the morning with three gendarmes, the guard with rifle and umbrella, and a civilian carrying our rucksacks. Passing the little stone church where the bells are hung from a tree we climbed steeply and continuously for three hours in drizzling rain which shut out the view. Going over wide-sweeping pastures we crossed Çafa Gjarpenit into a bleak upland valley of grey shale and coarse grass, then up again to Çafa Ponikut (6,790 feet). The rain stopped and the sun came out, filling the air with sweetness from the newly-washed earth. Going through a forest of giant beeches, many of them burnt and gaunt and dead, we descended by Çafa Berdelecit, having a view of cloud-wreathed peaks above a velvety-green valley and dark pines. Water was everywhere plentiful. We met nobody throughout the day. There are few wayfarers in the Albanian mountains, and except shepherds the mountain-folk prudently do not wander far from their homes.

Round a spur we came into the Vermosh valley, a gentle dale lying west to east across the frontier to Gusinje and shut in by beech-wrapped mountain-sides, its soft turf mauve-tinted with crocuses. But we were glad to reach the gendarmerie post and a cluster of houses at the head of the valley, for we had scoured along for eight hours from Vuklë.

Pal and Djeto Preloci threw their house open and gave us a splendid room. A fire burnt on a hooded hearth, there was a ceiling of wood, and a shelf high up laden with bright crockery. On the floor, down one side, carpets and rough embroidered cushions were spread and a metal lamp gave light. We sat on the floor contentedly with our hosts and their sons and their friends and the elder brother's wife gave coffee— she was an intelligent creature in white blouse and black head-wrap. Generally the host manages the coffee, but here women had more rights in the home than is usual in north Albania.

An Italian military surveyor in camp close by, Lieutenant Buonerba, hearing that strangers had arrived, came over to find us—a jovial fellow who seemed intensely popular with everyone. He carried us off to his tents and cooked a meal beyond our wildest dreams in these hard mountains. But back in our room we found three gendarmes and two civilians laid in a row, sleeping noisily, the air thick with a stench from ten bootless unwashed feet. We flung wide the window, then hurriedly buried our noses in the quilts laid ready for us. *Zoja* Preloci tucked us up and put out the light.

Next morning was crisp as an October day in England. The leaves were turning yellow and red, the grass sparkled with dew and there was a faint autumnal mistiness. The valley bed is 3,325 feet above sea level. The gendarmerie post had not been visited by a gendarmerie officer, British or Albanian, for a year, yet was in very good order. The way these little outposts of authority carry on without supervision, from month to month, speaks passing well for the gendarmerie rank and file. Nor was it unusual that the telephone line from this post had been cut for six months.

The men here are tall long-limbed people who stoop to pass their doorways, and there was one man with us who stood quite six feet eight inches. Few places in Europe are so isolated as Vermosh, which belongs to the Selcë *bajrak* of Klementi and has sixty houses. For some twenty weeks each year it is utterly snowbound. Though there was a paper agreement with Yugoslavia whereby the Albanian mountaineers might cross the frontier to market, the Vermosh people might not stir "by the breadth of one finger" beyond the line, so they said. Gusinje is three hours away, easy going down the valley and not far over the frontier; but to Shkodër it is three days under the best conditions—and to Shkodër the people had to go to market when they could.

"Nor are our flocks safe," said they. "A handful of Frontier Guards is all our protection from raiders over the border. Many sheep are stolen and sometimes men are killed." I repeated these tales to one of the Yugoslav Legation in Tirana who replied impatiently that Vermosh "is a nest of brigands who are always raiding us." Probably both are at fault, for these mountaineers have always raided each other.

Possession by Albania of Mt. Vermosh, which commands the Gusinje region and stands beyond the eastern end of the Albanian part of the valley, was hotly contested by the Yugoslavs. The history of this dispute is that of the dispute over Shën Naoum. Both places were awarded to Albania by the Conference of Ambassadors and both abandoned by Albania as a friendly gesture towards Yugoslavia in 1925. The frontier is marked by numbered cement pyramids, too solid to be itinerant, which have stayed the line's vagrancy since 1926. But the Yugoslavs are still dissatisfied, contending—not without some reason —that the Vermosh valley is the natural course for a railway from Peç (Ipek) through Gusinje to Kotor (Cattaro), because the low wooded hills which close the western end alone break a direct and open route. A railway threaded tortuously round the salient involves far greater difficulties and costs. But the Albanians say that in the loop formed by the frontier north of the valley lie valuable summer pastures which have belonged to the Klementi clan from time immemorial, and flocks from Shkodër and the low country by Lesh, Mati and Kruja are brought there in early summer until the autumn. Having been trimmed of so much pasture elsewhere, Albania will not yield here, and on this point Italy backs Albania strongly, wishing to impede direct communication between the Yugoslav interior and the impregnable gulf of Kotor. Perhaps the matter may be settled one day by an exchange of territory.

From Vermosh to *Han* Grabom the frontier is the crest of the great rock wall which forms the north-

On the Way to Selcë.

(See p. 137)

western side of the Cem chasm and has been so since 1878. No land frontier more effectively separates two countries.

Reckoning our cost to our hosts and adding something, we distributed the sum to the women of the house when we took leave of them. That is the custom of the land. In a mountain *han* the *hanxhi* makes a charge, but in a house it would be insulting to offer payment or give the men money. You give a present—money, or something which you have and they want—to the women.

The direct road to Selcë is the way to Shkodër and as tracks go in these mountains it is a fair one. We climbed steeply through a beech forest and crossed *Çafa* Metohiçës, the rugged mountains of Shala towering above and beyond a jumble of forests and glades, gentler mountains and ravines to our left. Then we zigzagged abruptly out of the sunlight into the upper end of the chasm in which Selcë lies—the valley of the Cem. The rock scenery is dramatic. There is a steep step in the bed of the canyon and Selcë clings to the slope of it, an oasis in a lean wilderness where an oath on the rocks is the most sacred of oaths. Aqueducts of hollowed pine trees bring wayward water down to the maize plots and little white-washed houses nestle under fruit trees, betrayed by curling wisps of smoke.

Lec Cuni, president of the commune, and his secretary gave us a warm welcome in their little white-washed headquarters. A man took off our boots and washed our feet while we sipped coffee. Then they spread a splendid meal of bacon, meat and potatoes and made us take their beds. "It is our duty," said Lec, "to be hospitable to travellers in our country." He was an efficient young man, devoted to his dog. One of his brothers was a captain of gendarmerie and another a chef at Bexhill!

Lec had been stung by a scorpion and was in much pain, so Hill dressed the place with permanganate of potash which he carried in case of snake bites. A poultice of mashed scorpion, applied immediately, is thought a good remedy in these parts, but better still is oil in which the creatures have been soaked. It is said that if you surround a scorpion with a circle of burning embers and he finds he cannot escape he commits suicide by stinging himself on his back, but I never gave a scorpion this trouble.

That night I dreamt of bacon for breakfast and the dream came true. Then we called upon Father Dema in his little church-house. He was a kind old man who had been in these parts eighteen years and knew much about Klementi. In 1909 the church was burnt by Turks who were trying to force military service and taxation upon the stubborn mountaineers; but Austria-Hungary, which claimed the right to protect the Porte's Catholic subjects, forced the Turks to pay for its rebuilding. In September, 1914, Montenegrin troops rushed into neutral Albania, overcame the Selcë men after three hours' fighting, sacked and burnt the place. Seventy-five men were executed for resisting. Vuklë, Tamarë, and Niksh were also burnt and fifteen men executed at Vuklë, but Vermosh saved itself by yielding at once. Ten thousand sheep, goats and cattle were driven from Klementi by the invaders who remained until the Austrians came in 1916. In November, 1918, came the Yugoslavs who stayed until 1921. In September, 1924, an Albanian band raided across the border to lift cattle. Though beaten back its incursion gave a pretext for a raid into Klementi from the Yugoslav side, so Selcë, Tamarë, Vermosh and Vuklë were again sacked before Albanian troops drove off the invaders.

The tall rock cliffs to the west were harsh in the glaring sun though Selcë lay still in shadow when we set off for Tamarë. At a twist where the Selcë canyon narrows it is partly choked by great boulders which seem as if thrown there by giants; and boldly drawn strata slope upwards from north to south as if the heights had been built up by layers pressed and stuck together. The crest of the right-hand wall above us was the frontier.

Tamarë is nothing besides an old bridge and the gendarmerie post. The post commander flicked the flies from his honey and eggs and tomatoes which he set before us on his office table; and we ate because you eat when you can in the mountains. Then we tramped on to *Han* Grabom, following the green Cem between great walls which drew the heat into the canyon and held it there.

Han Grabom is at the bottom of the *han*-scale and no place can have a blacker character. As it is so near the frontier the *ḥanxhi* is probably wise to do nothing about it for it has been looted more than once in the past. It is also close to the notorious *shkallë* to Rapsh, 2,000 feet above, an advantage which outweighs its sordidity because every wayfarer stops to fortify himself before ascent or restore himself after descent. We fortified, with coffee, within the lesser heat of the *han's* fly-blown shadow.

The *shkallë* begins at the mouth of a deep-cut re-entrant ending abruptly by the cliff on which Rapsh stands. A very stiff climb brought us to a shoulder of the mountain; and crossing it, we looked down upon the frontier line, so steeply that it seemed as if a stone could be flung upon a Yugoslav house in the canyon (which is here crossed by the frontier and pursues its course in Montenegro).

Then our way zigzagged through trees. Approaching the brow we heard a gendarme's whistle and soon the others of our party, who had seen us climbing, came down to meet us. Together we climbed to the lip of the canyon, then turned to look our last upon the Great Mountain Land. In the failing light sheep were coming up the *shkallë* with tinkling bells. The depths from where we had climbed lay in dark purple shadows between the great cliffs which yielded their harsh glare to a pink flush as the sun took leave of them. It was a grand, mysterious scene.

Our camp that night was in a shallow hollow of the open upland valley which leads back from the chasm to the rocky slopes towards Lake Shkodër. It is strewn with rocks and bushes and water is scarce, but a woman from one of the three hovels which are Rapsh brought us a cask of it. The people of Rapsh claim descent from one Gheg Laz, who came into the land about 1530 with a very poor idea of land values—unless this part was all he could get. Hoti and Gruda, which were handed over by the Powers to Montenegro in 1878, also claim him as their forbear.

The great autumn migration from Klementi to the lowland pastures had begun. In the first dark, as we lay by our fire in the hollow, ringed by a near low sky-line ragged with sharp-broken rocks and clumps of bushes and fragrant with the night's coolness, there passed us flocks of bleating sheep or goats with tinkling bells, and here and there a cow or two, and ponies laden with modest household goods and babies, and the owners too—a silent trickle of refugees from the winter snows. They came slowly, almost furtively, on to the skyline and hung there a moment—dark silhouettes between the low-flung stars—then melted down into the plateau to bivouac till the dawn called them to their way again.

Between Rapsh and Shkodër are fifty dull kilometres only half redeemed by the view of Lake Shkodër; and to Shkodër we went next day in nine hours of blazing heat.

Through Hoti the track dropped steadily over a stony waste to the frontier post called Brigjë on the road from Shkodër to Podgorica and there, for the first time in twenty-three days, we saw a car. The scattered houses of Brigjë were burnt by Yugoslavs in 1921, and in the low frontier hills beyond took place a massacre of Hoti and Kastrati men after the abortive rising of 1883 which an Austrian agent had provoked in a political game.

Baizë, half way to Shkodër, is a shadeless village of close-grouped houses huddled like sheep for fear of the highland wolves. But Tirana's heart was glad, for here he was among his own lowland folk who are impudently rid of the cringing of Turkish days. To Baizë he had looked forward happily—in Baizë, he said, we should find much pleasure. We found flies and dust and tepid beer. We told him here, as we always did, half an hour beforehand to begin re-loading the ponies and prepare to start again. "Ah," he answered, "there is time enough. People are watching me here so I work much more quickly." We and the mountain folk had not been worthy critics of his skill! But curiosity is incompatible with dignity in Albania, even in Baizë. Had it been an English village a crowd would have collected and gaped but these people just glanced as they passed on their affairs.

We limped through the Orthodox Serb village of Vrakë and reached Shkodër after dark, sad that our trek was done.

CHAPTER VI

THE LOW COUNTRY

IT was late November and rain had fallen heavily in Tirana for a month. It had rained until the mud ran fluid in the gutters and the air seemed sated with yellow moisture. The yellow had got into my bones and for three weeks I had been gripped by jaundice, a complaint common in Albania. So I was glad to escape from Tirana's winter dreariness and go south.

There were three primitive ferries on the way to Vlona in 1930, for the fine bridges which now carry the road over the Shkumbini, Semeni and Vjosa rivers were unfinished. Between the Shkumbini and Lushnja lies an unfenced agricultural plain too bored with itself to say anything to the traveller, sweeping seaward from the foothills, a-shimmer with steaming heat in summer or forlorn and sodden with winter's dreariness, pulled up short of the Adriatic by a line of very little hills. Mount Tomori, which redeems it when in the mood, too often wraps itself sullenly in cloud.

Lushnja's humble houses, mostly single-storey, cluster round a cobbled market place or slink away down muddled alleys; and on the shop-front shutters which, when lowered, become the shop-front counters, sit the tradesmen cross-legged among their wares. On a butcher's counter a ram placidly chews away his last hours, and turkeys gobble or are gobbled everywhere. There is an agricultural school with about seventy pupils. Most townsfolk are dressed in nondescript clothes; but the peasants come in wearing woollen *capotes*, heavy and brown, with open sleeves and hoods: baggy brown woollen trousers narrow at ankles, red socks and *opinga*. Some wear *xhurdini* like the Tirana plainsmen, and most wear dark blue high-necked waistcoats and coloured sashes. Head wear, white and woollen, varies from the fez-like to the polo cap or close-fitting skull cap of the north. As elsewhere in the Moslem lowlands women are rarely seen and always veiled—they shuffle along like lame black crows.

At the Semeni ferry there was a congestion of buffalo waggons. From Berat to Durrës is 58 miles and these carts take three days to make the journey and three days back, each earning about 4*s*. a day. There is something satanic about those great black, placid, wide-eyed buffaloes which move with an incredible slowness, their massive heads held low as if weighted down by their horns and swaying from side to side like clockwork toys. The carts they draw groan upon inebriated wheels which lean till you wonder how they stay on. Their creaking is an Oriental protest against progress.

Beyond the Semeni we crossed a Decauville line, a relic of war days, then bore right suddenly over low ridges and skirted the Myzekija plain, between the Semeni and the foothills, to Fieri. During the later part of the World War the Semeni was the battle-front; and in August, 1918, Austro-Hungarian and Bulgarian troops won for the Central Powers their last success by driving the Italians out of Fieri and Berat. The plain is dree, though agriculturally the richest part of Albania, but the tyranny of the beys—the privileged landed aristocracy—is stamped upon the very soul of it. Among the trees on the hillsides are beys' big houses, while down in the fevered plain are mud and wattle huts sheltering peasants—serfs or *rayahs*—who live in the squalor of cattle. The government's agricultural reforms look well on paper but application is slow, for reforms in the East are a slow business and the spirit of many beys is of the East.

The beys acquired lands by tyranny, or in default of taxes, or by main force, and the Porte's feeble show of protecting the oppressed barely checked their rapacity; and in idleness they grew fat on the half their cringing tenants coaxed from the soil by toil and sweat in the antique way. The reforms would let a bey do what he wishes with a hundred acres, surrendering a third of his other lands for a nominal sum and cultivating the remainder as the government directs. Most of the beys are unprogressive people who oppose change and take patriotism like castor oil, so Albania has a big trade deficit through importing what her own soil might yield readily.

The government's aim is to split the low country into small holdings, so communications have received much attention and the protesting waggons and the wooden pack-saddles borne by sorry beasts are yielding to motor transport. But this is only half the matter. The Albanian will not be told, yet from example he will learn. So skilled farmers must be trained and settled to compete with and shame the peasants' antiquated ways and indolence. Under-population is another difficulty, nor can the poverty-stricken mountaineers support the climate of the plains.

Fieri, a wretched place with about 1,500 inhabitants, was the centre of the Anglo-Persian Oil Company's brief activities in Albania until 1931. The Italians first found oil, in 1919, and tried to keep the discovery dark, planning to annex Vlona and its hinterland; but the news leaked out and an undignified scramble for Albania's "riches" began. In 1922 the Anglo-Persian Company was granted a prospecting commission over a wide area, but French, American and Italian competitors fell over one another in trying to prevent its ratification; and in 1923 the French hysterically refused to agree to the appointment by the League of Nations of a British Financial Adviser to Albania because of the oil question. When at last the Anglo-Persian concession was ratified in 1925 Mussolini, thinking the British had a monopoly, protested to the British Government. In the end the Italians and French were granted concessions too and the Italians, after much patient prospecting, have some success.

The countryside round Fieri is strewn with ancient fragments and ruinous buildings. Between Fieri and the sea rot the walls of *Apollonia*, or what was left of them by the builders of a *serai* at Berat over a century ago. At this *Apollonia*, a Greek oasis of literature and philosophy in an Illyrian waste, young Octavius (to be Augustus) had studied for six months when the news of his uncle Cæsar's death recalled him to Rome. The city was founded in 588 B.C. by Corinthians upon low hills beside the *Aoos* (now Vjosa) and for a time bore the name *Gylacia* after the leader of the expedition. Soon it grew rich from the yield of the fertile plain. The sacred sheep of Apollo pastured by the river and Euenius, for supposed negligence, was blinded when wolves destroyed sixty of his charges. But *Apollonia's* wealth excited Illyrian greed so in 229 B.C. the Apolloniates sought Roman protection, proving faithful allies of Rome against King Gentius and opening their gates to Cæsar when he marched to crush Pompey. At the mouth of the *Aoos* too King Philip V of Macedon lost his fleet to the Romans. But with the rise of *Aulon*, *Apollonia* sank; and sank still further with the decline of Rome (though it became a bishopric in the fifth century). Then Alaric came with his Goths, laid waste the land, and was acknowledged Master-General by the feeble Emperor of the East. Earthquakes did the rest, shaking the place to ruins and shifting the river's course, and the sea receded, leaving only a marsh which sheltered pirates in medieval times. A French archæological mission has brought to light many remains of the dead city, among them the foundations of a Doric temple: and in Fieri a modest museum shelters many fragments.

From the ruins has risen the monastery of Pojan, built mostly of the ancient city's stones and adorned by its sculptures. The monastery is not newer than the fourteenth century. Here, one Easter Sunday thirty years ago Miss Durham saw

"tall men in dazzling white fustanellas, dark blue leggings, crimson waistcoats with two bands of silver chains crossed on the breast, and white coats with hanging sleeves embroidered in black; women in long-skirted sleeveless coats striped diagonally with scarlet—brilliantly aproned and a-dangle with coins—who flashed and glittered like parrots in the sunshine."

But this magnificence is passing, for the Albanian is ashamed to be Albanian.

There are seventy Orthodox monasteries in Albania, thirty-six in the diocese of Gjinokastra and many of them earlier than the fourteenth century, but they are shells guarded by one, two, perhaps three priests and the communities they sheltered in lawless days are gone. The monastery of Shëngjon at Elbasan has 900 years of history and was rebuilt by Charles Topia in 1380. Ardenica monastery, eight miles north of Fieri across the Semeni, bears the date 1474 on the archway through its encircling wall, though its church was restored in the eighteenth century. It, too, has stolen some of *Apollonia's* bones and like Pojan has venerable cypresses, frescoes on its church walls, peace, and a wide view.

From here the Austro-Hungarians during the war carried off everything of value but a large eighteenth century bible. This, though the villagers entreated, pleading that it was a sacred treasure, a looter finally took away too. But at Lushnja he became mad. The villagers, sure this was punishment for his sin, brought back the holy book triumphantly.

Near Ardenica is Kolkondasi monastery, sheltering martyrs' bones and more of *Apollonia's*.

At Margellic, eight miles south-east of Fieri, are the remains of an acropolis. Ballsh, a small group of houses some way beyond, was once a place of consequence, founded in the fourteenth century by the Balshas, which had a bishop who fled to Berat when the Turks destroyed the place at the end of the fifteenth century. A few fragments mark the site of its cathedral. There is magic in one marble pillar, for if a bit is powdered and drunk in water it increases a mother's milk.

South of Ballsh, on the right bank of the Vjosa, stands Gradishta village below the site of the ancient *Byllis* (or *Bullis*). The ruinous walls are upon a plateau connected by a neck of land with the high ground behind and in ancient warfare must have had formidable strength. Holland writes much of its *enceinte* walls and fragmentary remains, saying the walls were built at two distinct periods, a rougher structure being imposed upon Greek Cyclopean foundations. An inscription carved upon a rock outside the walls tells that during the reign of the Emperor Trajan the Roman officer Valerius Maximus repaired the public road from *Byllis* to a place illegible. *Byllis* was important enough to give its name to a bishopric in the fifth century. Until the time of Ali Pasha the people of Gradishta, who owed nominal allegiance to Berat, were renowned for lawless ferocity, but Ali curbed their wildness.

West seven miles from Gradishta, on the left bank of the Vjosa, stands Selenica. Hot springs with inflammable gases bubbling through their basins here made place in ancient times for an Oracle which pronounced upon all matters except death and marriage. Frankincense was cast upon the flames and if unconsumed the Oracle was unpropitious. Round the fiery springs lay soft green sward where Pan and the Nymphs piped and played; and a silver coin of *Apollonia* bears, on one side, the head of Apollo and on the other three Nymphs dancing here. Holland was told the gases often ignited spontaneously after heavy rains. Ali Pasha rented bitumen mines close here, paying the Porte 10,000 piastres yearly. Romans and Venetians worked the mines before him; and in 1868 a concession was given to Ismail Kemal Vlora, passed to an English company in 1875, then to a French one which sold it, in 1922, to Italians who work it very profitably.

The road from Fieri bore us roughly over low hills to the ferry across the wide Vjosa. It was an eerie crossing in the dark. The car's lit inside seemed a refuge from the still blackness without and only the clanking of a chain or the gentle resisting of the water broke the silence. On the road beyond a jackal in the car's headlights fled before us. Our driver swung us wildly in his pursuit of it, whooping with hunter's glee. Soon venerable olive trees framed in their ghostly branches the twinkling lights on Saseno island—a string of them, like a dropped constellation with a belt of empty night beneath, where the sea was. Then we glided down to the sparse lamps and dust-muffled streets of Vlona. A mosque was lit outside by hundreds of candles guttering in an unsuspected breeze which made the shutters on the houses creak. We went to the Hotel Adriatic, well-managed by a Swiss who had been in English service.

THE LOW COUNTRY

My sound sleep was disturbed by a violent shaking. The hanging electric light was cutting capers in the air. I leapt out of bed and staggered across the heaving floor to the door. It was a bad earthquake shock, but it was over in a few moments. The landlord hurried up to reassure us, saying earthquakes were commonplace, but we dressed and went out to see how Vlona had taken it. Every house was lighted but few people were in the streets and only some tiles had fallen. Nevertheless an English newspaper reported the town wholly destroyed, multiplying its houses for sensation.

Next morning came wild rumours, slowly followed by the facts. Eighteen people had been killed by falling boulders up towards the Logara Pass; but a preliminary shock had given warning, so the list of killed was short though the damage very grave and many injured. Vlona had been in the fringe of the shock.

We went down to the port which a receding sea has drawn a mile from the town. There is a warehouse or two and two wooden jetties on the edge of this magnificent landlocked bay. Saseno island, the ancient *Saso*, lay ten miles across the water, a dark silhouette in the bay's mouth; and the Karaburun mountains of Cape Linguetta were reflected darkly in the glassy sea, seeming to give warning of the squalls they beget.

Pirates lurked by Saseno in Roman times though it was once held by Rome as a port of call; and Dodwell noted the remains of a Greek fort which the Venetians had repaired in medieval days. The Venetians, in dispute with the Balshas, seized the island to protect their shipping and remains of their watch-towers may still be seen. There are ruins too which indicate that the island once held a settled population, though settlers were unable to withstand for long the attacks of pirates; and by St. Nikolo bay was an Orthodox church evidently used by shepherds who came there in summer, but it was destroyed by Albanian Moslems from Vlona in 1788.

Saseno is three miles in length and at widest one and a quarter. It consists of two conical hills, respectively 1,086 and 1,017 feet in height, and three miles of sea divide it from Cape Linguetta, the nearest mainland. Ali Pasha took it from Ibrahim Pasha of Berat, but on Ali's death it passed under direct Turkish rule. When in 1864 Great Britain ceded to Greece the Ionian islands Greece claimed Saseno as one of them; but a Turkish commission of enquiry under Ismail Vlora found from archives that in the sixteenth century the island had been ceded by the Vlora family to the *vakuf* of Kanina. So, though Greece claimed ownership, the Turks held that their right to keep it was proved and would not give it up; but on the outbreak of the Balkan War a Greek detachment took possession. Soon after the Greek landing General Ghilardi seized it for Albania with a hundred Albanians and in June, 1914, Greece formally yielded her claims to it.

But guns had grown (in range) and so had Italy, so barren Saseno grew in strategic importance. Guns upon Saseno might command the Gulf of Vlona which can shelter the biggest fleet; so on October 30, 1914, Italian marines seized it to forestall Austria, finding only a few shepherds upon it. By the secret Pact of London of April 26, 1915, the Entente Powers made it over to Italy as part of a scheme for the partition of Albania and part of Italy's price for making war. Under the terms of the Agreement between Italy and the Albanian nationalists on August 2, 1920, the Italians withdrew their war materials from Vlona and its hinterland to Saseno, which they formally annexed soon afterwards.

Saseno is Italy's Gibraltar, strongly fortified and garrisoned, with a harbour for light craft, an aerodrome and roads. No doubt the hills are honeycombed with tunnels and concealed emplacements, so it ought to be impregnable. Its drawback is that there are no springs, so drinking water must be brought from shore or distilled or stored. None but Italian soldiers and officials—not even their wives—may land there. The Albanians are sore at losing Saseno—though it is of no value to them; but they are silent about it for policy's sake.

The whole story of Albania for thirty years has been influenced by the Gulf of Vlona which, being at the narrowest point in the Strait of Otranto and only forty-seven miles from Italy, is the key to the Adriatic Sea (a consideration which much influenced King Alphonso of Naples in his relations with Skenderbeg). From its shelter a hostile fleet might command the Adriatic and threaten the vulnerable Italian coastline, but possession of Saseno gives Italy that command provided always the hinterland of Vlona remains in friendly hands. So the Italians have worked to secure a constant Albanian ally that may bar Vlona and Durrës from the Yugoslavs who might, in war, attempt to throw open those ports to a fleet hostile to Italy. Vlona is naval, but Durrës is military, and at Durrës Italian troops would land in war to strengthen Albanian resistance. If they were not effectively opposed by the Albanians, Yugoslav troops could reach the Albanian coast in two or three days, whereas the Italians' crossing of the Adriatic and disembarkation in effective strength would take far longer; so the Italians have worked hard to train the Albanian Army to hold up a Yugoslav advance until Italian forces could land and deploy.

General Pariani, former commander of the Italian Military Mission in Albania, explained to me the Italo-Albanian defensive plan. There are, he said, several main *trouées* and various subsidiary ones by which an invader might come. Elsewhere the mountains are defence enough, particularly if held by clansmen. Of the main *trouées* the Bojana forms one, but the river would be hard to bridge because of its width and marshes even if not under fire from warships off the coast. By Hoti and the flat land between the mountains and Shkodër Lake there is another *trouée* which the Montenegrins used in the Balkan War and this would have to be held unless Shkodër was abandoned. The invader might come from Prizren by Kukës to *Çafa* Malit which the Serbs used in the Balkan War and in retreat in 1915, but all this country is well adapted for defensive operations from Burelë and Miloti. From Dibra there is the difficult *trouée* of *Çafa* Bulçizë, but south of Bulçizë is *Mali* Kaptin, a carefully planned key position with only three ways across it; and it also effectively commands the route by Martanesh and Shëngjerçë. Between *Çafa* Bulçizë and Librash is the main strategic area of Albania. From Librash to Elbasan is the most vital *trouée* of all, because once the enemy reached Elbasan they would be through the mountains and have turned the main defensive line; but it is a route easily defended. At Librash the road from Elbasan forks, one road leading north by *Mali* Privalit (an extension of Kaptin) to Dibra but passing close to the commanding Kaptin positions. The other prong of the fork goes by many defensible positions to *Çafa* Thanës and Struga. There is another *trouée* by the Lower Devolli valley, but invaders using it would have to pass south from Okhrida town between Lakes Okhrida and Presba to Shën Naoum and follow the Devolli through extremely difficult and trackless country before reaching the wider valley.

Thus the two key areas in a war with Yugoslavia would be Librash-Kaptin-*Çafa* Bulçizë, and Bregumatit (by Miloti); and between them, by Martanesh and Burelë, lies a deep depression providing a natural defensive line on its south-western slopes. This, said Pariani, would be the main line of resistance if the Yugoslavs forced their way through so far. The left flank is secured by well prepared positions on the hills (which no unauthorised person may climb) between Lesh and the Mati bridge, and the mouth of the Mati river has been sounded for the landing of troops and supplies. The right and more vital flank is equally well planned and secured. The Albanian Army is concentrated at Shkodër, Tirana and Elbasan, covering respectively the Miloti-Burelë, Kaptin and Librash sectors. Durrës is the Italian base for this defensive line, with roads radiating to these points.

Vlona, the ancient *Aulon*, held the country northward to the Vjosa and traded with Greece and Illyria long before the Romans came. Its coins, dating from 400 B.C., are found in plenty. It supported Cæsar in the civil war and repelled Pompey's general Octavius. In the fifth century it became the seat of a bishop, had its part in the wars between the Normans and Byzantines in the eleventh and twelfth centuries, and in 1258 passed with Berat to King Manfred of Sicily as part of the dowry of his bride Helen. But Manfred lost both towns, and his life, to Charles of Anjou between 1266 and 1272.

Vlona was recovered for Byzantium by Andronicus II, but in 1345 Dushan's Serbs took it. The Balsha princes held all southern Albania; and on the death of Balsha III's widow her son Rugina, threatened by the Turks, in 1417 offered his heritage to the Venetians for 9,000 *duckats*. But while the Senate talked the Turks walked in, though the Venetians recovered Vlona and kept them out of it until 1464. The Turks restored the fortifications, but they were dismantled by the Venetians who held the place again for a few months in 1690. "An apology for a fort—a square enclosure of ruinous walls, with towers and a few cannon" commanding the wharf were all Leake found there. Vlona was ruled under the Turks by the Pashas of Berat, and Pouqueville complained that (about 1810) its inhabitants were "men whose manners are like those of the Algerines, and its port is far from presenting the same security to vessels of other nations as to those of its own." Ali Pasha took Vlona in 1812—his lie that Ibrahim Pasha was Francophile brought him the help of two English frigates which blockaded the gulf.

At Vlona on November 28, 1912, Ismail Vlora proclaimed Albanian independence, an act which conflicted with Greek plans, so Greek warships blockaded and shelled the place. Their irregulars advanced to Logara but were held up there by Albanian volunteers. The Turkish Army, in the Lushnja-Fieri area, was too preoccupied with the Serbs to care about Albanian affairs. Vlona was the seat of the first Albanian government until January, 1914, and Prince Wilhelm paid the place a visit at the end of July. It fell unresisting to insurgent central Albanians in August.

But Albania was a tom-tiddler's ground of warring factions and foreign agents, a situation which might have turned out badly for Italy, so on December 26, 1914, Italian troops occupied Vlona which became their base of operations in the country. By the Pact of London Vlona and a strategic hinterland were made over to Italy by the Entente Powers who added a clause providing that Italy "should not oppose" the partition of the remainder of Albania between Serbia, Montenegro and Greece. But when the idea of a powerful Yugoslavia was adopted by the Entente, Italy took alarm at the prospect of having her old rival Austria-Hungary replaced by another, so in 1917 she proclaimed Albanian unity and independence under her protection.

All went well between Italians and Albanians until indications at the Peace Conference that Albania would be partitioned according to the Pact of London after all stirred Albanian alarm. So the nationalists resolved to be rid of the Italians, and the Albanian provisional government at Durrës (which in August, 1919, had agreed to give Italy certain mandatory powers) was overthrown. Then Albanian irregulars and militia from all parts poured down upon Vlona where the Italians had only 5,000 war-weary men sick with malaria. Some sharp fighting during June and July, 1920, went badly for the Italians in spite of their warships' guns, while Communism at home stopped the despatch of reinforcements. On August 2 an agreement was reached and within a month all Italian troops had been withdrawn. The Albanians are very proud of this triumph.

In 1913 there were at Vlona about 100 Italian families and three Italian schools. The town has now not many more Italians and its population of 9,100 is well coloured with Turkish and Gypsy blood. It is a pretty place with half a dozen mosques (one of them originally a Byzantine church) snuggling at the feet of easy hills with grassy glades among their olive trees and seeming to shrink from the marshy flats towards the sea where there are salt works and a fishery. Above the dull-white houses and dull-red roofs towers the ornate Italian consulate like a sacred bull among sacrificial sheep.

Two miles south is a high and steeply rising hill crowned by the ruinous walls of Kanina, so called from *Chaonia*, the antique name of all these parts. An *enceinte* wall and a tower still stand, but the place was much damaged by Italian guns in 1920. Below the walls there are a few houses and a reasonable road leads up to them from

Vlona. A Decauville railway climbs over these hills from the shore to Selenica for its bitumen. The Normans who fought the Byzantine Emperor Alexius Komnenus (1048-1118) knew Kanina. The Angevins held it, then the Serbs, and under the Balshas the Topia family ruled it. In 1368 the commander of the castle was one Kastriota, the first of that great name to be written in history. The Turks took it in 1417, lost it to the Venetians, then took it finally in 1690.

As the velvet shadows came through the olive groves, stealing down like panthers to water in the first dark, night ran chilly fingers up our spines so we withdrew from it to the hotel. But Albanian hospitality soon dragged us from our proper restaurant to a smoky, sordid, noisy place to eat grease and gristle off dirty plates with a simulated gratitude for this good-hearted treating.

Well past midnight I was writing in my room. Suddenly I caught a faint sound as of a distant underground train. In the instant it came, rushing from the south through the still night, the noise of it swelling to an awful clattering rumble full of menace. The jugs danced and the ground heaved as if a big wave had passed beneath. But this earthquake was less than last night, though faint tremors continued at intervals.

CHAPTER VII

THE HIMARA AND THE LION

"Tambourgi! Tambourgi! thy larum afar
Gives hope to the valiant, and promise of war;
All the sons of the mountains arise at the note,
Chimariot, Illyrian, and dark Suliote!

"Shall the sons of Chimari, who never forgive
The fault of a friend, bid an enemy live?
Let those guns so unerring such vengeance forego?
What mark is so fair as the breast of a foe?"
(*Childe Harold's Pilgrimage* : Byron.
Note: Chimari=Himara.)

THE sun had cut sharp the black shadows of Vlona and saturated its dusty air with heat when we drove from the town, past the air-port, upon a fair road close above a rocky shore. The water barely stirred and the dawdling gulls made a stipple of themselves or their reflections on the bay's glassy sea, tearing the still day with their sad cries.

Ten miles southward we came to the head of the gulf where *Llumi* Dukatit, the ancient *Celydnus*, empties into the sea. Before us the valley lay like a cleft in the mountains, the bed of it rising to blotches of dark pines. Its scarped old rocks re-echoed the blare of Cæsar's trumpets summoning the men of *Oricum* to bring forth their keys, and they have watched *Oricum's* decay and sinking till the sea flowed in over its bleached stones. These parts were the land of the Amantes (as they called themselves on their money), who sprang from the Abantes of *Euboea* and Locri from *Thronium*. Returning from *Troy* in eight ships they were driven by a tempest to this coast where they established themselves as rulers from the Apollonian border to *Panormos* (Porto Palermo); but the Apollonians early took from them their most northern settlement which they had called *Thronium*. Their capital was *Amantia* (now Plotsça village) and *Oricum* a notable port. Near *Oricum*, in 214 B.C., Philip V narrowly escaped the Romans; and at *Oricum* Paul Emilius embarked his army for Italy in 167. In Roman times a great road from *Nikopolis* passed by *Buthrotum*, along the rugged Himara coast past *Oricum* to *Apollonia*, and thence joined the *Via Ægnatia* at *Clodiana* (Pekinj); and along this route the Italians built the existing road during the war—so history repeated itself.

Crossing a little plain we climbed steeply from the valley till opposite Dukati village which so impressed Lear's artistic eye that he wrote:

"Shut out as it stood by iron walls of mountain, surrounded by sternest features of savage scenery, rock and chasm, precipice and torrent, a more fearful prospect and more chilling to the very blood I never beheld."

But now Dukati, till yesterday prosperous with well-built two-storey houses and 1,800 inhabitants, lay shattered by the earthquake. There had been many injured by crashing boulders and falling walls; and the terrified people were straggling miserably towards Vlona, away from those rocks, with their most valued goods.

Here we met black-bearded, warm-hearted, General Leon de Ghilardi, a great character whom Albania lost tragically in the Fieri rising in 1935. He had been sent from Tirana to direct relief work and had called out 1,000 of his militia in Vlona to help him. Of Croat origin he had served Prince Wilhelm faithfully, for an adventure. His brother is a Colonel in the Mexican Army.

GENERAL GHILARDI   (*See p.* 158)

Climbing by awkward hairpin bends we reached the huts of Logara which had escaped damage by being wooden. The place is a refuge for the well-to-do from Albania's summer heat. Ghilardi made us share his lunch. Every few minutes the ground trembled but Ghilardi ignored it and told tales. While fighting for the Austrians during the war he had hidden 7,500 gold pieces in the ground under his tent in military water bottles. Soon after, he left hurriedly, leaving the gold so safely hidden that he had never been able to find the place to dig up this fortune again. He talked proudly of the militia which he commanded—18,000 youths well clothed in Italian grey, with white wool skull-caps. They make a pretty sight swinging along with their colours, their rifles and their band, in splendid style, these young men who will create a new Albania.

An unkempt peasant, seeing Ghilardi, rushed to him with a glad cry, flung his arms round the general's neck and kissed him warmly on both cheeks, then smothered his hand with kisses. The man had served as a sergeant under Ghilardi who was well pleased and remarked merrily that he had not been kissed for three years.

With a boy and donkey to carry our kit we pushed forward on foot to the long narrow col which carries the road over the pass at 3,000 feet, pausing to look back through the blue haze at the gulf of Vlona, laid like a map in the frame of the valley's scarps. To our left as we went on were the flanks of *Mali* Kjorë and *Mali* Cikës which tower to 7,000 feet, and on our right the ridges of Atanasia and Shën Ilia—lower, and dark with pines. Here the road was scored by cracks in places a foot wide.

Ragged spectres of mist rushed past us through the dark pine branches, tearing themselves to shreds which the sun-steeped air of the valley behind caught and threw upwards. Behind them we came upon their main body, cold hollow billows which surged and boiled like ghostly breakers, casting forth a wild man in a big cloak who cried to us fearfully (in American) as he fled past: "Go back! The mist is terrible, and the mountains are alive with falling boulders. It is awful down there." And sure enough there boomed a sound, now and then, as if the phantom billows were breaking on the heights.

Our road twisted sharply downward into the heart of the clouds. Before us we sensed boundless white space, cold and still, where a kicked stone's clattering seemed an irreverence and the coarse water-beaded grass the last known thing on a strange world's brink. Then the grass shivered in an eddy and there came from far below the plaintive murmuring of waves against a rocky shore. We looked down through a rift at a glint of silver. A moment more, and the cloud thinned and wisped up from us like a tattered veil revealing sparkling sea far beneath. The slopes about us had heaved mightily, for the stones had been flung from their sockets in the turf and the outer edge of the road was chipped away like a broken biscuit by bounding boulders.

As we sank lower our eyes ranged ever further down this untravelled coast, this ragged line of sandy bays and rugged cliffs—and capes, the toes of Acroceraunia's horny feet; and the sharp-rising slopes behind them, ribbed and scarred, scored by mountain torrents and mottled by olive groves and terraced vineyards, swept upward to beetling crags and screes and high-flung forests here and there which raked the sky. This was wild ground a century ago, dangerous for the lonely traveller; Leake was the first and Lear the second lettered Englishman to come this way, though Lear met a well-born compatriot, a fugitive from justice, living at Himara in a torture of remorse. Dodwell speaks of the people as predatory Christians notorious for their attacks upon ships becalmed off their rocks whose crews they sold as slaves. He came sailing by in *Lo Spirito Santo e la Nativita della Madonna*, a ship manned by Dalmatians.

"As the wind seemed to forsake us on this treacherous coast," he wrote, "the crew were ordered out to prayers; the names of a great many saints were invoked, particularly St. Nicolo, the Neptune of the modern Greeks. Among the many terrific tales which they recounted respecting these fatal rocks, there was one circumstance upon which they laid particular stress and of which they would not permit us to question the reality. They said that loud voices were always heard upon the rocks at midnight; and that a short time before storms and sirocco winds, lights are seen dancing about upon the crags. The latter part of this story is probably less fabulous than it would at first appear";

and Dodwell suggests the lights are due to gases like those of Selenica. So rightly was this coast sometimes called the Chimaera. Pouqueville adds that the Acroceraunian mountains have trembled upon their bases, but always in autumn and in the night; and he quotes Pliny who says the greatest earthquakes here happen early in the morning, or in the evening, after violent changes of temperature.

In ancient times these parts were well peopled. Strabo mentions eleven different nations near the Acroceraunian mountains, each ruled by a sovereign prince; and each had two or three towns or villages, a tract of mountains for their flocks, a narrow valley or two for cultivation. And so they remained more or less, fighting and marrying one another and absorbing fresh stock that the sea threw up, reduced by the Romans and swept by other invading waves but ever recovering the independence their mountains made easy till Ali Pasha drove his sword through their coast and cleft a way for the Turks; but the Turks let well alone, and no Turkish soldier dared stray from the range of his nation's guns among them, so they never paid taxes and cared for the Turks not a fig, proud of their association with Skenderbeg in the days when they were good Catholics. The Orthodox faith has come to them since. They have taken hardly to central government, fearing Moslem preponderance and giving ear to Greek propaganda which sounded more cultured than Tirana's ranting—for they are the most advanced of all Albania's peoples.

Ghilardi came down the slopes from the clouds, pausing every few moments to watch the avalanches crashing down the trembling mountain's scarred face. We went down with him towards Zrimadhës, a place of good houses and 1,800 people. The road is good though the hairpins need a motorist's care. The sun sank in a blaze of red and gold and purple, blackening the far islands and near cypresses against its glow. Palasa, we heard, was a mass of ruins but Zrimadhës not so damaged.

Short of Zrimadhës a well-built house near the road received us. Its courtyard was packed with women, rocking babies in cradles, children piled among household goods, and knots of gossiping men—refugees from Zrimadhës' cracked walls beneath the crags. A stone's throw from us was Caesar's landing place for his campaign against Pompey; and a little the other way stood *Palaeste* (now Palasa village), walled city of antique *Chaonia*.

We went upstairs to a well-furnished room, its walls hung with faded portraits in ornate frames, among them Prince Wilhelm and King Zog impartially. All the notables of the place straggled in afterwards. Ghilardi harangued them mightily and dramatically in the King's name, urging them to bear their misfortunes bravely. Then he led the conversation wide of earthquakes, though it was hard to forget them for the squalling

EARLY MORNING AT ZRIMADHËS *(See p. 162)*

of infants in the yard below and the shocks which came every half hour or so. Citrons, large as coconuts, drew our attention, for Zrimadhës does a big trade in them to the Jews. The Jewish tradition is that when the Israelites came from Egypt they found in Palestine trees laden with citrons. Moses declared this bounty a sign of God's love for His people, so, ever since, the Jews have wanted citrons. But the fruit must be unblemished and undamaged, so the Zrimadhës traders must wrap them in paper on the trees and in cotton for exportation.

Supper came after we had fretted three hours for it. Then we went to bed among bugs which positively sang for joy at having our new meat.

Sea and sky were a riot of colours when we rose at sunrise to a spoonful of citron jam, a glass of water and a cup of coffee for breakfast. Then we took leave of Ghilardi and edged from the house by twenty handshakes.

The road turned sharply into the deep cleft where Zrimadhës clings, a fantastic place split by the ravine into which the sun cast sharp black shadows from the heights. Its neat houses, square and wide and windowed in both storeys, are terraced on steep slopes below precipices and above precipices; they are like two flocks of over-bold sheep which have scrambled downward until pulled up by the ravine's brinks, where they stand looking across at one another. From the stronger ones, which chose to ignore earthquakes and carry on their daily business, rose slow wisps of smoke blurring their outlines and hanging lazily in the crystal sunlight. Here and there were citron and orange trees gay with fruit. The narrow road was blocked by rocks which men were clearing. One house lay smashed like an egg by a big boulder and most of the houses on the northern side of the ravine were untidily cracked.

Beyond Zrimadhës the road thrust over a hill through oak and olive groves on carpets of rich grass, then crossed a wide gulley with bare earth cliffs riven and fluted by wind and rain and offensively red in the green and blueness. There were vineyards and cypresses and a taste of the sea. A peasant woman came by bearing her infant in a wooden cradle slung upon her back and, unlike the women of the north, posed readily for my camera.

Then we came to Vuna, a big village terraced up a hollow in the mountain's flank and threaded by steep flights of steps and cobbled alleys, dark-shaded by archways and vine trellises and cool as a church with the sea's breezes between the stones. The Venetians were intimate with all this coast and created an atmosphere of sun-bleached antiquity which lingers in Vuna and its neighbour places; and they left in Vuna a Lion of St. Mark, a hideous beast rough-hewn in stone which people still call the *Sammarco*. Later came Neapolitan influence, borne across the sea by returning Albanian mercenaries to take root again in the old stone walls and lazy shadows and wine-presses and the peoples' blood. We went to the girls' boarding school with an introduction to *Zojusha* Lezha, its head, a Shkodër girl vivacious with the English she had learnt at the Kyrias school, attractive and well-dressed and dazzlingly fair with pretty bobbed hair. Her school was as bright as herself, clean as a new pin, its windows wide-flung to the glittering sea a thousand feet below. The notice boards and neat beds and desks told of efficiency. There were three girl teachers and eighty pupils—twenty-seven of them boarders.

Our donkey boy now put us in a fix by saying he would come no further. Nor could another be found. So finally, Miss Lezha would have us take her old servant, a seemingly decrepit old woman, to carry to Himara

WOMAN FROM VUNA CARRYING HER CHILD IN A CRADLE
(See p. 164)

what gear we could not bear ourselves. I demurred at burdening a woman, but Miss Lezha replied that fetching and carrying were the old thing's job—and off she went, setting us a fair pace on the good road. Lear's guide in these parts explained to him of women that "although certainly far inferior to mules, they are really better than asses or even horses."

Himara (which gives its name to all this coast) is a romantic place crowning a hill which rises from the olive trees at the end of a spur, and shrinking from defiant precipices on two sides. A cleft ravine guards its northern side and puts forth a tongue of rich flat land; and below its precipices towards the sea are gentle hills patched with vineyards and maize plots and olive trees and spiked with cypresses like great black tacks pushed up from below. A mile to the south is a little sandy cove where are the sub-prefecture and gendarmerie post and new houses for which old close-packed Himara has no place. Corfu shows clearly across the sea. But Himara's steep alleys were manure heaps, putrid with dung both animal and human, banqueting halls for flies which rose in their legions as we passed. This dirt is Ali Pasha's fault for populating the place with Greeks. We hurried to reach the brink of its precipices and pure air, but the abandoned place loves alleys leading nowhere.

At the gendarmerie post a ragged old man who had been to America would explain us to authority in his better Albanian. When he had done I asked him what he had said (for his version had sounded rather wild). "I tell him, Mister, you good fellah—you run around into every kink and getta much good informations," he flung forth in reply. The post commander attached a gendarme to us—"as a friend, not because there is any danger." Nor is there in these peaceful parts.

Before the coming of Ali Pasha Himara was a proud place as its strong position indicates. Dodwell says there was once a castle built by Justinian—but Justinian only rebuilt the ruin of a walled Chaonian town. It was the seat of a bishop in the ninth century and in the tenth century the Bulgars under Tsar Simeon held it with all these parts. During the Turks' first years in Albania they garrisoned a fortress here with 300 men but the Himariotes threw them out in 1570 with Venetian aid.

Leake's host at Himara in 1805 had served Naples as a captain and his son had lost his life fighting for the wretched King Ferdinand. Leake met a Colonel of *Cacciatori Albanesi* in the Neapolitan service, whose second in command was a native of Vuna, and there were perhaps a hundred pensioners of the King of Naples in Himara alone. Naples had many attractions to offer the Albanians. They were given long leave and good pay—better pay than that of the Neapolitans themselves; but they had to find their own clothes and arms. Foreign military service was the Himariotes' chief trade and one told Leake that at Trieste he had been questioned about Albania by Napoleon himself. They were keen to serve the British if the British would have them. Their pride was their freedom from the Turks whom they would have at no price and they paid no taxes but thirty *paras* a head yearly to the Pasha of Berat for the liberty of trading to Vlona. Fishing off their coast, and pasturage, were the common property of them all. Greek was spoken by most of the men and Italian by those who had been abroad, "but the women in general know little of any language but the Albanian." There were 300 families in Himara, divided into five principal alliances, and feuds between these groups were as readily begun as ended. The price of blood was 2,000 Turkish *piastres*—at Vuna it was just half that amount—and until it was paid a feud would continue. Though the Himariotes often intermarried with the Vuna people they were generally on terms of suspicion or open hostility to one another—the normal state in Albania in those days (so two villages separated by a third were usually in alliance). Every house was prepared for defence and Ali Pasha their greatest fear. In 1801 Ali's men had fought with the Himariotes on the hill above Palermo; and more recently, when visiting Palermo, Ali had tried in vain to buy land from them to build a castle.

But Ali was not to be denied. In the spring of 1810 his men attacked in force from Porto Palermo and the Himariotes, when their ammunition was exhausted, fought on, sword in hand, for three days. Ali's victory came by treachery. He bribed four brothers of Vuna who let his men through in rear of the gallant defenders. At first he was content to carry off 250 hostages; but in the hard winter of 1816–17 he fell upon the district again, drove out most of the inhabitants to Prevesa and other remote parts of his domain, and sent unwilling colonists from Prevesa and Thessaly to take their place. Hughes tells that only Kuç, a village in the mountains above Himara, was spared; and Leake says Kuç was a Turkish village. It is, by accounts, a place of strange traditions and beliefs—among deep forests and high pastures roved by wolves and bears and scattered near the clouds with the stones of antique places. It lies high on Skivovik, a mountain rising to near 7,000 feet.

At the "Adriatic Hotel" we climbed by a steep ladder from a cafe noisy with men, and by a trap door passed with their unwashed bibulous smells into a large bare room beneath the tiles. The young *hanxhi* was Greek in blood and sentiment and dishonesty and amiability. His military service had been spent in Tirana as servant to Baron von Kirchner (assistant to the Chief of General

Staff) which was just another proof of the Baron's widely-known courage. Only his *raki* was good and he told how he made it. The grapes are crushed and stand for eighteen days; then most of the juice is drained off for wine. The residue is boiled in its juice and the steam from it, condensed, is *raki*, which must stand for forty days more. A hundred kilograms of grapes yield ten kilograms of *raki* and thirty-five of wine. *Raki* may also be made from plums or figs.

There is magic in this coast's still dawn. The stars dim and go out, the night-shadows are diluted evenly by the stealthy first light into pallid, dewless grey like wan moonlight, and the black, lonely sea changes in a few moments to a miracle of fragile powder blue. Then, in an instant, the sea's distant plane is decked with a golden thread which widens and grows till the orange of it is flowing shoreward, pursuing the retreating mountain shadows towards their proper battlements. Here and there among the still-sleeping olive trees a slow spiral of smoke, stretching itself lazily upward to find the sun, tells of a stirring household. Then a donkey bell tinkles through this fairyland, linking dreams with man's toil; and the sun looks over the heights, painting a pattern under the trees and cutting sharp-edged shadows against the full light. The earth springs to life again and a sun-baked day has come.

With a pony and a lad to care for it and a Dibrani gendarme we set off early next morning between the shore hills and the heights. We met two women laden with rosemary, who fled past me crying that my evil-eyed camera should not look upon them. Then we climbed steeply to a col thick with daisies and dandelions and looked down upon Porto Palermo, a land-locked bay of rare perfection. Vaguely it suggests the forepart of a crab. Its fat mountain body is steep to the water, bare of trees. On either side a cape projects into the sea like a great in-curling claw; and in the middle, where the head should be, is a little round treeless island ending in a cliff and linked with the body by a slender neck of sand. On the island is a massive castle built by Ali Pasha in 1814 and well-preserved. On the neck or at its base are a tiny gendarmerie post, a tiny church, a two-roomed cottage giving the wayfarer his indispensable Turkish coffee, and the ruins of barracks built by the Italians during the war and afterwards destroyed by them. There were three little sailing boats in the bay and the population not above six. British warships used it sometimes during the World War.

When Leake came here in 1805 there was "nothing more than a small square enclosure containing a house, a church, and two four-pounders," with a garrison of five Moslém and five Christian soldiers. There were a few vineyards and corn-fields and sheep on the slopes, tended by the soldiers. The hills to the north were well cultivated but belonged to free Himara which had exclusive right to the fishing in that part of the bay. Ali Pasha, who gained Palermo in 1798, was emphatic about the fitness of the harbour for British warships, thinking their coming would facilitate his subjugation of Himara.

"A gale accompanied with rain," wrote Leake, "which comes on at night from the south-east, brings a ship of Dultjuni, in Italian, Dulcigno, into the harbour, bound to that place from Alexandria. As the Dulciniotes have the reputation of being inclined to piracy the garrison is alarmed and prepares for defence. Indeed they had already been put upon the alert by our arrival, for our boat being from Corfu the governor suspected some Russian treachery, and before my cot was conveyed into the castle it was searched, lest it should contain concealed arms."

One may imagine the suspense as the *Dulciniote* lowers her flapping sails, then swings to anchor against the breakers and the driving rain; but she had no harmful intentions, though Dulcigno (now Ulcinj) was said to be a place of 6,000 pirates who gave no quarter. Her predecessor had been a French privateer, and there was ever danger of Barbary corsairs.

Of earlier records there are few, except that the place was anciently *Panormos*. But the minds of the old folk, as everywhere in Albania, are stored with tales of the past. Some tell of a Prince of Taranto who came here to claim his bride, the daughter of the feudal lord; and they describe in sharp detail the medieval ships that brought him, the wedding feast, and the dress he wore.

The castle is a silent place given over to lizards. We passed through its yawning entrance and almost lost ourselves in its cavernous belly, cold as the tomb. It is low and wide, massive in everything, and the light from its loopholes is lost in passing through the deep embrasures. There is a seemingly interminable succession of arches and halls, a well in the earth floor, and its flat roof is heavily battlemented. Italian military notices are everywhere, for the Italians used it as a barracks during the war.

Going on we met a man on his donkey and a woman—black as a widow in the local dress—walking beside him. He was dressed *alla Franka* and hailed me in American. Reading my look, he remarked it was the English and American custom to let the woman ride, but that here it was not the way.

We cut across the southern cape and came to wide Grava bay, the mountains rising from the sea beyond it more steeply though less loftily than before and bearing on their flanks groups of white dots which are villages. Two valleys meet the sea here and the first we crossed by the shore. Cypresses pointed to Kypero's distant houses clustered on the brink of a thousand-foot precipice like a village in a fairy tale—as indeed it is, for all this coast is a fairy tale. Here and there were cacti by the shore, and in the valleys grew burdened orange trees and cotton plants with bursting pods. Wild pig teem and pastures are rich. From Borshi a new road was being built by the Sushica valley to Vlona, so avoiding Logara. Beyond Borshi we passed Sopot (which is barely a place) on our way to Piqeras (or Pikernion). Early in the sixteenth century the Turks built a small castle by Sopot, on a rock, but in 1570 the Venetians took it by storm. Leake found it garrisoned by some of Ali Pasha's men and says the place was one of the rare Turkish settlements on this coast.

Long shadows were drawing across the wandering road from wayside oaks as we wound higher and higher above the sea. Piqeras is of roughly the same size as Zrimadhës and Himara; it has 165 houses and perhaps 1,000 inhabitants. It is drawn out along the crest of a spur, which falls abruptly at its western end to the sea nearly a thousand feet below and on either hand slopes away steeply under the billowy greyness of dense olive trees.

As Piqeras came into sight the sun went down behind the black island of Merlera which floated in an opalescent sea. Its last rays smote the untidy cloud-wisps into a tattered veil of gold and crimson and laid a glowing trail across the still water for the feet of night. The cypresses and figs and olive trees stood beautifully against this glory, and through the twilight's hush came the tinkle of donkey bells and the barking of a jackal. Then the last light forsook us, fleeing to its sun. The purple dark welled up by us and flowed seaward in pursuit and the earth paid homage to the stars with the incense smells of night.

We came to a little lamplit café by the wayside where the village notables were fortifying themselves in a practical way against the chill of night. They called us in to join them. There was Pericles (of Frasheri) the commune chief, and the mayor Sokrat, and the post commander—a smart and taciturn sergeant. Rugged countrymen, but courteous and overflowing with kindness. One of the two gendarmes who manned the local post—a broad-built cheerful Dibrani—was put at our disposal to serve and mark respect for us. Our boy and donkey we dismissed, paying 8 shillings for their day's work.

Pericles said Piqeras was proud of its hospitality, as we should see. With the four of them we went over the cobbles of a little alley—their main street—between the low houses which sent forth, here and there, a chink of light, or restrained voices, or a friendly greeting to our companions. They led to a little restaurant where a young man with the rolling gait of a seaman came to us with a bright smile.

"You are English, sir?" he asked. "I am very glad to see you here—I served as a steward aboard a British merchantman. George Nakos is my name."

His was a rough place of rickety tables and benches, odd advertisements on the walls (chiefly for cognac), the dim light of an oil lamp to show its poverty; but Nakos knew our likes in food (such as he had) and in manners (which he had). There were ten men of Piqeras, he told us, who had served or were serving on British ships. Most men of the village seek work elsewhere for there is not enough among their olive groves.

Our friends showed us to a pin-clean room with four windows, well scrubbed boards (unfavourable to lice) and two iron beds with soap-washed coverings. This, said Pericles, was the village guest room, and the charge

THE HIMARA AND THE LION

for the night was 2s. 6d. if we wanted to pay. There was a woman to bring us water and the gendarme would sleep in the next room to ours. We sank thankfully to sleep—unbitten.

The next day's sun streamed in to wake us to the sight (from our beds) of great oranges among their dark leaves within arm's length of our windows, while the soft breeze bore up the sea's murmuring from far below. Across the sparkling water danced Merlera, Fano and Samosraki in their haze like animated chips of Corfu—each is peopled by descendants of adventuring Piqeras folk. Nakos conjured up fried eggs and tea, then Pericles and Sokrat showed us round.

At the village fountain by the roadside the women were at their household washing, bare-footed and clean and free to move in their light skirts and blouses. Here and there, wide-flung massive double doors under a stone-arched porch gave a glimpse of a little courtyard under a trellis of vines which let the sunshafts pass to splash the flags. But life in Piqeras was an easy one, unhurried and contented, for no one fussed and no one shouted and few stirred in the alleys, so our clattering on the cobbles seemed a sacrilege. Even the fowls appeared to be idle in their searching among the weeds and the very stones—saturated with heat—were greedy for sleep.

The Commune office, workmanlike and spotless, was painted fresh blue and white, the Greek colours, and thereon I remarked. But Pericles explained this was a relic of the old days when the Himara looked to Greece for fear of Tirana's Moslems and the older people, born to it, are Grecophile still; but the younger ones care nothing for Greece. Moreover Piqeras is Albanophone whereas Zrimadhës is Greek-speaking, though further from Greece, and its people call it Dhirmi. The keen young head teacher of the Piqeras primary school was a graduate of the gymnasium at Prevesa (in Greece). At his school cleanliness was the rule too, and the children looked trim in their red and black. The walls were hung with diagrams—natural history and other subjects; and there was a big map of the Balkans marking Albania red and her irredentist dreams (from Prevesa to Mitrovica) pink. There were three (male) teachers and ninety children in five mixed classes.

Bent on bathing we parted from our cortège and scrambled seaward by slopes thick-clad with luxuriant heather and drowsy with the hum of bees. A praying mantis seemed pathetically to crave our mercy with apprehension in its great eyes. Low down on the slopes there were little meadows and walled-in maize plots and vineyards. Below them a clear stream flowed beneath the trees of a tiny valley to meet the sea in a little cove rimmed by a narrow belt of smooth hot sand between the shrubs and the water. At the door of a square house by the shore a well-dressed man with a look of refinement addressed us in nearly faultless English. Fourteen years ago, he explained, he had emigrated to the United States where he came to own a string of restaurants and ticket agencies; but the noise and bustle had wearied him, so at length he had sold his business and come back to enjoy the peace of his native place.

We had said we would go on to Saranda that night if the mail van came through, as our time was short and our money too. The van passed thrice weekly, but to-night the road might be impassable on account of the earthquake. Nobody in Piqeras owned a car for no car could get into its narrow alleys. Nor was there a telegraph and the telephone was not functioning. At last Pericles and Sokrat came to say the van had come; but must we go? I said we must, and their goodness to us called for reasons. As for money, they replied, they would be glad to lend all I wanted; and Saranda would be there another day unless there came an earthquake—and if it was destroyed it would be well if I had spared myself trouble with it. We had given them no chance, they complained, to show their hospitality, for last night we were tired but to-night we would spend feasting and merrymaking in their houses.

But we had to go. So we walked sadly through the moon-cleft shadows of the village street to the road where a little crowd of these kind people watched us climb to the benches beneath the van's canvas awning with a real sadness they made us feel. As the van rolled away down hill they stood in the splash of light from the roadside café's door and waved to us farewell.

Downhill we went at first, through the olive trees' black shadows; then the engine hummed and the van strained as we drew clear of the trees and began to climb. Up and up we went, twisting and turning and bumping and lurching along a thread of a road where the least swerve would have sent us plunging a thousand feet over bare steeps to the sea. The beams of the headlights lost themselves by the faint stars, but the moon was good; and across the leagues of black and silver sea the islands lay dark and mysterious. The road is good (for the Balkans) if the light and driver and car are good, but I was not happy to be driven by an unknown man who might be drunk and might be careless and whose van was heavy and ill-sprung. We passed Lykova and Shën Vasili, then lost the sea and reached a col where Nivica Bubarit stands. Here we stopped and I sighed relief. But worse came to me, in the form of a large fat woman who climbed in and sat opposite me, wedging her feet against the drums of stinking olive oil between us; and with each lurch she slipped further down, pushing those drums harder and harder upon my shins. I could not move, for there were others beside me—men in enormous *capotes*—so I was glad when the journey ended.

Nivica was once large and prosperous, the most important of the independent Christian communities on this coast, and was able to defy all Ali Pasha's efforts to capture it until 1798. From attack by land it was protected by the strength of its position high on the mountains: and by sea, by treaty between Venice and the Porte whereby no warship might sail through the Straits of Corfu nor any fort be built within a mile of the Ionian coast. But by the Treaty of Campo Formio the Venetians forfeited their rights in these waters to the French who, anxious to stand well with Ali, let him send his ships through the straits and put ashore troops at Saranda and Spilja (Nivica's landing beach) on Easter Sunday, 1798, while the people were disarmed and at prayer. Nivica and Shën Vasili fell to his men after a short unequal struggle and soon the whole coast to Palermo was in his hands. Many of the inhabitants were deported to Trikkala, and Nivica put to flames; and to secure Spilja landing Ali built a little fort above it.

From Nivica the winding road took us downward through the black shadows of the hills which divide the plain of Delvina from Cape Kefali. The plain is wide and rich, parted on the east by bleak mountains from the valley of Gjinokastra. Vlach shepherds set up their mud and wattle huts in it during summer while pasturing their flocks; and there are ruinous walls at the head of the valley—in fact all these parts are littered with the bones of dead places.

At last we saw before us, through the frame of a col, the lights of Saranda strung out along the shore and doubled by reflection in the sea. We rolled down to them; and at the Pirro Pallas we flung wide the windows to catch the gentle lapping of the moonlit water against the rocks beneath and to gaze through the brilliant night at the gloomy mass of Corfu's mountains, so near now that they seemed an easy walk across the polished floor of the North Channel.

But Saranda itself is a cheerless place, though it is the ancient *Onchesmus*, the port for *Phoenice*. It gave its name to those favourable winds, the Onchesmites, which filled the sails of ships bound for Italy, and derived this name (through the form *Anchiasmus*) from Anchises, the father of Æneas. It was a place of consequence in Epirot and Byzantine days and there were bishops of *Anchiasmus* in the fifth century. Through the ages it has been linked with Corfu by trade—Corfu sent over lemons, figs, rice and oil and took grain, fish, cattle, wood and *botargo* (the roes of mullet, a fish plentiful in Lake Vivari). Under the Turks it was the property of the Sultans and now belongs to the Albanian crown; but its population has dwindled to 1,900, though it ranks second only to Durrës among Albanian ports and many vessels call on their way from Corfu. There is no quay and none but small craft can come within 300 yards of the shore.

Much of Saranda's *enceinte* wall still stands, though it is disfigured now by new villas against it. It formed an exact semicircle with the beach as diameter and was flanked by about twenty towers. Within it are the remains of houses and two churches.

Immediately behind Saranda rise low bleak hills covered with herbs and boulders, and crowning one are the massive ruins of the Byzantine church of the Forty Saints from which the place takes its Italian name—Santi Quaranta. From this church subterranean passages are said to lead down, perhaps to within the *enceinte* wall, though I have heard of one outlet only—half way down the hillside. The tale is that there dwelt forty saints in forty rooms in a monastery which adjoined the church; and the church had three domes and seven semi-domes. (At Mesopotamo village is a fine Byzantine church still in use, standing on the ruin of a much earlier building.)

On the opposite hill, divided from the other by the road, are the ruins of a village. Ali Pasha built it in 1801, populated it with shepherds and farmers who paid him a third of their produce, and in 1804 added a small fort with two round towers.

Some twelve miles south of Saranda, at the southern end of Lake Vivari, stand the ruins of *Buthrotum* (now Butrinto). As the road was still on paper and the trip by sea costly we put off going and returned next day to Vlona and Tirana. But a friend who went told me of it afterwards. Down the coast a little motor tub carried him across the blue water to the bar at the mouth of the river linking the lake with the sea. Then a sailing boat bore him three miles up the glassy river between silent hills and wooded banks and by a plain that once belonged to Cicero's friend. There is utter solitude here, for the springs have dried up and malarial mosquitoes reign in summer virulently. Suddenly there comes into sight a little jetty and a cluster of huts like a pioneering settlement—quarters for the Italian archaeological mission; and amid the silent groves stand wondrous statues and impressive fragments of an ancient glory. My friend never so nearly captured the atmosphere of the classical times as here, he said, for the Italians have contrived to make the place live again.

Buthrotum was founded by the Greeks upon a peninsula bounded on the west by a small bay in the lake and from the north to south-east by the windings of the river. It was a miniature Troy, with Trojan names for its gates and the streams in its neighbourhood. In a sacred wood close by, on the banks of the "false Simois," Æneas, the Trojan hero, found Andromache, her hair dishevelled and her eyes welling with tears, sacrificing to the shades of her dead husband Hector. She welcomed him, and told him the city's name, and that the country was called *Chaonia* after Chaon, who had been killed by accident when hunting, by Helenus, son of Priam, her new husband and the ruler of the land.

"Virgil, who has in so few words transmitted to us the topography of this town and its neighbourhood, may still serve as a guide to the traveller. If he no longer sees the gate of Scoea, nor the vast galleries in which Helenus received Æneas and his companions, he will find the lake of Anchises, with the little streams which then bore the celebrated names of Xanthus and Simois, now called the Pavla and Bistrica."

So wrote Pouqueville 130 years ago. And to-day archaeologists have uncovered the glories which Pouqueville missed when he landed here, a Barbary pirates' captive, for Ali Pasha's pleasure.

In the first century B.C. *Buthrotum* fell to the Romans who rebuilt the mighty walls (about a mile in circumference) which the Greeks built first in the fifth century B.C.; and Caesar's legionaries, languishing here under a tyrannous sun which glinted on their arms and made them thirst and sweat and shrink into the fly-blown shadows of the walls, let their eyes range across the blue straits to Corfu, over the shining lake, and down into the plain close about them—a plain better cared for then than now. Next came the Byzantines and the Bulgarians, fighting one another; and in the tenth century *Buthrotum* was a bishopric. Then a Despot of Epirus ceded it to Manfred of Sicily. Then the Angevins took it and withheld it from Dushan's Serbs. In 1386 it fell to the Venetians, but in 1502 came the Turks; and Turks and Venetians played a game of ball with the poor place— Venetian diplomatic documents hold many references to it.

In 1716 Marshal Shulemburg retook Butrinto for Venice; but by the Treaty of Campo Formio it passed to the French who garrisoned a little triangular Venetian fort on the right bank of the Pavla where that river leaves the lake. Their connivance at Ali Pasha's seizure of Nivica helped them not at all, for at the end of 1798 Ali went to war with them and marched upon Butrinto, so the French garrison blew up the fort and withdrew before he arrived. In 1800 Ali had to withdraw again because of the pressure Russia brought to bear upon her Turkish ally; but when the breach between Turkey and Russia occurred Ali (who had helped to make it) reoccupied Butrinto (in 1805). When the French had gained the Ionian isles by the Treaty of Tilsit General Berthier, the Governor of Corfu, threatened to retake Butrinto in retaliation for the aid Ali gave to the British blockading squadron. So Ali garrisoned the place with 6,000 men and wrecked it in the hope that the European Powers would take no interest in its ruins. But the fishery was rich, so Ali let it to the Bishop of Janina for £4,125 (of that period); and the bishop sub-let it to the Corfuotes who depended upon it largely for supplies of fish during the long fasts. The place is infested by jackals which howl hideously at night, and wild pig abound. It has long been famed for duck and snipe and woodcock, so parties from British warships often go ashore to shoot there.

Archaeological discoveries there have been very notable. Stone Age axes and knives and Bronze Age buckles have been found. Fine sections of the Greek walls still stand, and the ruins of a theatre; and there is a pagan altar, beautiful statues, and a perfect Roman mosaic of many colours and rare beauty, repaired in Byzantine days—it stands among trees beneath the stumps of fourteen columns of a Byzantine baptistry. And there are the remains of many Roman buildings, Byzantine frescos, glass, inscriptions, porcelain, coins. Yet a vast field for archaeological research, here and elsewhere in southern Albania, remains untouched. There is *Phoenice, Kalivo* (an ancient Greek town near Butrinto), *Hadrianopolis, Phanote, Amantia, Byllis*—a dozen ancient towns in fact, either partially or wholly unknown.

Konispoli, on the Greek border, is a Vlach settlement. In summer most of the population scatter to pasture their flocks. In Ali's time there were 400 or 500 families in two factions, and Ali exploited their feuds to gain power there. Near Konispoli are the ruinous walls of another Greek city.

Five miles north-east of Saranda stands a long, isolated, flat-topped, rocky hill with fluted flanks. At its foot is a village partly destroyed in 1913 by either Greeks or Albanians—each says it was the other. On the plateau stood the proud city of *Phoenice*, once the richest, strongest and most important place in all Epirus. Its acropolis was one of the largest in the classical world, being seven times greater than that of Athens!

Although it was so strong the Illyrians gained *Phoenice* without a blow in 230 B.C. King Agron was so elated by the victory of his ships over the Ætolians and by the spoil they brought back that he feasted himself to death. His widow, Teuta, had caught his madness and ordered her officers to plunder every ship they met and every place they could. Her fleet anchored off *Onchesmus* to get supplies; and the commander, winning over 800 Gallic mercenaries whom the Epirots employed to garrison *Phoenice*, occupied the city. Thereupon Epirot forces marched upon *Phoenice* and took up a position beyond the river Bistrica, removing the planks of the bridge to secure themselves against surprise by the Illyrian garrison, then sent reinforcements to *Antigonea* (Tepeleni) to oppose Scerdilaidas, Prince of Illyria, who was marching south with 5,000 men. Thinking themselves secure they

kept no watch and indulged in the plenty of the land.
But by night the Illyrians made a sortie, replaced the
planks, surprised the Epirots and routed them. Scerdilaidas reached *Phoenice* unopposed. But the Epirots,
reinforced by Ætolians and Achaians, again marched
upon *Phoenice* and the opposing forces met at *Helicranum*
(? Delvina). But no battle took place because Teuta,
alarmed by a defection of Illyrians to the Dardani, had
sent to recall her forces from Epirus. So Scerdilaidas made
terms with the Epirots whereby *Phoenice* was evacuated,
but the slaves and loot were embarked upon Illyrian ships;
then he retired northward by *Antigonea* (probably crossing
Çafa Skarfica). Soon afterwards Illyrians and Epirots
together were plundering the Ætolians and Achaians.

In 205 B.C. peace was concluded at *Phoenice* between
Philip V and the Romans, bringing to an end the First
Macedonian War; but not many years afterwards Philip
was crushed and *Phoenice* fell to the Romans. It became
a bishopric in the fifth century and the Emperor Justinian
repaired its walls. Thereafter it shared the strange
vicissitudes of these parts until the Turks came, when it
fell to ruins. Archaeological excavations have exposed
Greek works dating from the fourth century B.C. and
repaired in Roman times, the ruins of a Byzantine church,
inscriptions, and many other treasures.

Mustafa Pasha of Delvina blocked the pass to Ali
Pasha for seven years; but at length Ali overcame his
successor and built a fortress. Leake found Delvina
Moslem, with no more than thirty Greek families. The
population is now about 3,000. Delvina stands high
at the western end of the pass and is rich in olives, oranges
and vines. The road beyond passes through a defile
on its way down to the Gjinokastra valley, then turns
right to the Greek frontier at Kavakia, twenty-eight
miles from Saranda and forty from Janina; thence it

climbs to Delvinaki which, so Hobhouse wrote, was always thought the boundary of Albania proper; and he added that the people to the north spoke Albanian —not Greek. Hughes adds that the Gjinokastra valley had, in Ali's day, a population of 80,000 and nearly 100 towns and villages; and both he and Holland were greatly impressed by the view of it.

Janina was Ali Pasha's capital. Ali—"the Lion"— whose family name was Hushuf, was born at Tepeleni in 1741, son of the bey of that place. Tepeleni was held by his family in feudal tenure under the Pashas of Berat. Ali's grandfather, Mukhtar, was killed in the siege of Corfu by the Turks; and Mukhtar's son Veli, Ali's father, trapped and burnt alive his two elder brothers so that he should inherit the property.

In those days Turkish authority in these parts counted for little, and the country was a seething mass of petty chieftains and more or less independent towns and villages in a state of perpetual guerilla warfare with each other. Over them the Pashas of Shkodër, Berat and Janina held nominal sway and in little more than name represented Turkish authority; and they were as bad as the little men, fighting each other fiercely for power and land. But their fighting was a shedding of money rather than blood for their armies had to be recruited in feudal style through the lesser men (whose sole aim in taking any part at all in any dispute was gain). The lesser men would bargain with the house lords—they would buy the services of so many men, or a position, or a house, bidding against the other side. Sometimes a house lord would sell his services and his men's for a price arrived at by much bargaining, then give the services of half the men paid for until he could strike a bargain with the other side. But generally treachery on a small scale was not done, though on a big scale it was done whenever profitable and held to be all in the game. Houses, if destroyed, were easily set together again. The fighting was chiefly a dodging behind trees and firing from behind cover at the enemy before he came too near, so it was seldom decisive; and in the end the stronger treasury won.

Ali succeeded his father who was killed by neighbours, and with the help of his mother Khamko (a daughter of the bey of Konica) tried to hold his own. But in vain. In 1771 he had to fly, penniless, before his enemies, and his mother, and his sister Shainica, captured by the men of Gardiki, were outraged and brutally treated. That put a stain upon the family honour and Ali's long deferred vengeance was rich and red. His luck, so goes the tale, was changed by his finding a cask of Venetian *sequins* in a ruin. He recovered the family property, then enrolled under his cousin Kurt Pasha of Berat, the powerful Vizir of central Albania. In war against the Pasha of Shkodër Ali so distinguished himself that Kurt was urged either to put him to death or to give him his daughter in marriage. But Kurt, a fine character, thought it enough to dismiss Ali.

As a brigand and cattle lifter Ali showed no mean ability and practised it whenever the occasion offered; and he fought to extend his power round Tepeleni. His methods were practical.

"What did Ali do with the men of your village?"

"Nothing at all. He made friends with our chief man, persuaded him to come to Tepeleni, and then roasted him on a spit; after which we submitted."

Once Ali fell into the hands of the Pasha of Janina but the Pasha soon released and helped him. Then he had an affair with Kurt's married daughter and had to escape from Berat by scaling a high wall. Soon after he joined the Pasha of Negropont and reaped such advantage that he was able to conceal the enormity of his later activities by posing as the Porte's executor. By cunning and treachery he rapidly widened the bounds of his authority and Hormova, Libohova, and other places about Tepeleni fell to him. He married Ermineh, daughter of Kaplan Pasha of Delvina, who bore him two sons—Mukhtar and Veli. Much later he had a third son, Salih, born by a slave.

Meantime Kurt Pasha had gone to war with him, but Ali held his own, and for his services in the war against Russia of 1787 the Porte made him Pasha of Trikkala and Derwend-Pasha of Roumelia. These appointments set him firmly on the road to power. The Porte encouraged Ali, thinking to check the bigger chieftains.

Janina, capital of a *sanjak*, was in a state of anarchy, so Ali sent agents to put it in a worse state; then, when the time was ripe, he marched against the city, defeated the beys who opposed him, and entered with a forged *firman* appointing him governor; and this *firman* he induced the Porte to confirm.

Ali now worked to extend his power by every conceivable means, secretly aspiring to the crown of Albania, and he justified his misdeeds by declaring they were for the glory of the Porte and the subjugation of infidels. He kept up a steady flow of bribes and tribute to Constantinople where he maintained many agents; and he acted readily as the Porte's mandatory against rebellious chiefs (even so far as Vidin and Sofia). He built fortresses, roads, and bridges, attempted agricultural improvements, suppressed his brigand friends, and kept such an excellent police force that the country became safe for merchants and travellers—so many distinguished travellers were attracted to this classic ground. In fact Ali subdued many districts never before under the Turks.

In July, 1792, began Ali's famous struggle with the

Suliotes, whose epic resistance was not overcome until December 12, 1803. In 1798 he gained the coast north of Suli as far as Porto Palermo; but the French held Prevesa, Parga, and Butrinto, so Ali joyfully obeyed the Porte's command to drive them out. He wiped out a small French force at Prevesa and occupied Butrinto, but Parga he did not gain until the unworthy British evacuation in 1819. Nelson congratulated him on these efforts, and the Sultan made him a Pasha of Three Tails and Vali of Roumelia. The French were driven from Corfu by the Turks and Russians.

But Ali, feeling none too secure from either French or Russians, called for British aid; so Colonels Leake and Church were sent to see what could be done in the event of a French invasion. Leake made a military survey of the country, while Church raised an Albanian regiment in which served many of the men who afterwards led the Greeks in their War of Independence.

After Austerlitz (December, 1805) and the cession of Dalmatia to France Ali played French again. Napoleon sent him some valuable presents through Marshal Massena (and afterwards offered, it is said, to help him win the crown of Albania) and the French Ambassador to the Porte got for his two sons the Pashaliks of Lepanto and Morea. In 1807 Marshal Marmont sent Colonel Vaudoncourt to win the support of the beys and pashas of Herzegovina and Albania; Vaudoncourt stayed with Ali to superintend operations against the Russians in the Ionian islands—operations stopped by the Treaty of Tilsit. The Ionian islands passed to the French; but Ali wanted them, so he played British again, taking a big part in patching up the breach between Turkey and England—for which he was presented by the British with a fine park of artillery and several hundreds of the newly invented Congreve rockets. Ali's support of the

British led the French to consider the invasion of Albania, but the British successes in Spain put an end to their plan.

In 1808, Ibrahim Pasha of Berat, Mustafa Pasha of Delvina, Mehmed Deliani of Konispoli, and other chieftains, fearing for their security, combined against Ali. But Veli defeated Ibrahim (his and Mukhtar's father-in-law) and the others went down before Ali who then gained Delvina and Gjinokastra. In 1809 he took Berat, Himara in 1810, and Vlona in 1812. With the single exception of Parga Ali now ruled from a little south of Durrës to the Gulf of Salonika, and south to Corinth—excepting the Athenian peninsula. He was never able to make headway against the Bushatis of Shkodër. Though alarmed by his power the Porte, unable to crush him, continued to issue his annual *firman;* and in return Ali paid over the Christian capitulation tax and customs revenues—but beyond that he did as he pleased and England, France and Russia had representatives at his court.

In the ante-chamber of Ali's great *seraglio* at Janina were to be seen Turkish and Moorish soldiers, Albanian irregulars from every part, Turkish officers, Ali's Ministers, Greek and Jewish secretaries, Greek merchants, Tartar couriers, pages and black slaves, petitioners seeking audience, astrologers, alchemists, poets and many others. His audience chamber was large and gaudily decorated. Ali himself (in 1812) was richly dressed, corpulent, about five feet nine inches in height, with a forehead remarkably broad, an eye penetrating yet not expressive of ferocity, a long white beard and a moustache. His complexion was fair. Byron wrote of him:

"Yet in his lineaments ye cannot trace,
While Gentleness her milder radiance throws
Along that aged venerable face,
The deeds that lurk beneath, and stain him with disgrace."

Though fiendishly cruel, Ali lived in a land and in times where mere death was held of small account, so that perhaps his roastings and drownings and tortures were necessary to strike terror into his subjects. Though there were three hundred concubines and slaves in his luxurious harem he had only one wife, in the strict Moslem style; and even his favourite, an Albanian girl, had to make obeisance to his sons' wives. Sometimes, from among all these women he would reward a favoured officer with a wife, a gift which had to be accepted however little desired! And he would dispossess a man of his property for refusing to give his children for the harem. He was very hard-working, for he trusted no one and would never decentralise. He allowed no political differences between Moslems and Christians —he even built churches for the Christians, who outnumbered the Moslems in his domain. He would accept invitations to dine with Greeks and Turks alike (with precautions against poison), and he would tolerate all manner of insults from *dervishes*. He was temperate and not fastidious. He was impatient (hence some of his castles were too hurriedly built for care) and disgustingly avaricious (a failing which proved his undoing). He could read and write, but his geography was sketchy. In the art of low cunning he was unrivalled; and if, for example, he wished to be rid of a man he would send a common prostitute into that man's house, then, discovering her there, hang him. Infidelity was ruthlessly punished. Unfaithful women were tied in sacks and thrown into the lake after dark. There was the case of Phrosini and sixteen other girls of Mukhtar's harem who were accused of infidelity and drowned by Ali's order. Only lower class women—Moslem or Christian—were to be seen in the streets of Janina at any time. At night nobody might walk about without

ALI PASHA, THE LION OF JANINA
(From an old Print)

Below—ALI'S IRON CASTLE AND ROUND TOWER TO-DAY
(See p. 188)

a lantern and the bazaar was patrolled by ferocious dogs.

Ali's army was but a mob of picturesque ruffians going as they pleased for hope of loot or pay. They were armed with long heavy unbalanced muskets which could not be aimed without supports. Ali gave all his military offices to Albanians, who respected and admired him and gloried in his deeds as one of them; but he employed many foreigners for technical services and the Great Powers were ready enough to send him such aid in the hope of winning him to their respective sides—so Ali, in true Albanian style, took what he could from each and then did as he pleased. The Albanian part of his domain was the most populous region of the Turkish Empire and in the country round Tepeleni he had 16,000 men armed with muskets. He reckoned Albania 200 hours in length, in half of which (before he took Berat and Vlona) he held sway, the other half being divided equally between the Pashas of Berat and Shkodër; but he admitted there were some chiefs who acknowledged the authority of none of the three.

In Ali's day Janina had a population of 40,000 but it has dwindled by half. It already had an eventful history when the Turks first came to it in 1430—and they stayed there, nominally at any rate, until March, 1913, when it surrendered to the Greeks after four months' siege. It stands beautifully on gentle slopes by the side of a lake six miles long, perhaps two broad; and on the other side the lake is bounded by bare limestone mountains. The lake's only outlet is by long underground channels. In the middle of it stands an island upon which, in Ali's day, were a fortress, 200 houses, and seven convents where Ali used to keep his state prisoners.

On a rocky promontory stand the decaying walls of Ali's great fortress—the Iron Castle. In his time it was a small town in itself, crowded with the wretched hovels of Turks and Jews, two mosques, and the old *seraglio* of the Pashas—an irregular mass with wide eaves, long rows of windows, and walls richly painted both within and without with patterns and scenes. The Christians forfeited their right to live in the fortress after a revolt in the sixteenth century. Ali greatly strengthened it by forced labour—even the Greek Archbishop had to do his bit; and the labour gangs were encouraged by a band. A moat, cut round the walls, was filled by the water of the lake—which must have sunk in level since those days. Round the town he threw up military lines. He built a new *seraglio* by the edge of the lake in the southern part of the town, almost adjoining his two sons' *seraglios*. Outside the fortress there were, too, seventeen mosques, six Greek churches, five *tekkés* and two synagogues. On the north of the town was a park with red deer and an ostrich and a pavilion in which an organ played when a fountain flowed.

In 1819 Ali was scheming to attack the Pashalik of Shkodër. But times were no longer good for him. Europe was pacified, the Sultan was consolidating his Empire. Only the two great Albanians, Mehemet Ali of Egypt and Ali Pasha of Janina were unsubmissive. Then Ali overreached himself. In February, 1820, he tried to bring about the assassination of his enemy Ismail Pashou Bey in the precincts of the palace at Constantinople, "the residence of the Caliph and the centre of security." The Sultan resolved to crush him and made elaborate preparations. So Ali rallied his chieftains. The fortresses at Okhrida, Berat, Këlcyra, Permeti, Tepeleni, Gjinokastra, Delvina, Vlona, Porto Palermo, Saranda, Parga, Prevesa, and in Greece many other places were garrisoned. His sons Mukhtar and Salih were at Berat, and at Tepeleni Mukhtar's son

THE HIMARA AND THE LION

Mahmoud. Ali himself was at Janina, and Omer Vrioni —a veteran of Mehemet Ali's wars—commanded a striking force of 15,000 picked troops. The Greek guerilla leader Odysseus commanded Ali's irregular bands. Ali now proclaimed he would grant his people a constitution. The Greeks were enthusiastic, "but the Albanians only asked if a charter would ensure their pay." The Turks were contemptuous.

Meantime Mukhtar drove back the Pasha of Shkodër (who was embarrassed by a revolt among the Montenegrins) and occupied Elbasan and Kruja. But the Turkish fleet gained all the Albanian ports so Mukhtar, faced with rebellion at Vlona and Kanina, fell back on Gjinokastra. Then Ali's power crumbled away. His people, sore at his tyranny (and many at his discipline), forsook him directly it seemed safe to do so. Omer Pasha and his lieutenants went over to the Turks, one by one the fortresses surrendered: even Veli (at Prevesa) and Mukhtar (at Gjinokastra) surrendered on promise of Pashaliks—but afterwards they were both suspected of planning to aid their father and were executed. Only little Mahmoud stood firm at Tepeleni.

But Janina was held by 8,000 faithful Albanians, with over 200 cannon under a skilful Italian named Caretto, many Congreve rockets and supplies for some years. A strong flotilla held the lake and the island was garrisoned. Nevertheless Ali was seriously alarmed and thought of flight. He was told that some British gunboats would lie off Butrinto; these he might seize and thus escape to Corfu, but that no open protection could be given him while he stayed on Turkish territory. But while hesitating to leave his treasures his retreat was cut off. So first he gave Janina over to his soldiers to loot, then destroyed the town by bombardment from the fortress so that it should not shelter his enemies.

Those of the inhabitants who escaped this destruction were either slaughtered by the advancing Turks or perished in the mountains, and the ruins of the town were still smoking when the enemy arrived. On August 20, 1820, Pashou was proclaimed Pasha of Janina.

But the proclamation was premature. Soon, defection among the investing forces led to the raising of the siege; so Pashou was relieved of his command and ultimately beheaded. Now Ali encouraged the Greeks to revolt and they did so, in the rear of Khurshid Pasha who was sent against Janina from the Morea with full powers and promotion. The siege began again in February 1821, though it was not closely pressed until November. Ali resisted gallantly. On July 24 the fortress on the island was accidentally destroyed by fire. Then Caretto deserted. Finally, Ali blew up the fortress of Literica and shut himself in the round tower of the Iron Castle, near his beloved wife's tomb. Here he kept his treasure and below it a magazine; and in the magazine he posted his faithful servant Ahmed with an ever lighted torch and orders to blow the place up if the Turks broke in. Then, at last, the old Lion of Janina surrendered—on condition that he might retire to the island with half his fortune. For several days he was treated magnificently, so upon assurance that the agreed terms would be observed he sent his ring to Ahmed as a sign to hand over the tower. That day—February 5, 1822—he was treacherously assassinated. His head was embalmed and sent to Constantinople, and the faithless Omer Vrioni reigned in his stead.

So ended the career of one of the most picturesque scoundrels of modern times, who had caused the death of about 100,000 people. His atrocities were soon forgotten, but his courage and achievements live on in many a wild ballad, many a crude portrait, many an Albanian heart.

A Market Scene in Tirana, 1931. The Parliament Building is Seen Beyond

(See p. 193)

CHAPTER VIII

KING ZOG AND HIS CAPITAL

TIRANA, in 1930, was an untidy place, though the Albanians were making great efforts to transform it from a quaint Turkish town into a capital that looked modern. Its Turkish body with 10,000 inhabitants had put forth straight wide boulevards till it sprawled loosely over two miles and held 32,000 people. More streets were cut through its houses and gardens and mosques, happily leaving the concentrated chaos of the bazaar intact in the very middle. The plan is a good one, drawn up with Italian advice, and in the end Tirana will be a pleasant place; but it would have been a pleasanter had the Albanians listened to the Italians in the matter of architecture and adopted a native style. But anything which looks Albanian the Tirana people would not have; and they were proud of the great double-barrelled "Boulevard Mussolini" which seemed to rush resolutely and dustily towards the distant Military School between scattered derelicts of the old and skeletons of the new.

The Municipality and new Ministries were being set up in a circle by the mosque of Ethem Bey. Before they were opened in 1931 the various Ministries were all over the town in ramshackle Turkish buildings which seemed to glory in the antiquity of their dirt and their cracked woodwork and the stink of their disgusting latrines. By the new Ministries is the Parliament, like a child's toy theatre; it was built in 1923 as an officers' club and is as quaint within as without.

The bazaar, a maze of cobbled streets winding between single-storey crazy houses with open fronts and mysterious interiors filled with primitive needs becomes on market days a boiling swell of peasants in *xhurdini* and *dolama*: donkeys weighed down by their clumsy pack-saddles: soldiers in misfitting uniforms and unpolished leather who would scare any crow: groups of women like old black hens, squatting by a wall, heavily veiled, their embroideries spread out before them: foreign or emancipated Albanian women, dressed *alla Franka*, hunting for the cheapest as the housewife will: their servants too: and among all these feet an indescribable chaos of charcoal and vegetables and chickens and eggs and fruit and firewood and pots, and heaven knows what besides. Rain would banish the *alla Franka* folk but otherwise business would go on.

The *Rruga Mbretnore* (Royal Street), the main shopping street, has blocks of single-storey concrete shops selling foreign goods and overcharging foreigners to raise money for their second storeys. Northward, this street strayed away to mud heaps between the ragged ends of mud walls which had given way before its intentions; southward it ends at the Old Mosque, a beautiful place with quaint mural paintings of Constantinople beneath its wide eaves and dark cypresses to set off its minaret. Beyond is a little public garden which grows roses as big as cabbages. Here the band plays on Sundays in summer and everyone who has *alla Franka* best parades up and down in it. Close by is the square old Turkish house which is the King's palace, standing in a garden of concrete paths and flower beds. It is simply furnished. The audience chamber, which runs the whole length of it, has a highly polished wood floor, and one time when the King received me it was strewn with little Persian rugs like an archipelago. The King stood smiling at my efforts to avoid skidding on them as I withdrew backwards; but they were the cause of the undignified downfall of one British officer and his wife, who collapsed in a floundering heap of spurs and frock.

Behind the palace are some ruinous walls of the old fortress built by Ahmed pasha Toptani in the eighteenth century and destroyed during the struggle between Kaplan pasha Toptani and the Pashas of Shkodër and Kavaja. It stood on the site of an older fortress repaired by Justinian. The Toptanis first built a road to Durrës; and they imported agricultural implements, and Italian experts to teach the people how to use them. In Leake's time Tirana, Kavaja and the plain were an appanage of the Sultan-Mother. Lear found Tirana "as wretched and disgusting as its fellow city (Elbasan)—horrors I had made up my mind to bear in Albania, and here, truly, they were in earnest."

In hot weather the Llana stream, which bounds Tirana to the south, is a succession of stagnant pools which would pullulate with malarial mosquitoes were they not sprayed; and here the bull frogs fill the still darkness of summer nights with their voluptuous croakings, a fit accompaniment to the plaintive music from the Gypsy quarter.

Against the old Ministry of the Interior is a compound which served as the state prison until a concrete and cold and thoroughly modern prison was built; and some prisoners once cut their way through the mud-brick walls of the Ministry into the Press Bureau and so escaped. Thereafter a filing cabinet was put against the wall which had so softly given, and a light kept burning all night in the office so that the night patrols could look through the window to see the same was not happening again.

Between the old Ministry of the Interior and the Italian

Legation is a graceful Venetian bridge across the Llana beneath a gigantic plane tree; and close on the other side is the Gypsy village, a cluster of neat white cottages. These Ciganes, as they are called, being no longer nomads, have lost their language, though they still tell the tradition that their forbears came over the sea from the direction of the sun (meaning Egypt). Their type is very swarthy and quite unlike the average Albanian, but in common with the nomadic Romanies their physique is poor. The men, when they must work, become *hamals* or blacksmiths or executioners or scavengers—it is the Gypsy who drowns the stray dog and carts away the refuse—tasks to which the Albanian will not stoop. There are many of them at the ports, where they work as stevedores and boatmen and porters. The women are stocky, hard-working, far neater than the Tirana Moslems, and they are often employed as servants, for the Albanian dislikes charing. Their noses are markedly Semitic. Their intelligence is average, but they keep their simple houses much cleaner than the lowland Albanians. Nevertheless, the latter despise them, so the old official class is very much afraid foreigners should think them Albanians; and once the Minister of the Interior prohibited the taking of photographs in the Cigane quarter in case it should be represented as typical of Tirana!

The nomadic Romanies are well represented in Albania too, the grammar of their language being very close to that of our British gypsies (according to S. E. Mann). They believe in a supreme God (called, in Romany, Devil) and various nature gods symbolised by the sun, moon, dawn, the sea, and so forth. They live in tents—near towns in winter. Their women, as everywhere, practise fortune-telling and are most lascivious; and the men make baskets, ropes, and deal in horses like their kind in other lands.

IN THE GYPSY VILLAGE AT TIRANA
(*See p.* 196)

KING ZOG AND HIS CAPITAL

South and west of Tirana is a little plain (over which the town is expanding), divided from the rich green valley of the Arzen by a range of low hills beautifully covered by scrub and olive trees. North and east of the town is a soft full countryside of olive groves and almond trees and little farms and meadows—a glory of flowers in springtime; and further still towers *Mali* Dajti, five miles away and often mantled with snow in spring. Several roads lead out towards Dajti, boldly at first, then degenerating into antique Turkish roads—narrow cobbled ways which were cheap because nobody ever used them when it was possible to go beside them, so on either side there generally is a deep-worn track, a muddy ditch in the rains; but their cobbles were handy for building. This way stand the new military and civil hospitals, both large and ultra-modern.

Tirana has an air mail and passenger service, electric light and electric bakeries; on the other hand it has no sewerage, no water laid on, no buses or trams and no railway (though a railway from Durrës was once begun). Here you may see dancing *dervishes* piercing their cheeks with knives: decapitated hens flapping in the restaurants: lumbering buffalo waggons and pack trains: sheep slaughtered in the streets for the Bajram feast: turbaned Moslem priests and bearded Christian bishops: pierrot-like peasants gravely discussing the respective merits of wooden ploughs in the market: Moslem women who turn their backs and draw their black robes over their faces for fear of your polluting gaze—and others who walk boldly in semi-transparent veils and flesh-coloured stockings: half-naked beggars who run whimpering at your heels in the main street: water carriers with their ponies and their petrol tins: tall mountaineers in national dress arm in arm with officers in shining boots and spurs

—in fact there are still, in Tirana, endless contrasts to amuse and delight.

A friend of mine once remarked to an Albanian shepherd upon the absence of brigands in the countryside and the security which travellers now enjoy. "True," said the man, "because all the brigands have gone to Tirana where they wear collars and rob with authority from behind office desks." That is precisely what happened during the transition stage from which young Albania is now emerging. The magnificent characteristics which so impressed those who watched Albania's struggle for independence are still held by the mountain men, who won that independence while the bastard Turks, fanatical Sunni Moslems of the low country, cringed in cafés or stood for the Sultan; and when Prince Wilhelm came to Albania these miserable fanatics rose against him, swearing they would have none but a Turkish Prince. After the World War the least uneducated among them combined with the dregs from every corner of Albania to exploit the land, finding that robbery in a peaceful way was profitable; but now a new generation is thrusting out the old, a generation brought up with national ideals and national pride and an enthusiasm for national improvement.

It is idle to pretend that the people of Albania are a homogeneous race, for widely dissimilar types are seen; and the difference, both in character and physique, between the lowland peasant or townsman and the mountaineer is as clear-cut as the line which divides the mountains from the plains. The strength, nobility, simplicity, pride and honesty of the mountaineers are the qualities of men of ancient stock geographically beyond the contamination of invading armies and civilisation's vices (though when they do become contaminated they prove, often, that "the sweetest wine

BOY OF THE LOWLANDS—NEAR TIRANA

(*See p.* 198)

makes the sourest vinegar"). Successive waves of invaders poured into the plains but the mountains defied them more or less successfully. Last came the Turks, good horsemen but poor mountaineers. The best Albanian stock went into exile or retired to the mountains rather than stay beside them; only the worst remained. Turkish influence gradually soaked deep into the lowlands, melted in by the sub-tropical heat of the plains and valleys which wilts resisting powers and breeds fevers. Peasant blood was diluted by the soldiery, while many who became landowning beys and pashas were of eastern blood and took wives and concubines from all parts of the Sultan's domains. So many lowlanders and townsmen and beys are scarcely Albanian at all, well steeped in Oriental indolence, corruption, deceit and suspicion.

King Zog has always realised that centuries of backwardness cannot be spanned in a year—that the modernisation of Albania must not be hurried. This attitude led to his eviction by the progressive but impatient supporters of Fan Noli in 1924. To Zogu adhered those who feared that progress would rob them of their privileges—the landowners and fanatics. With their aid he returned in December, 1924, enjoying the sympathy of the Powers and supported by his own clansmen, by clansmen who were ready to serve anyone for money, by the enemies Noli's regime had made, by a detachment of Wrangel's Russians and by Yugoslav troops at the frontier. When in 1925 the Russians' pay fell into arrears their commander drew them up before the Ministry of Finance and demanded it. They were paid —and paid off; but some of the officers were naturalised and remain in the Albanian service.

Noli was surprised that Italy did not support him against Zogu, then Yugoslavia's protégé; but when he proposed an alliance with Italy in 1924 the Italian Government were bound (by their Treaty of Friendship with Yugoslavia) to refrain from interference in Albanian affairs. When, however, the Yugoslavs themselves interfered by supporting Zogu, Italy held herself absolved; and Sola (afterwards Italian Minister in Albania), who had seen Zogu in Belgrade, had reported well of him. So the Italians resolved to back him; and the revolt in the north in November, 1926, alleged to have been stirred up by Yugoslavs, provided the occasion for the Pact of Tirana. Hitherto Zogu had been reluctant to commit himself so openly.

During 1927 the Treaty of Alliance and proclamation of the Kingdom were discussed. Zogu preferred to postpone the latter step, but the conclusion of the Franco-Yugoslav Pact in November, 1927, was taken as suitable cover for the signature of the Treaty. Mussolini had discussed Italy's Albanian policy with Chamberlain, who apparently agreed to it provided it did not threaten international peace; so the Italians stood behind Zogu while he proclaimed himself king. Though the demonstrations at this event were carefully organised there was genuine enthusiasm—not, perhaps, for the man but for the monarchy, a form of government the Albanians understand.

Inevitably King Zog must have a care for his life, for he has political enemies, and private enemies too (those to whom he owes blood), and some think the Yugoslavs would be glad to see him dead. So he is seldom seen. When he does appear, every precaution is taken, and his Royal Guard camp all round his little summer bungalow on the beach near Durrës while he is there. Since his accession this incarcerated King who works from dawn till dusk has never been anywhere in his own country except Tirana and Durrës; and his

BOY OF THE MOUNTAINS—NEAR TIRANA *(See p. 198)*

mother, while she lived, supervised the preparation of his meals (for fear of poison). Even Osman, kavass at the British Legation, was to a point a blood enemy of the King's! Osman, who was trained at a Turkish Officers' School, fought with Hassan Prishtina for Albanian independence in 1911–12. He joined the Legation in 1921; but when Zogu returned to Albania in 1924 there was some alarm because Osman, as Prishtina's man, was bound to shoot Zogu, his chief's blood enemy, if the chance came to him. However, the feud seems to have been "compounded" somehow.

A London periodical told its readers in 1931 that King Zog employed as his personal bodyguard an Englishman known as "Battler Smith." This doughty man kept off a frontal attack by the King's enemies, being handy with a gun, but they got round the flank through the kitchen, so the King had to seek medical advice. We six Englishmen in Tirana—Sir Jocelyn Percy and his son, Hill, Stirling, Mann and myself—eyed each other with grave suspicion! I, at any rate, played no such role.

Of the six Princesses (the King's sisters), three are married—Adilé to Emin bey Hyssejnagoll of Dibra: Nafié, whose husband, Cena bey Kryeziu, was assassinated in Prague in 1927: and the eldest, Senije, born in 1903, an energetic worker for the Red Cross, who married a Turkish Prince in the Spring of 1936, somewhat to the annoyance of the Turkish Republican government. The King himself remains unmarried—as he once said, what has he to offer a foreign Princess, living as he does? Though nominally a Moslem his faith is lightly held; and polygamy, never much practised by pure-bred Albanians at any time, is illegal. At one time Zogu was betrothed to the daughter of Shevket Verlaci of Elbasan, most powerful bey in Albania (now a political fugitive in

Italy), but when he came to the throne he broke that off for he dared not so ally himself with the landowning class or rouse the jealousy of other beys. While he was in Vienna in 1931 the Press discovered he had a mistress, a well-born Austrian girl who had been his friend for a number of years. The Vienna papers so eagerly pretended they had discovered something unusual that the Austrian authorities reprimanded them for "insulting the institutions of a friendly state."

So King Zog has no heir, though it is said he has nominated his young fair-haired nephew, Kryeziu's son. Some believe he thinks Prince Wilhelm—or his son Karl Viktor—might succeed him now he has nationalised the country somewhat; but if this should be his plan there are obvious reasons for keeping it to himself. Prince Wilhelm is a quiet, tall, handsome man of great personal charm, with a ready wit and keen sense of fun. He lives near Munich, very modestly, driving his own car and enjoying simple pleasures. His son, born in 1913, has his father's goodness and much ability. Prince Wilhelm's metal was too fine for Albania in 1914, nor did he know Albanian ways, so his courtesies were often mistakes. He told me once that when visiting Tirana he helped his wife from their carriage and allowed her to walk before him, an action which the people interpreted as a sign of feebleness! But now he—or his son—might fare well on the rising tide of the younger generation; and among the older people, particularly the mountaineers, there are many who see in him their legitimate King to whom they gave their *Besa* (which Zogu well kept until the obvious need of his country led him to overlook it). Until 1928 Prince Wilhelm held an Albanian passport, but when Zogu became King the passport was not renewed, so the Prince begged one from Lichtenstein!

When Zogu became President and Dictator in 1925

Prince Wilhelm

(*See p.* 202)

his task was no easy one, for the men at his disposal represented the worst reactionary elements; but as time went on he amnestied his political opponents, so the better elements are rising to the surface and the appointment of a government of younger men under Mehdi Frasheri in the autumn of 1935 inspired great hopes. King Zog has told friends he knows he has been surrounded by rogues; but he argued that only they had the experience to govern, so their corruption had to be overlooked until the younger men had learnt the discipline of responsibility. Perhaps, too, he felt it safer to have the rogues under his eye; and the worst were the most loyal to him, for they knew their positions and lives depended on him.

Though Italy has loaned large sums of money and numerous technical advisers (military and civil) to Albania with obvious benefit to the country, the Italians are disliked, their intentions suspected, and all misfortunes invariably attributed to them. Partly this is due to the evident stranglehold they have gained over a nation fiercely proud of its independence, partly to Yugoslav political propaganda, and partly to individual Italians' tactlessness. But there are other reasons too. The old official class bitterly resents the power which Italy acquired to interfere with their corrupt practices, so they pose as patriots and denounce the Italians while greedily taking their money. Again, these same elements cannot bear criticism, will not take advice, and are excessively conceited. There is probably no other capital in Europe where so many simple acts are held undignified—the carrying of parcels or the wearing of shorts for example; and an Italian officer's Albanian orderly was arrested once for giving his master's children a ride upon a donkey —because it was undignified for a soldier to be with a donkey.

The wildest rumours about the Italians throve on ignorance. I was always told the Albanians were paying the salaries of their Italian advisers and officers, whereas in truth (which the Albanians were too proud to admit) the officers, being on the Italian Army active list, were paid by their own government as a matter of course. The number of Italians in Albania was constantly exaggerated too. The Albanian census gave 2,074 in a country with a million inhabitants, of whom 245 were officers and advisers, and most of these had their families with them. When in June, 1931, Italy agreed to subsidise the Albanian budget provided she had enough financial control to check corruption, rumours were put about that as her condition 15,000 Italian families were to be settled on the land, that Italian officers were to command the army, and that the British Minister had made a *démarche* against these arrangements. There was no truth in these tales. Yet I met only one Albanian official (though many not officials) who ever expressed concern at the budget deficit or the weight of debt and the impossibility of repaying the Italian loan. The Italian-controlled National Bank was gravely suspected. "The Bank is robbing us—it must be because it pays interest. The Italians would never pay interest with their money, so they must be paying it with our own money to make us think it is a good Bank."—That from a responsible official.

The Albanian Army is like an illegitimate child that nobody will own. On a peace footing it is about 12,000 strong, but King Zog told me (in January, 1931), he would reduce it to three battalions: and later he is alleged to have said it serves Italy, not Albania—"which," said an Italian, "is untrue. It serves nobody." The Italians are divided on the question of its worth, their only care being that in war the passes should be held for fifteen days.

Italy is often blamed for saddling Albania with an army, but this is unfair because the army was on much the same footing long before there was any agreement with Italy; and if Yugoslavia repudiated all designs upon northern Albania and collaborated in helping Albania to her feet the army would be unnecessary. It is commanded by an Albanian, General Xhemal Aranitas; but the Chief of the General Staff is an Austrian, General Gustav von Myrdacz, a quiet man devoted to music and his garden. He commanded an Austro-Hungarian battalion in Albania during the war, met Zogu in Vienna, returned to Albania in 1922, became naturalised, and undertook to pull the army together. He and his wife were the first foreigners of any note to live in Tirana. The Assistant-Chief of Staff, Colonel Erebara, has an Austrian mother; while the luckless General Ghilardi was a Croat by birth.

"If you need advice don't ask a friend, ask your enemy, then do the opposite of what he says," is an Albanian proverb. Too often Albanian officials look upon all advisers as enemies; and so, if the British are better liked than the Italians, it is largely because there are fewer of them and they have less power. But they are equally obstructed—more so, because it is easier since the British Government is not behind them. Percy is a man of vast experience, well liked among the rank and file, who took pains to pick his officers. So if the gendarmerie is not all that it might be the fault must lie with the Albanian authorities; and though the lips of the general and his officers were always tightly sealed in professional silence, all Tirana knew that corruption was still rife, pay still irregular, and the general constantly obstructed or ignored. The truth is that the corrupt do not want a strong gendarmerie for it would mean an end of their corruption. The renewal of the

British officers' contracts always entailed months of laborious negotiation over petty details. Even an English butler engaged through the Legation to train the King's domestic staff was so hampered that at length he fell to drink in despair. It seems, in fact, that many Albanians are congenitally obstructive—perhaps through habit of constantly obstructing the Turks.

Sloth and suspicion made foreign business in Albania maddening except for the Italians, whose Legation looked upon their enterprises as a political matter. But even for the Italians it was hard enough because of the shortage of competent Albanian workmen; and though it was laid down on paper that one third of the skilled labour employed for execution of Italian contracts might be Italian, advantage was never taken of this condition and the Italians tried to train native labour, providing staffs for an agricultural and four technical schools. Feasts and fasts made small business an agony. Values, moreover, were queerly estimated. A glass inkstand was charged by weight, and the price of six wineglasses asked for two because the other four had been broken in transit. Bartering in Eastern style is still the general practice.

Administrative corruption was from the top downwards, though there were many shining exceptions among higher officials. But so much dishonesty, indolence and injustice in high places was a pernicious example to the miserably underpaid junior men—and the peasants too —who learn to think in terms of graft. The younger men cried out bitterly; and though some of their bitterness was due perhaps to lack of opportunity, most was genuine shame at their government's state. The corrupt and reactionary elements were headed by a small camarilla whose mysterious power seemed out of all proportion to their importance. They dominated the Chamber and pulled the strings which swayed a cabinet of marionettes—for the cabinet is still nominated by the King and Albania has not yet attained to freedom in elections. Their only interests were robbery, and the suppression of rising youth which threatened them. Their position with the King seemed to be secured through one of them, Abdurrahman Krosi, known to patriots as "Albania's Black Spot." His position was, and still is, that of a medieval favourite. No more than an illiterate servant while Zogu was a chieftain, Krosi rose with his master and is now deputy for Mati (by the King's command); but some declare he is the only man the King can really trust, while others whisper that in truth he is the King's father—a slander I repeat merely to show how his power seems to the people. An Albanian once told me a story of Essad Pasha's servant to show how, in his view, Krosi gains his power. When Essad became powerful he told his faithful henchman he would be supported and well treated but would have no influence. But the man craved one favour—which the Pasha granted; it was that whenever Essad saw him in a street or café he would call him and whisper in his ear: "Go to hell." When the people saw Essad whispering they concluded the servant had great power, so he was able to grow rich and prosperous.

Krosi's name is a by-word on the lips of Albanians and foreigners alike. Ministers hate him; the people fear him: yet still he reigns in Tirana, having a hand, or money, in any number of enterprises which succeed accordingly, for his word is law so it is policy to have him as a partner or friend or director at any price. Those few who dare oppose him think they risk assassination. He ought to be shot, his interference is intolerable, he tried to sell anthrax-infested sheep to the butchers, he had bad fish sold in the streets, he was interested in an hotel so a rival establishment was commandeered as a government office—and so forth: comments or tales by most credible people. The source of Krosi's power is the mystery of Tirana. It was for criticising him in the Press that I had to leave Albania; and it was his camarilla which ousted Colonel Stirling from his post as Inspector-General of Government Services because they would not tolerate his reports to the King upon their corrupt practices, making Stirling's position so impossible that he had to leave the country two months before me.

Having undertaken to prepare a section upon Albania for the *Near East Year Book* (for which the Albanian authorities were very keen) I paid an exorbitant rent for a rickety mud-brick bungalow with leaking roof and innumerable scorpions upon the outskirts of Tirana, and set to work throughout the summer heat of 1930. It was like working in a Turkish bath. And even behind gauze-covered windows there would be flies—they would come in about each visitor till they mustered a legion and buzzed from my face to my legs, from my legs to the window, then back to my face again, looking innocently like our common flies but far from common in the way they pricked and pricked.

But physical irritations were nothing to those occasioned by necessary contact with officialdom. The Ministry of Education furnished statistics of schools and pupils but there were seven mistakes of simple addition in the totals. After weeks of patience I obtained an elaborate sheet giving the numbers of foreigners in Albania; there were, it stated, only three British in the country—whereas there were nine, well-known to everybody, in Tirana alone! The census taken that summer (for which the entire population was shut up throughout one Sunday by troops) gave the total British as seventy-nine—of whom not more than thirty were of British blood.

Then there was the ordeal of interrogating idle or ignorant officials in stuffy offices filled with unwashed smells, and the exasperation of having correspondence opened or parcels lost—for which, of course, the Italians were blamed.

The other side of the picture was revealed by a boy from the American Technical School who came to type for me sometimes. A ragged creature, he spoke with patriotic fervour, saying often: "We must all work night and day for our country: if I work all the time my body will get stronger and stronger: sleep is a waste of time when I might be working for my country." This school, established by the American Junior Red Cross soon after the war, reflected, on the whole, much credit upon the two Americans who ran it for so many years, and turned out splendid lads sometimes—among them some astonishingly wise for their age. Another notable institution having American support, a large building near Tirana, is the Kyrias school for girls, the private enterprise of three Albanians from Korça, who have several American girls to assist them. There are 150 girls, Moslem and Christian—for the younger generation takes no account of religious differences and there is Moslem fanaticism only in the central plains. Officials are indiscriminately of all religions and Christian Skenderbeg the national hero. Unhappily the plains are populous so the fanatics are many; and when the Bektash Mehdi Frashëri (then Minister of National Economy) wrote denouncing the seclusion and idleness of Moslem women as uneconomic he was so attacked that he had to resign. At balls, too, some girls of the best families might not dance for their parents' prejudices, though they hated the restraint and showed revolt by dressing in western style.

The occasional state balls at the Tirana Club—to celebrate some national event or honour a distinguished foreign visitor—were gay affairs, however, the concentrated essence of diplomatic functions as Seton-Merriman saw them, a riot of decorations and uniforms and with a strong flavour of intrigue. In Tirana, as in all Balkan capitals, intrigue and rumour enliven visits and dances, supper parties or tennis at the club which might otherwise be commonplace; and the town is so small that one may be in easy touch with everyone, meeting all from the highest to the lowest in the cafés, the streets and at social functions. Of gossip there is a steady stream, for the bickerings of a small international community with nothing else to do but be scandalous or jealous may be imagined. Visiting was often a hot and irksome duty, but Tirana's social life is a serious strenuous business in which only the very hardiest conventionalists can hope to shine.

There were many comedies. Once there came to Tirana a man calling himself Professor, his card smothered with degrees from obscure universities, who showed daring books on art, literature and love which bore his name as author. Some (unheard of) university of which he was vice-president, he said, admired Albanian brilliance, so he had to offer degrees to those most distinguished—only there were very substantial fees which several very high Albanian officials paid! Then the police, smart for once, discovered he was one of a gang who found this trade very profitable. Next there came—the rumour of the coming of a fabulously rich though wildly eccentric American. He made sure the rumour preceded him, so a policeman was attached to him to honour his money. He threw cash about—and freely exposed substantial cheques. It was said he would buy up the National Bank, pay off the Italian loan, build an immense hotel; and he presented fat cheques to the Albanian Red Cross. So the King decorated him and the Minister of Economy gave him papers saying certain concessions would be his if he raised capital—which were what he wanted for raising money. Then he feigned illness and went—just before the cheques were dishonoured.

Terrific thunderstorms are common in the Tirana plain, and the sirocco is a visitation I experienced once in Durrës. A stuffy, burning wind came moaning mournfully from the south-west, then shrieked as it fell upon Durrës and swirled the sand and dust into choking clouds which blinded our chauffeur as we crawled from the town seeing barely a yard beyond the car; and the windscreen saved us from decapitation by a fallen telegraph wire. Then the thunder came, and terrifying forks of blue lightning which rent the night-black clouds and once or twice played horribly on the car's metal parts.

The plateau of *Mali* Dajti is a grand refuge, near at hand, from Tirana's summer heat, and there is a log cabin for shelter at night. The plateau is a magic Alpine place in summer, bounded on one side by steep scrub-grown slopes downward (to the plain), and on the other by steep slopes upward, thickly covered with immense beeches. The summit of the mountain (about 4,000 feet) is a long knife-edge, precipitous to the valley on the east, complicated by trees and rocks and having a view of the sea and Durrës and the mountains and valleys north and south and east, and the Tirana plain below—where, at night, the capital sparkles like an enchanted city. The plateau is sweet with hay, a glory of flowers, and only the tinkling of cow-bells breaks its sleepy peace. There are groups of haymakers and a cowherd or two, but rarely anyone besides; and in the evening a myriad fireflies flit like fairies among the ghostly tree trunks.

But among the many enchanting spots near Tirana, Petrela is probably the most notable. A range of hills divides the upper part of the smiling Tirana vale from a turbulent country (to the south) of bare grey clay ridges, scrub-covered irregular hills, meadows, and patches of corn which are emerald green in August. At one end of the range is the Krraba Pass; at the other stands Petrela. An abrupt hill (1,600 feet high) is crowned by a precipitous rock and on the rock is a ruined castle. Among the olive trees on the upper slopes are little wood and mud-brick houses with dark balconies and high latticed windows. At the foot of the hill is the wide stony bed of the Arzen, and beyond the river the new Tirana-Elbasan road.

Close below the castle is the "village green"—an open space among the olives flanked by a quaint mosque and several red-tiled cottages. One is the gendarmerie post. And there is the "village club"—a wide-spreading plane tree. Passing through an archway in the *enceinte* wall a steep cobbled way leads to the citadel which is triangular with a circular tower at each angle. Two sides are protected by a sheer precipice. It is a small place, and swallow-tailed butterflies flitting from weed to weed among its ruins were the only life when I was there. On one tower lies a rusty cannon.

It is not known when a castle was first built here, though the natural strength of site and walls indicate importance in ancient times. Knolles describes its capture by Skenderbeg in the autumn of 1443. It was, he says, a

"citie strongly scituate upon the top of a steepe rockie mountaine, as all the rest of the cities of Epirus be, and was by the Turks well furnished with men, munition, and other things needfull."

Skenderbeg sent a "faithfull and wise fellow" to tell the garrison that if they surrendered they might either join him or go in safety with all their goods. Either way,

PETRELA CASTLE: LOOKING FROM THE ENTRANCE
(See p. 212)

they would be rewarded. The "faithfull fellow" added artfully a grim account of their compatriots' fate at Kruja and of

"other their fellowes abroad in the countrey, whose dead bodies as then lay in everie corner of Epirus for a prey to the hungrie dogs and greedie wolves";

and he warned them that the Sultan (defeated at Nish) was in no state to relieve them. As refugees had already brought them such tidings, they surrendered, and Skenderbeg fed them and gave them money and sent them on their way with an escort for their protection. Petrela passed again into Turkish hands after Skenderbeg's death; and it probably resisted siege many times by insurgent Albanian chieftains in later years.

The tomb of Balabanus Badera, who was killed at the siege of Kruja in 1466, is at Petrela. By local legend Balabanus, who was decapitated while fighting before Kruja, took his head in his hand, and rode to Petrela, and set it where his grave now is. Another time Skenderbeg, cut off at Petrela by the Turks, mounted his white horse and leapt from the walls—across the plain of Tirana—into Lesh, and the imprints of the horse's hoofs in both places may still be seen. Balabanus set a fashion, for there are the graves of sixteen or more Turkish generals and notables beneath Petrela's olive trees, though whether or not they all chose their last resting places in the same decided manner as Balabanus is not known. Their descendants sometimes send money for the care of the graves.

Once, in talking with a Kruja peasant lad, I remarked that I disliked Tirana—thinking of the people and their petty conceits. He thought a moment, then agreed: "Tirana is a bad place—the water is bad." For drinking water is the chief criterion of places in Albania. All drinking water in Tirana was brought in petrol tins by picturesque water-carriers with their donkeys; but for washing there was water from the well which each house had.

In the autumn I took another house, rather less crazy than the other, but like it in the absence of all comforts such as bath or kitchen range or light or heating. However, it had a fireplace in the sitting-room, though the smoke poured into the room from cracks in the mud and plaster wall and the price of wood was high. But anything was better than the cheerless copper braziers in which charcoal is burnt, which give off deadly fumes. There was a large garden—a wilderness of tall weeds—enclosed by a high mud-brick wall with tiles on top. A massive double wooden door under a tiled porch gave into a little alley with other doorways, which led into a deserted lane; and the stillness of the night was broken only by the shrill whistles of the night patrols. In the garden were an immense walnut tree haunted by doves and magpies, a cherry tree, a fig, a plum, a thorn tree and several vines growing as they pleased. There was a stoned-up well, but the water was fit only for washing.

Beyond the garden wall was an open space dotted with olive trees, and among them a little mosque with a rickety wooden tower as minaret. As the sun went down the *muezzin*, leaning from this minaret against a deep orange sky, would cry mournfully to the Faithful, the last syllable of his weird dirge drawn out in a tragic wail the length of a deep breath. And going out, I would see silent figures coming slowly through the furtive dusk to obey the summons.

Albania has an infinite number of public holidays, religious or national—feasts, fasts and fears are a great impediment to the traveller, wrote Leake over a hundred years ago. There being no state religion there are holidays for Moslems, Roman Catholics and Orthodox alike. Most exasperating of all are the Moslem Big and Little Bajram, about two months apart. Then, whether you are Christian or Moslem, it is the fashion to call on Moslem friends to wish them *Për shumë vjet Bajram* (meaning: for many years Bajram). No more need be said, but you must eat a sticky sweet and a spoonful of jelly, wash them down with water, sip Turkish coffee and smoke a cigarette; but the rising generation are sticking out against this fashion and call only on those of their chiefs who are fanatical when they feel a call tactful.

Autumn is the time for national holidays. There is the anniversary of the proclamation of the Kingdom, the King's birthday, Independence Day, and the "Triumph of Legality"—anniversary of the King's triumphal return to Tirana in 1924: but many feel this last is in bad taste since so many of Zogu's former opponents now fill government posts. On these days the police see that all shops are shut and Tirana smothered in flags. In the morning there is a military parade or a reception of the uniformed diplomatic corps by the King; and in the evening the streets are gay with strings of coloured lights, bands play, there is a show of fireworks, and everyone walks up and down the streets.

In January, 1931, Tirana was disturbed by news that forty high officials had received letters accusing them of ruining the country and threatening their lives if they did not resign: and by the imposition of a new law depriving the Press of all liberty to criticise the corrupt camarilla. The Press law was violently and gallantly opposed by Nebil Cika, who launched a furious attack, through his paper, upon the corrupt and was brought to trial in consequence—but, to the indignation of the camarilla, he was acquitted.

But the two events which most stirred Tirana while I was there were the assassination of the Italian Lieutenant Chesti at Shkodër on June 26, 1930, and the attempt upon the life of King Zog at Vienna on February 21, 1931.

Chesti was murdered by a corporal of the Albanian Frontier Guard who afterwards found asylum in Yugoslavia. Such incidents may have incalculable consequences, so for two days the atmosphere was tense and the danger of war freely talked about. Rumours circulated that the affair had been planned by the Yugoslavs to provoke Italy, and the absent Italian Minister rushed back to Albania in a destroyer. Then calm was restored as swiftly as it had been disturbed, for war for a corpse was not in the Italian programme.

The attempt upon King Zog, had it succeeded, would probably have precipitated an international crisis ripe with danger of war. The King left Albania on January 25 in great secrecy, sailing from Durrës on an Italian cruiser and travelling to Vienna to consult a specialist, for it was thought he was suffering from tuberculosis. It was the first time he had left his country since 1924 and none but a few high officials knew of his going until he had gone. Great precautions were taken to keep order in his absence, the Tirana garrison was strengthened, and the frontier troops reinforced in case Gani Kryeziu, chief of the Albanian emigrants in Yugoslavia and a blood enemy of King Zog (whom he held to account for the assassination of his brother Cena, the King's brother-in-law), should attempt to lead bands over the border to stir revolt. The King's going had a quaint effect upon the camarilla who became suddenly polite to their critics—though Krosi himself felt it better for his health that he should go with his master.

Everyone knew the King risked his life by going to

Vienna, centre of revolutionaries and headquarters of his Albanian enemies; and everyone whose opinion mattered was positive that if the King was killed, there would follow immediately a bloody revolt against his entourage, the camarilla. Nor was there anyone who could succeed him, but many who might try; and the armed forces would split up to support their respective patrons, for not many officers and men were free of someone's patronage.

News that the King was suffering from nothing worse than over-smoking was received with much scepticism —and no little disappointment among those who felt he alone protected the camarilla. Nevertheless deputations came (by order) from the chief towns to congratulate the Queen Mother (and impress each other with their loyalty); but the King still lingered in Vienna.

Three weeks later came the startling news. The attempt was made as the King was leaving the Opera House. Three men rushed up and opened fire. The King was already in his lighted car and his A.D.C., Topallaj, getting in. Libohova, the Minister of the Court, was about to follow. The first shot killed Topallaj, who fell upon the King and probably saved him by stopping another bullet; and Libohova was struck down by a bullet in the leg but drew his revolver and opened fire from the ground. The King also emptied his own revolver, then called to Topallaj for his, not knowing Topallaj was already dead. Krosi stayed in the Opera House—and Tirana lamented he had not been in poor Topallaj's place. The police rushed up and the two most determined assailants—Albanians—were overpowered.

All shops in Tirana were closed immediately the news came, and the town beflagged. The Queen Mother's house was open to the public all day and everyone was free to walk in and congratulate her upon her son's escape. The post office surged with people sending telegrams of congratulation to the King in the hope of winning a good mark.

Grave reports now began to pass among high officials pointing to Yugoslav complicity in the affair. The King's assassination, it was said, had been planned by the Albanian Revolutionary National Union under the presidency of Angjelin Suma, and was to be followed by an invasion of northern Albania by armed bands, organised among the Albanian minority upon Yugoslav soil, which were to exploit existing disaffection and the confusion which would arise. At the end of January the Yugoslav Minister in Tirana had warned the Albanian Government of a plot—but this warning had been given, said the mischievous, so that Yugoslavia might afterwards protest her innocence of the affair. According to reports, leaders of the Revolutionary Union had paid a long visit to the Yugoslav Legation in Vienna on February 7; and on February 11 rumours of a plot against King Zog had begun to circulate in the frontier districts. Though the Italians were keen that the worst should be thought of Yugoslav intentions, impartial observers formed the opinion that the Yugoslav government had no hand in the affair, though individual Ministers or officials may not have been entirely innocent of it. Once the bands had passed the frontier the Yugoslavs would have closed it and declared (as when they helped Zogu over) that the affair was an Albanian domestic matter in which nobody should interfere; but Italy would probably have landed troops to protect her interests and restore order, whereupon the Yugoslavs would have protested that this was Italy's aggression and they were obliged to intervene for the protection of Albania's independence. Therein lay, and lie, all the elements of a grave international crisis, so much so that the British government had called the Yugoslav government's attention to the rumours of preparations against Albania.

King Zog returned to Tirana on March 20, being loudly acclaimed by those who realised his life meant peace and by others who believed in his good intentions. Before leaving Vienna he had with King Alexander an amusing exchange through the Press. King Alexander declared Yugoslavia cherished the most friendly sentiments for Albania—to which King Zog answered that such declarations, while bands were formed on Yugoslav soil to attack Albania, were rot. Since bands may assemble and disperse again in twenty-four hours, it is hard to prove or disprove their reality.

The trial of Zogu's assailants Ndoc Gjeloshi and Aziz Cami was held in September, 1931, at Ried in Upper Austria where attempts to assassinate them would be less easy than in Vienna. The accused had known that in Austria political murder is punishable only by imprisonment. Though the proceedings were *in camera*, enough emerged to indicate a premeditated crime and that the accused had received monthly salaries from Zogu's enemies in Yugoslavia. They protested they had met on the fateful night by chance and had acted upon impulse—"When an Albanian has not got himself in hand," explained Gjeloshi, "he has a revolver in it." They declared Zogu had sold Albania to Mussolini and was oppressing the Catholics. Gjeloshi was convicted of killing Topallaj, Cami of wounding Libohova, and both of attempting to kill the King, so they were sentenced respectively to seven and three years' hard labour.

Meantime my own affairs drifted to a climax. Before coming to Albania I had drawn up, with expert advice and Stirling's collaboration, a scheme for a tourist organisation. It entailed a small subsidy to a British

Agency, the opening of an Albanian office, the publication of a periodical, regulations for the control of hotels, the erection of mountain huts, and so forth—the whole requiring a trifling outlay by the Albanians who would reap a rich return from tourists and propaganda.

When I reached Albania many people—from the King downward—discussed the scheme enthusiastically. I was urged to hurry my other work and be free to put it into effect. But when I was ready to begin, every conceivable obstacle was raised as pretext for delay, though I was encouraged to do any amount of preliminary work (for the authorities' benefit). The authorities evidently imagined that because I had proposed the scheme there must be some great gain attached, so they took me for a donkey and dangled it before me like a carrot in the hope that, in my anxiety to get the carrot, I would not kick them through the Press. They thought this subtlety worth while, for I was the only foreign correspondent (except Italians) in the country; and when they found this method did not work with me they gave it up and me up too.

At the end of April, the Automobile Association cabled stating they proposed sending representatives to Albania if I would guarantee a basis for discussion of a tourist organisation. The Minister of Interior, Musa Juka (a fanatical Moslem who had once been brought to trial upon charges of corruption laid by Stirling but had been reinstated by the King) had said he was preparing proposals, so on May 2 I called on him to discuss them. They were fatuous—dealing chiefly with passports for "tourist groups"; but that, he said, was all the government would do. Then he opened upon another matter.

My articles in *The Near East and India*, he said, had offended, particularly two statements lately. I had written there was a budget deficit, but I must know that if the government chose to collect certain taxes amounting to 18,000,000 gold francs—presumably he had in mind that 75 per cent of Tirana escaped direct taxation through influence or bribes—there would be no deficit. I replied my figures were from the Ministry of Finance and asked him to say plainly whether there was or was not, in fact, a deficit. He replied that there was; so I asked what the other offending statement might be. I had written, he answered, that a certain official occupied a position analogous to that of a medieval favourite and presumed (correctly) that I meant Krosi. But Krosi, he said, had no real influence—he exploited his intimacy with the King and the Ministers but did not sway them. Many people, he concluded, would hang Krosi were it not for the King's protection. I answered that those who would *not* hang Krosi (outside his own camarilla) might be counted on the fingers of a hand, and that he (Juka) was *not* represented by any one of those fingers. The thrust went home, for it turned him to riotous mirth and we parted with much cordiality.

But a week later I was called urgently to Juka's office again. Without preliminaries he declared, scowling, that he had reconsidered my articles which were too insulting to be tolerated—I had even suggested the rejoicings when the King escaped assassination had been organised! I must, therefore, leave the country within ten days. The government, he concluded, were aware of Albania's faults and capable of remedying them without remarks in the foreign press.

I am convinced Juka was pushed into this action by Krosi, who held over him the knowledge of Stirling's charges against him for corruption (though the King had stopped his trial) and had twice brought them up in public to force Juka's hand in other matters. I was afterwards told some suspected me of being a Yugoslav spy, though I was at loggerheads with the Yugoslavs (over my Press reports on the attempted assassination of King Zog) and friendly with the Italians. Others had me Prince Wilhelm's spy! But spy is the term commonly applied to foreign critics of a Balkan government, just as Communist is the name for native critics.

Our Minister at Durrës, Sir Robert Hodgson, had been told on the previous day by Juka that I had become *très indésirable* and would be asked to leave the country. Sir Robert stood by me with a firmness which is not always (unfortunately) displayed by British representatives on behalf of British journalists, as I was to learn in Bulgaria. He said he could not deny the truth of my articles which had caused the trouble; and though he did not contest the Albanians' right to turn out of their country whomever they pleased (and even had he done so successfully, the authorities would have made my life intolerable) he strongly objected to "the procedure he (Juka) had in mind of summarily ejecting a British subject who was a friend of this country and had only written what he thought to be fair criticism of its institutions." Finally, after much negotiation, it was agreed I should remain to complete my travels in the south (of which the ensuing chapters are an account), though I had to forego all work as a journalist while I stayed. In these last days I found how many good friends among the Albanians I had—though for their safety I had to ignore them in the streets. The government kept the affair dark, though having me watched; but when I returned from my travels I was warned again to go and the police scared my servant into leaving me as a hint of what they could do.

In an article in *The Near East and India* of August 6, 1931, the Editor wrote of my affair:

"He conceived it to be his duty in his zeal for Albanian progress to draw attention to incompetence and other shortcomings among Albanian officials. . . . It was this side of the activities of our correspondent that embarrassed a certain clique in the Albanian official world, the more so as it was realised that his stand for public honesty and efficiency was endorsed by the better type of Albania's public men, and it appears to have been feared that with this, so to speak, outside support the progressive elements in the country might prove too strong for the forces of medievalism. The climax came when the man who is regarded by many as Albania's evil genius was indicated by our correspondent as the focus of reaction, and the diagnosis was so far confirmed that the elimination of our correspondent became a trial of strength between the old and the new school in Albania."

CHAPTER IX

WHERE ALI RULED

CLIMBING through the olive groves behind Vlona we came into a shallow valley green with new corn and splashed scarlet with poppies. The radiant sun flowed into our car's metal parts till they were scorching hot. Passing the oil derricks of Penkova and glimpsing the snow-streaked Logara peaks we climbed again, over the rocky shoulders of *Mali* Kuçesi (6,266 feet), bare of trees but sweet with herbs, until we reached a wayside spring under a great plane tree close above the Moslem village of Sevaster. Far below stretched the stony bed of the Vjosa (the ancient *Aoos*—or *Laos*)—and beyond, wrapped in haze, the rolling hills of Malakastra, in olden times a rich district famed for its oxen. Over the ridge behind us was the village of Plotsça, the ancient *Amantia*, its houses standing within the half-buried remains of an *enceinte* wall.

The houses throughout these southern wilds are well built of stone, with thick rough tiles; and they dare to have openings high on their walls which are nearer to windows than to loopholes. The people of this part—Liaperia—between Vlona and Tepeleni, were notoriously lawless until disarmed in 1904; and before Ali Pasha's time they acknowledged no authority.

Presently we zigzagged down again steeply to trees and meadows near the Vjosa—which flows past the remains of several forts (between Tepeleni and the ruins of *Byllis*) dating from Byzantine or Roman times. At last, rounding a spur, we sighted Tepeleni, the ancient *Antigonea;* and as we crossed the Bença stream by a wooden superstructure over a fine old single-arch bridge, a peal of thunder boomed round the heights as if to remind us that this place is immortalised.

> "The sun had sunk behind vast Tomerit, [Tomori]
> The Laos wide and fierce came roaring by;
> The shades of wonted night were gathering yet,
> When, down the steep banks winding warily
> Childe Harold saw, like meteors in the sky,
> The glittering minarets of Tepalen,
> Whose walls o'erlook the stream; and drawing nigh,
> He heard the busy hum of warrior men
> Swelling the breeze that sighed along the lengthening glen."

So came Byron in October 1809 to visit Ali Pasha. But Tepeleni's glory has departed long since and now the great walls stand mouldering, enclosing only heaps of stones and weeds and dung and chickens. Ali's fortress (built at the end of the eighteenth century) stands on a shelf, its wall to the east and south upon the edge of a cliff 200 feet above the river. To the north the shelf falls away to the Bença stream, to the west the mountain rises precipitously. The Bença flows down a forbidding valley from the heart of dark Kurvelesh—a wild district of crag and forest. The village of Bença was founded in 1775 by a family which fled from Pregonati because of a feud—a cause to which several other villages in the district owe their existence; and nearby, crowning a hill, are the ruinous walls of a castle. At Nivica Lovës too are the ruins of some antique Chaonian town.

Below Tepeleni's cliff are the pillars of a fine bridge built in Byzantine times. Ali spent much in restoring it, the restoration being directed by one Selim Agha, son of an Englishman named Bailey who had been sent abroad to forget a love affair; but Bailey became a

Moslem, married a beautiful Turkish girl who bore Selim, and eventually died at Tepeleni. Selim's efforts, and even the sacrifice of lambs upon the bridge, were in vain, for the river soon swept it away again, leaving only the antique pillars, and we crossed later by a ferry.

The present village of Tepeleni—of perhaps fifty houses and 300 souls—straggles across the shelf between the fortress walls and the mountain. It is a poor place which was seriously shattered by an earthquake in November, 1920. There is a tradition that Tepeleni's houses may not exceed a hundred and that if more are built they are soon destroyed.

Several travellers have described Tepeleni in Ali Pasha's time. Of Ali's courtyard Byron wrote:

> "Richly caparison'd, a ready row
> Of armed horse, and many a warlike store,
> Circled the wide-extending court below;
> Above, strange groups adorn'd the corridor;
> And ofttimes through the area's echoing door,
> Some high-capp'd Tartar spurr'd his steed away;
> The Turk, the Greek, the Albanian and the Moor,
> Here mingled in their many-hued array,
> While the deep war-drum's sound announced the close of day.

> "The wild Albanian kirtled to his knee,
> With shawl-girt head and ornamented gun,
> And gold-embroider'd garments, fair to see;
> The crimson-scarfed men of Macedon;
> The Delhi with his cap of terror on,
> And crooked glaive; the lively, supple Greek;
> And swarthy Nubia's mutilated son;
> The bearded Turk, that rarely deigns to speak,
> Master of all around, too potent to be meek,

> "Are mix'd conspicuous: some recline in groups,
> Scanning the motley scene that varies round;
> There some grave Moslem to devotion stoops,
> And some that smoke, and some that play are found;
> Here the Albanian proudly treads the ground;

Half-whispering there the Greek is heard to prate;
Hark! from the mosque that nightly solemn sound,
The Muezzin's call doth shake the minaret,
'There is no god but God!—to prayer—lo! God is great!'"

Hobhouse wrote:

"The court at Tepeleni, which was enclosed on two sides by the palace and on the other two sides by a high wall, presented us at our first entrance with a sight something like what we might have, perhaps, beheld some hundred years ago in the castle-yard of a great Feudal lord. Soldiers with their arms piled against the wall near them were assembled in different parts of the square: some of them pacing slowly backwards and forwards and others sitting on the ground in groups. Several horses, completely caparisoned, were being led about, while others were neighing under the hands of the grooms. In the part farthest from the dwelling preparations were making for the feast of the night; and several kids and sheep were being dressed by cooks who were themselves half armed . . . we saw the court Fool, who was distinguished by a very high round cap of fur; but, unlike the ancient Fools of more civilised monarchs, the fellow is obliged to confine his humour to gambolling, cutting capers, and tumbling before the Vizir's horse when his Highness takes a ride."

Leake, describing a ceremonial visit of chieftains to Ali at Tepeleni, wrote:

"They all come attended with followers armed to the teeth, in numbers proportioned to the power and rank of the chiefs. Their array in approaching, and their introduction to the Vizir, afforded some fine pictures of feudal life which carry one back in imagination to Europe in the tenth century; for the Turkish conquest of Albania has not merely prevented this country from partaking in the improvement of the rest of Europe, but has carried it in manners some centuries further back than it was at the time of the conquest."

Hughes was entertained at Tepeleni, in Ali's absence, by the Governor Ibrahim. At bed time

"a party of slaves came into the room bearing in their hands and on their heads silken mattresses, rich coverlets of embroidered velvet, pillows of the same material, with a species of fine Constantinople gauze for sheets, and all the apparatus of bed furniture, magnificent enough for princes"; —and so they slept, "in splendid misery."

In 1818 the *seraglio* in which Hughes was entertained was accidentally burnt.

"In the horror of this scene the Sultana (the mother of Ali's youngest son Salih) with the other ladies of the harem, endeavoured to escape through the doors of their apartments, but were actually met and driven back by the yataghans of the eunuchs appointed as their guards; these wretches would rather have seen them all fall a prey to the devouring element than exposed to the lawless gaze of public curiosity: such is the force of Mohametan prejudice! In this extremity they let themselves down through the casements of the windows, which they broke and tore away for that purpose. . . . Ali now set his head at work to contrive some plan for restoring the edifice without incurring any expense. His first care was to issue proclamations throughout his dominions stating that the vengeance of heaven had fallen upon him, and that Ali had no longer a home in the place of his ancestors: he called therefore upon his loving subjects to assist him in his distress, and fixed a day on which he expected their attendance. At the time appointed, Tepeleni was crowded with deputies from various districts: with his old associates and friends: with his children and relatives of every degree. . . . At the outer gate of the seraglio the Vizir was seen seated upon a dirty mat, cross-legged and bare-headed, with a red Albanian cap in his hands to receive contributions. He had been cunning enough to send beforehand to several of his retainers, from whose poverty little could be expected, large sums of money: which they now brought and restored to him as if they had been voluntary presents from their own stores. When therefore any bey or primate offered a sum less than his expectations, he compared his niggardly avarice with the liberality of others, who must have deprived themselves even of the necessaries of life for his sake. . . . Such a hint was quite sufficient to double or treble the contribution; and by these means he collected a sum of money which enabled him not only to rebuild the seraglio, but to add very considerably to the treasures in his garden."

Ali kept treasure valued at £2,000,000 in a big building within the fortress, three storeys high, and always carried the key himself. His *seraglio*, as large as that at Janina, was built upon the site of his ancestors' *seraglio* and stood in extensive Italian gardens laid out by two Italian deserters from the French at Corfu; Ali gave these men a house, a good salary, and a wife apiece from his harem.

The name Tepeleni means Helen's Hill, the legend being that once the place formed an alliance with the neighbouring villages of Damesi and Dragoti under a woman named Helen. Here, on June 12, 1920, 400 Italians surrendered to Albanian forces; but the ancient *Antigonea* looked upon a great Roman triumph.

A mile south of Tepeleni the Vjosa, flowing westward between mountains known anciently as *Aeropus* (to the north) and *Asnaus*, emerges to meet the Zrinos, a smaller river which runs past Gjinokastra. At the confluence the Vjosa bends sharply and flows north-west. In the bend is a little plain, and beyond it the mouth of the cleft Këlcyra gorge, the ancient *Fauces Antigonenses*. Here, in 198 B.C., the Consul Titus Quinctius Flamininus defeated Philip V of Macedon.

Flamininus, newly appointed and eager to outshine his predecessors, hurried with a reinforcement of 9,000 men to take over command of the Roman army which was encamped five miles from the enemy. Philip's army held the gorge, all weak points being strengthened by entrenchments and military engines. First, Flamininus met Philip to discuss terms but no agreement was reached. So a bloody but inconclusive action was fought next day—at first on the little plain, then in the gorge to which the Macedonians retired. Then there came to Flamininus a shepherd who proposed leading the Romans by mountain ways to Philip's rear; so 4,000 foot and 3,000 horse were sent with him, marching only at night by moonlight. Flamininus, with his main body, made feints to occupy the Macedonians' attention until the prearranged smoke signal was seen; then he advanced, his wings flung forward. The Macedonians, moving out to meet him, were driven back to their lines; then, discovering the Roman detached force moving down upon their line of retreat, they broke and fled. They were saved by the ground, which hampered pursuit, and lost only 2,000 men; but they retreated up the Vjosa into Thessaly and in the following year were routed utterly at *Cynoscephalae*.

Close here is the monastery of Kodra, scene of a frightful massacre of Albanians by Greek irregulars in 1914; and beyond it is Hormova, scene of one of Ali Pasha's massacres. Ali had a particular grudge against the Hormoviotes who had combined with the men of Gardiki to insult his mother and sister when they were made prisoners; and he was irritated by Hormova's stubborn resistance to his expanding power and by the brigandage of its inhabitants. (One of their priests used to hide in a hollow tree—near the bridge of Subashi between Tepeleni and Gjinokastra—while colleagues forced wayfarers to consult this oracle and pay handsomely for his words.) So Ali induced about a hundred Hormoviote notables to come for a conference in the monastery of Tribuçi nearby, having previously paid a friendly visit to their village. The notables left their arms outside the monastery as was customary, whereupon they were seized and bound. Then Ali marched upon the village and put it to flames. The Hormoviote leader, Prifti, was spitted and roasted alive and every man slaughtered.

"The dark Hormova became a ruin,
 And Tzans Prifti became roast meat in the frying pan,"

wrote the contemporary poet Haxhi Seret.

But Ali's worst massacre happened at *Han* Valiare, between Tepeleni and Gjinokastra. About six miles west of the road here, up the Belica valley, stood the proud town of Gardiki on a conical hill in the centre of a perfect amphitheatre.

"Few cities," wrote Hughes, "could boast so superb a site." Holland found a "castle crowning one summit of the hill; on the other, nearly a thousand houses, all built of stone, lofty, and deriving an air of magnificence from their situation . . . it appeared to me one of the finest towns I had ever seen in Turkey."

The castle was said to have been built, or rebuilt, by the Sultan Bayazid; and there were over 5,000 inhabitants, most of them Moslems.

"It's constitution," wrote Hughes, "was a species of republic, each family sending a representative to the Council, out of which thirteen members were chosen by vote to form the executive government: their office was annual, and they had power of life and death, though it was necessary for eight of them to concur in cases of capital condemnation. No person was allowed to carry arms within the city walls, and a murderer not only forfeited his life to the state but also his property, both personal and real, to the family of his victim."

Thus Gardiki was exceptionally well governed, most towns being in a turmoil of inter-family feuds. But it was nervous of Ali, who secretly planned a dreadful vengeance for the insults to his mother and sister forty years before though he waited until the whole of the surrounding district was in his hands.

Early in 1812 Ali besieged Gardiki which was soon induced to surrender upon very favourable terms; but thirty-six of its chief men went to Janina as honoured hostages. Then Ali called before him the entire male population (unarmed) and from among them personally picked out without regard for their religion 730 who had been (or whose parents had been) in Gardiki while his mother and sister were captives there. In *Han* Valiare all these wretched men were massacred in cold blood.

For this deed Ali's Greek troops served, for his Albanian Moslems and Mirditi declined to carry out his order, the Mirditë chief declaring he would attack the condemned men only if they were unbound and armed. That same day the hostages at Janina were tortured and slain. Then Ali ordered his Greeks to go up into Gardiki which they sacked utterly, raping the women and putting the place to flames. Those of the inhabitants who were not slain were deported to Prevesa and Vonica or driven into the mountains to perish.

Over the door of *Han* Valiare an inscription in sixty-four verses was set, written in the form of a dialogue between the *han* and the dead men. The men explained that they were killed because, while Ali was a youth dependent upon his mother, they tried to crush him and his family. Of the real cause there was no word, for it was a stain upon the honour of Ali and his family. At the end of the inscription Ali himself spoke, expressing hope that he would never have to repeat such a deed and warning his neighbours to give him no cause. This grim mausoleum was abandoned to the vultures.

Ali forbade the rebuilding of Gardiki, so it lay in ruins; and when Hughes came to it "no living beings disturbed the solitude but serpents, owls, and bats ... one expects to meet a spectre at every step." Hughes was appalled by the desolation of its gutted and deserted walls.

Gardiki was the ancient *Phanote*. In the winter of 170-169 B.C., Appius Claudius, hoping to make good his defeat in Illyria, marched into Epirus and laid siege to *Phanote*; but when he heard Perseus had entered Ætolia, he retired towards the plain of Elaeon (probably the wide valley by Gjinokastra). Clevas, who held *Phanote* for Perseus, followed the Romans, fell upon them at a difficult point on their road and killed a thousand of them; then he moved towards *Antigonea*, plundering and demonstrating, in the hope of drawing out the garrison into the valley where Philostratus was in ambush. The plan succeeded, and the garrison lost almost as heavily as Claudius had done.

Near the monastery of Cepo Albanian forces were defeated, on May 12, 1914, by Epirot bands reinforced by Greek regular infantry and artillery, though Greece was protesting at the time her innocence of the Epirot ravages which reduced more than 150 villages of southern Albania to blackened ruins, caused the death of thousands of innocent victims, and brought about such a state of frightfulness and terror that the British Government was seriously troubled. At the confluence of the Belica and Zrinos rivers are ruins of the Byzantine *Dhrynopolis*, which was probably built when *Hadrianopolis* fell to ruin; but there are many ruinous walls hereabouts, evidence of a once teeming population.

Immediately below Gjinokastra are scattered stones and traces of a small Roman theatre marking the site of *Hadrianopolis*, a town founded by the Emperor Hadrian, repaired by Justinian, and the seat of a bishop in the fifth century. Close by are the ruins of Shëntriada fort, built by Ali to protect his way through the valley before Gjinokastra fell to him. On a height opposite Gjinokastra are ruinous Hellenic walls, perhaps the remains of the town of *Elaeus*. South-east of Gjinokastra is the village of Libohova, in Hobhouse's time inhabited by a thousand Moslem and a hundred Christian families; and Ali built a large *seraglio* for his sister there. Behind is a pass which leads through the district of Zagori and over the Nemerçka range to Permeti; and the inhabitants of this district were noted, in Ali's time, for their travelling as tradesmen to remote parts of Europe.

The villages on either side of the Zrinos valley are well provided with churches and monasteries, some having two or three, and they might give many thrills to those with time to visit them. At Spilio monastery, north-east of Gjinokastra and about 1,500 feet above the valley, are large and partly artificial caverns in the limestone cliffs, evidently once used as refuges. There are natural curiosities too—at Vero, close to Gjinokastra, a subterranean river emerges from beneath the mountain; and between Goranje and Vanista to the south there is a subterranean lake.

Gjinokastra is said to have been founded in the fourteenth century by Gjin (or Gjon) Bua Spata, hence its name. The stones of *Hadrianopolis* were probably taken for its building. It became the seat of a bishop, and it fell to Ali Pasha in 1811. Until Ali's arrival it was a flourishing town with 20,000 inhabitants, the majority Moslems, though most of them belonged to the Bektash sect which is scarcely Moslem at all. It was a free town, ruled by the heads of families. Ali inveigled its bravest warriors into his service before attacking it, so it offered only slight resistance and thus escaped heavy taxation. It stands well up the mountainside, upon steep-sloping spurs and in the gulleys between them, a lovely place of climbing alleys, stone-arched doorways, and trailing vines, cypresses and minarets, wide views and striking architecture of the old style. The houses, scattered without plan, have wide eaves mostly, and rows of tall latticed windows for their second storeys (though windows low down are generally small and well barred). But its population has dwindled to 10,836, and though it is the capital of a rich prefecture times are bad and returned emigrants complain loudly.

Completely dominating the town is the great fortress built by Ali Pasha after his capture of the place. It stands on a long, abrupt ridge on the site of an antique castle. Two thousand labourers worked constantly until

Gjinokastra: Looking Northward Towards Tepeleni (*See p.* 234)

it was done; then young Salih, Ali's favourite son, was appointed governor and installed in a *seraglio* within the fortress which held also quarters for 5,000 men, subterranean magazines, 85 cannon, and a mosque.

In 1879 Gjinokastra became a headquarters of the Albanian League; and although it was a centre of the Bektash sect Greece hotly contended for it on the grounds that it was Greek, both during the settlement of the Albanian boundaries in 1913-4 and after the war. This strong place was chosen in February, 1914, by Zographos as the capital of his "Provisional Government of Autonomous Epirus," for its position in the centre of the strongly nationalist Bektashis (whom the Greeks were keen to destroy), its easy communication with Greece, and the readiness with which the townsfolk could be cowed by guns in the fortress, made it ideal for his farce. Zographos was well equipped, for the Epirots "attacked" the regular Greek troops who "abandoned" their arms and equipment. Gjinokastra was officially reoccupied by the Greeks in the autumn of 1914, but in October, 1915, they withdrew again before the Italian Expeditionary Force and on June 3, 1917, the Italians proclaimed there "the unity and independence of the whole of Albania under the shield and protection of the Italian Kingdom."

For five miles south from Tepeleni the valley is narrow, its slopes rising gently from the green river's banks and thickly wooded with planes, maples, oaks, figs and other trees. Then it widens somewhat, and there is a narrow plain with cornfields and rich meadows and grazing flocks; and away to the right are the cliffs which bound the Belica valley. At Gjinokastra we drove up the steep cobbled main street under trellises of vines and (shunning the cheerless hotel) accepted the generous hospitality of Major Coleman Smith (of the gendarmerie) when we had found the narrow ditch which was the only approach to his house. It was a pleasing Turkish house, well built of stone round a little flagged courtyard with a stoned-up well under a trellis of vines. The living room had eight tall barred windows at one end overlooking half the town. Round three sides of the room and under the windows stood a broad divan. The walls were panelled with wood and painted white, the wooden ceiling was carved and heavily painted in red, green, yellow and blue designs, and all over the house—on cupboards and walls—were crude stars and crescents. Another similar room had a large cupboard in the end opposite the windows, and above it a latticed gallery for the ladies of the harem. A trap door in the back of the cupboard gave access to the gallery, and it in turn gave into another gallery overlooking another room and opening into a third, upper, room which must have been the ladies' privy living apartment.

Clothes in Gjinokastra are *alla Franka* mostly, though white wool caps are often worn—shaped here somewhat like a tea-cosy. The peasants mostly wear thick rough knee breeches, cloth gaiters, nailed shoes fastened with straps, and long thick square-cut jackets of sombre colour. The bazaar is small and less picturesque than in most other towns. Returned emigrants have brought an almost modern touch to the shops, but they irritate by their abrupt questions: "What part America you come from—England? How long you bin in my country? What salary you make?" And so forth.

Driving back to Tepeleni we found at the ferry below the castle a band of Vlachs—men, women and children, their worldly goods and perhaps fifty horses, trekking to summer pastures; and as they were there first they held that we must wait till they had all crossed, a matter of several hours whereas we could be over in ten minutes.

But by dint of threats and cigarettes we blasted and bribed our way through them. A good road for ten miles through the great wooded Këlcyra gorge brought us to Këlcyra village. Ali gained the place in 1796 by murdering his nephew-in-law the bey, whom he enticed to Janina for Veli's wedding then accused of plotting; and thus he opened his way to Berat. He built a castle on a shoulder of the mountain above—a square enclosure of a single wall with a tower at each angle—having complete command of the pass; and between the castle and the river he built a *serai*. According to Hughes the old town, consisting of about 200 wretched hovels whose inhabitants were in a frightful state of misery, lay high up towards the castle; and he found ruins of several hundred more houses whence the inhabitants had emigrated to the mountains of Kolonia in the middle of the eighteenth century. The present Këlcyra is a miserable place of about thirty houses huddled round a bridge over the Desnica stream close by its confluence with the Vjosa, the old town having been finally destroyed by Epirot bands in 1914. Until 1903 the castle was held by the son of one of Ali's beys, but he so harried the neighbourhood that at last the people cried to the Turks—and cried so loud that the tyrant was taken to Constantinople for trial. Rumour had it that all the nails used in a room of his castle were of pure silver, and that his father had enough silver-mounted weapons to arm 300 men. Another tale is that high on the mountain lie ruins of a castle built by Pyrrhus of Epirus. Between Këlcyra and Permeti are the remains of another castle, said to have been built by a Tosk (Southern Albanian) chieftain who followed Skenderbeg.

The good road to Permeti passes through a soft valley of cornfields and pastures, an Arcadian vale where goats with melodious bells on their necks feed contentedly while the goatherds lie asleep on their *capotes* or smoke in the shade of walnut trees.

Permeti seemed a rather cheerless place for want of trees and the greyness of its walls and roofs, though a stubby minaret and a few cypresses break its monotony. "Permeti the infernal, little bread and much water," so an old saying goes. It stands entirely on the left of the Vjosa which here flows between rocky cliffs, the mountainside behind it rising steeply and stonily. The bridge over the river—slung across by the site of a Byzantine bridge—was so shaky that no car might pass over loaded. The most striking feature of the place is a pillar of rock on the river's bank with a ruin on top, said to be of a church in which St. Paul once preached. Within the ruin was a miraculous spring of the purest water which St. Paul is supposed to have blessed, so in Turkish times the governor of the town sold permits very profitably to pilgrims coming to drink it. Permeti has now about 3,000 inhabitants.

On a slope behind the town Ali Pasha built a fortress—a poor affair, an oblong quadrangle with towers. The walls were prolonged to include an old *serai* which parsimonious Ali would not pull down, though this extension spoilt the castle; but when the walls were built he found the old *serai* would not serve so built a new one, with extensive gardens, fine baths, and a marble-paved kiosk in which a fountain played.

South from Permeti the road continues by the Vjosa to the frontier, about five miles on passing an old Byzantine bridge. Presently the valley closes in, the Nemerçka range on the west breaking into towering crags with snow-filled gulleys and tremendous cliffs rising sheer to the sky from spurs thick-grown with shrubs. High above the river's right bank our road wound among bushes or beneath the shade of oak and plane and chestnut trees and was, until lately, notorious for hold-ups. In 1929 three men were shot and their car looted at a spot now marked by a cairn, so a gendarmerie post was built by the wayside. The river widens and narrows at the whim of the spurs, passing here and there by flats of turf and flowers or little plots of plough which add their red to the brilliant patchwork; and as we rounded each bend we looked far down the valley to the great precipices of Zagori in Greece, veiled in blue haze.

At last we came to Perati bridge which spans the Sarandaporos into Greece, barred at one end by a somewhat ramshackle Albanian post and at the other by a smart building painted blue and white. The bridge is antique, of a single high arch, bearing a wooden superstructure for cars to pass. Further on our road left the little river's valley and bore us up a long narrow ridge covered with box and oak scrub until we overlooked the intervening spurs to the Greek mountains on the one hand and the Nemerçka mass on the other; and presently we saw against the sky the grey stone houses and ruined clock tower of bleak Leskovik.

It is a big village (of 2,200 souls) huddled on a bare col between pine-clad heights, which mark the frontier, and a rocky cone-shaped hill called Malisin. This hill, towards the middle of the last century, was held by one of Ali Pasha's beys who defended it gallantly for several years against the Turks; but at last the Turks discovered and cut off his water supply so he surrendered. According to tradition the Turks once massacred 20,000 Albanians in a hollow close above the village—and so harsh a spot would seem a fitting place for such a deed. Though there are some Orthodox Vlachs, the people of Leskovik are Bektashis mostly, so the Greeks destroyed the place in 1914 and it is still suffering from this disaster.

But Leskovik is renowned for its vines which grow all over the hollows below it; and in its neighbourhood—notably at Postenani—are hot sulphur springs which attract many visitors from beyond the frontier in summer. Northward, the good road leads on to Korça by Ersek and the plain of Kolonia where the inhabitants, Moslems mostly, had until recent years a wide reputation for brigandage.

We camped outside Leskovik and returned next day to Permeti. Then, leaving Këlcyra on our left we went to the Bektash *tekké* of Suka in a narrow cultivated valley. The *tekké*, strongly built of stone by *dervishes* in 1920, is rectangular and somewhat like a Yorkshire dales farmhouse; it stands on a hillside, owning about fifty acres which are tilled by its ten *dervishes*. Passages and rooms were very clean but sparsely furnished. *Baba-i-madh* (*Grandfather*—or *bishop*) Kamber Ali who happened to be there, a portly jovial old man in flowing white robe and very ecclesiastical manner, has his seat at the *tekké* of Tahir Baba at Prishtë. He had been to America and spoke English. A *dervish* brought coffee and cigarettes and *lokoum*, and a rose each—for the rose is an emblem of Bektashism; but the *Baba-i-madh* would not let me photograph him because he had drunk no water for twelve days (a self-disciplinary practice)—though what that had to do with it he did not explain.

Bektashism was founded by one Haxhi Bektash Veli, a Persian, who died in 1338 (though some say the doctrine is really that of a sect called Houroufi, founded by a mystic named Fadlullah who was murdered in 1394). It is a philosophy rather than a religion, having a common base with Buddhism and Zoroastrianism, and was propagated in the Islamic world beneath the religious cloak of Mahometanism—though it has little in common

BERAT: THE LOWER TOWN

(See p. 240)

with that religion. Indeed the Bektashis are only partly guided by the Prophet and ignore many of his injunctions (notably in regard to abstention from strong drink, the veiling of women, and regular prayer). Though they have found it discreet to do so, they need not observe the Moslem feasts and fasts (which hamper evolution), they dislike Moslem fanaticism, pray only at sunrise and sunset, and do not turn towards Mecca when they pray. Nor are prayers obligatory—and their prayers are not for thanksgiving or supplication to some external power but rather a meditation or self-analysis. There is little outward ceremony; and the Bektashis have no ideas of penance, though abstinence at appointed times from drinking pure water or killing animals for food is practised for self-discipline. They have no mosques but pray anywhere, the *dervishes* of a *tekké* generally in the *Baba's* private room. They have secret signs whereby members of the sect may know each other in times of persecution or political danger.

The mysteries of Bektashism, closely guarded secrets, are revealed to adherents of the sect by stages as their knowledge evolves away from the dogmatic observances, prohibitions, and superstitions of popular religions and towards the enlightened philosophy which inspires the highest orders; but there are certain fundamental mysteries which remain unrevealed, and revelation will come only at the psychological moment in the social and political evolution of the world.

Though there is practically no literature upon the Bektashis, the main principles of their teaching are known. They hold that God is the Divine Spirit of Goodness, the life and soul of all, which manifests itself from time to time through different beings according to circumstances —for man is the highest expression of Divine power, with innate knowledge of good and evil. So Christ, Mahomet, and other prophets, saints and leaders too are all revered by the Bektashis as manifestations of that Spirit. Man does not die but is transformed; and there is no heaven nor hell but those man creates for himself by his deeds. The Bektashis are almost pantheistic; they find God in nature, on the mountain tops, in the smiling valleys, in animals, in human kindness and understanding. They live their philosophy from day to day with allowances for human frailties, teaching simplicity and brotherly love and gentleness towards all living creatures. Their beliefs are certainly confused with pagan superstitions and legends—many of these deliberately invented to identify (for gaining a hold over ignorant masses) some local saint or shrine or tribal deity with their own. St. Naoum, for one, they identify with Sari Sallteku, so the saint's tomb at the monastery of Shën Naoum is their place of pilgrimage. But tolerance is the essence of their views, for they see good in all creeds, perfection in none. Christians, Moslems, and others may join the order and share its secrets without being called upon to forswear their original faith; and Bektashis will marry those of other creeds without seeking to force a change of their partners' privy beliefs. They respect women who may visit their *tekkés*, they ignore social inequalities, and they hold work a duty whereby man earns his right to food. They teach that it is wrong to be full while others are hungry, evil to boast one's own righteousness while denying good in others.

Bektashism was introduced into Albania by *dervish* Sari Sallteku, who came from Corfu where Bektashism had taken root in the second half of the thirteenth century. Sallteku founded seven *tekkés*, among them that of Sari Salik upon the crags above Kruja—where he slew a dragon. According to Ali Tyrabiu of Tomori, Skenderbeg became a Bektash while in the Turkish service but reverted to Roman Catholicism (probably as a matter of policy).

In Albania the sect grew steadily in strength and *tekkés* were established early at Tepeleni, Gjinokastra, Konica, Mecovo and Janina. The Bektashis began to spread too in North Albania, but Kara Mahmoud Bushati dislodged them from Shkodër, Kruja and Tirana, destroying their *tekkés;* and at the beginning of the nineteenth century the Sultan attempted to suppress a sect which threatened his omnipotence within the Empire, massacring the Bektash Janissaries. The refugees from North Albania found a friend in Ali Pasha because their support was valuable to him against the Moslem Turks who persecuted them. Ali was himself secretly converted to Bektashism by *Baba* Shëmin of Kruja, and with his support Shëmin re-established the sect at Kruja and founded the *tekké* of Melçani at Korça. During his wanderings Shëmin spent a night with the Zogus in Mati and blessed the family.

The Bektashis led Albanian nationalism, their tolerance of all creeds making easy their co-operation with northern Catholics and southern Orthodox alike where Christian fanaticism did not supervene (as among some of the Orthodox during the struggle with Greece in 1913-14); and their principal adversaries were, and are, the fanatical Moslems of the plains. These fanatics did their best to wreck the Albanian national cause, rebelling (in alliance with Serbs and Greeks) in 1914 against Prince Wilhelm and persecuting the Bektashis, though the latter and the Christian nationalists kept them out of the mountains. Now that Turkey has "gone modern" the fanatics are no longer pro-Turkish, but they still hold a central position, geographically and politically, in Albania, and only time and education can shake their power. A Bektash leader told me the central Albanian Moslems remain the most retrograde and unenlightened of all Albanians, men debased and corrupted, who have neither loyalty nor honour.

In January, 1922, an assembly of 500 Bektash delegates resolved to break away from the tutelage of Ankara, hitherto the seat of the Supreme Bektash (an Albanian) who transferred himself to Tirana, which became the headquarters of the sect when in September, 1925, the Turkish Republican government suppressed religious orders of *dervishes* in Turkey and closed the Bektash *tekkés*. But Bektash relations with the Moslems of Albania remained anomalous until 1929, when the organisation of the Moslem religious community came up for consideration by the government. Supported by the Orthodox Prime Minister Kotta, the Bektashis demanded complete religious independence; but the Moslems were too strong for them and they gained only spiritual and executive autonomy within the Moslem community, a compromise which ill satisfied them, for they dislike such identification with the fanatics.

Their statutes were drawn up at Korça in 1929. The sect has clergy, confirmed members and laity; and their clergy consist, in Albania, of one "arch-grandfather," five "grandfathers," fathers and priests. There are said to be 7,370,000 Bektashis of whom 200,000 are Albanians—most of these in southern Albania. They are gaining ground among both Moslems and Orthodox Christians, their nationalism, the mystery of their philosophy and the absence of ritual making a strong appeal to the younger people, and their simplicity, hospitality and courtesy giving them much prestige. There is no doubt of their influence for good, for it is almost tangible in the districts where it prevails.

Five miles north of Suka we climbed from the valley into a complicated country of ridges and bluffs but almost

Berat: The Old (or Upper) Town

(See p. 245)

bare of trees. Our way led along the crests and over the summits, climbing gradually over 3,000 feet. To left and right were valleys and wide views, mottled beautifully by sunlight through the clouds and dotted with stone farmsteads; and to our right lay *Çafa* Bubesit, and Tojari, scene of many sanguinary engagements between Ali Pasha's men and those of the Pashas of Berat—for Ali's troops had to "break their knees and shoulders and buttocks" (as Haxhi Seret put it) before winning Berat.

Then we slithered dangerously round the ten narrow hairpins of the old Çiroçaf corkscrew and followed a ridge giving a view of Tomori's vast dark bulk towering from a chaos of soft hills into a cap of billowy cloud. Making a restrained descent to the Osum river (the ancient *Apsus*) we soon saw ahead of us Berat (of 10,403 inhabitants) the lower town nestling at the foot of a rugged hill which bars the valley and bears the old walled town like a crown.

The crumbling walls of old Berat, extending for about 600 yards along the crest of the hill, enclose more than a hundred inhabited houses, white-plastered mostly, with wide eaves and window-boxes and little gardens, built haphazard and threaded by alleys. This is a Christian quarter. Once, so it is said, there were thirty-two churches within these walls but now only five remain (dating from before Christ, so someone observed!), one of them being below ground. Here too are the ruinous walls of many more dwellings and fortifications and public buildings.

To east and west beyond the walls the bare hillside falls away steeply, with no place for buildings or cultivation, so the form of the old town is perfectly preserved. To the south the walls top a rocky cliff 300 feet above the Osum which narrows here to squeeze between the cliff and a steep hillside. Here the river is spanned by a fine seven-arched bridge built at Kurt Pasha's expense in 1780. The builder at first declared no bridge could stand, so Kurt threw a bag of gold into the water to show that money was no object; and a woman was built into the bridge to appease a devil opposed to its construction.

The lower town stands in tiers upon the slopes, beautiful for its architecture and its minarets and startling for its rows and rows of staring windows. Its antique mosques and rambling alleys, its hot dark shops and coffee-houses, its wide market square shaded by acacia trees, its river and its views of Tomori, its costumes and its pack trains together make it one of Albania's most fascinating places, though it is apt to be feverish in summer.

The importance of its position (commanding the narrow entrance to a valley leading from Illyria into the heart of Epirus) and the size of its foundation stones seem proof enough that the old walled town stands on a site of great antiquity, evidently that of *Antipatria*—a town captured in 200 B.C. by Apustius who had been detached by Sulpicius to lay waste the Macedonian frontier. The Romans knew it latterly as *Albanorum Oppidum* and built a subterranean passage to the river to ensure its water supply during siege. In the first half of the fifth century Theodosius the Younger repaired it and re-named it *Pulcheriopolis*—either because of its beautiful place or to honour his sister Pulcherie. The Byzantine Emperors sometimes made it their headquarters when chastising revolting Albanians; and in the ninth century it became the seat of a bishop. In 1205 it was partly rebuilt by Michael Komnenus and thereafter shared the vicissitudes of Vlona. In 1270 it was captured for the Angevins by a small force of Catalans, but soon afterwards was recovered for Byzantium by the Emperor Michael who defeated the Angevins before its walls. When in 1345 Dushan's Serbs took it they renamed it *Beligrad* (Beautiful Town) of which Berat is a corruption. For many years it held out for the Balsha Princes against the invading Turks and in 1438 a Turkish host besieged it for seven months in vain (losing 10,000 men). It stood for Skenderbeg; but the Turks finally took it in 1450, and in trying to regain it Skenderbeg suffered the worst defeat in his career.

Under the Turks Berat, capital of Toskeria, was ruled until 1811 by native Pashas who claimed descent from the Kastriotas. The most famous of them was Kurt, who fought fiercely with Kara Mahmoud of Shkodër and Ali of Tepeleni. He was succeeded by Ismail, who soon died and should have been followed by his son Mehmed; but Ismail's son-in-law Ibrahim seized the town, drove out Mehmed (who retired in poverty to Lushnja) and fortified the hills which overlook the walls. Nevertheless Ibrahim was a modest man of simple habits and only one wife. He governed well the shrunken pashalik (which now extended from Elbasan and Lushnja to four hours south of Berat), paid regular tribute to the Porte which appointed his son, Sulejman, Pasha of Vlona as a counterpoise to Ali Pasha, and tried to be peaceful with his powerful neighbours. But Ali wanted Berat.

In 1809 Ali sent 5,000 men against the town under Omer Vrioni. He carried the new forts on the overlooking hills and

"by him the siege was pressed with so much vigour and the bombardment so kept up against the citadel and town from the opposite heights, whilst the garrison and inhabitants were so terrified by those newly invented instruments of destruction the Congreve Rockets, under the direction of an English officer [Leake], that Ibrahim Pasha was obliged to capitulate upon condition of retiring with his suite and treasures to Valona"

(wrote Hughes). Ali waited upon the left bank of the river, and directly Ibrahim had passed out he took possession without even the knowledge of the Sultan. Then he explained to the Porte that a great part of upper Albania being in revolt, and Ibrahim too old and ill to restore order and strongly suspected of attachment first to Russia and lately to France, he (Ali) "had thought proper to secure this important fortress with troops that could be relied on." The Sultan acquiesced, giving the governorship to Ali's son Mukhtar, so Ali gained the strongest fortress and richest province in Albania; but he treated the people gently in case they should rise on behalf of their esteemed fallen chief. Berat was refortified; and some naval cannon presented by Nelson to Ali were used in defence of the town in 1914 against central Albanian rebels—but this Nelson touch did not save the place.

Curzon (in *Visits to Monasteries of the Levant*) tells how in 1834 he watched a Turkish force go from Janina for the relief of Berat which was besieged by insurgents; and in 1847 Spencer found the Turkish governor (who disposed of 900 men and 20 cannon) expecting an attack by rebels—there was an exodus from the lower town of

"the old and the young, the sick and the infirm, the suckling babe and the cat of the fireside; in short all included among the privileged class or who had the means"

struggled up to the citadel under a blazing sun with as many of their treasures as they could carry.

In 1879 Berat became the headquarters of the Albanian League; but early in the present century Greece strove to set her influence here, maintaining a school and a bishop, and Italy was at pains to counteract this influence, not wishing Greece ever to reach so far north. Until 1904 blood feuds raged and brigandage was rife in the district; but now the flintlock and the *fustanella* are relegated to the bazaar and the family chest and Berat dresses *à la Franka* mostly. In June, 1914, the town fell to central Albanian rebels. Three months later Greek bands occupied it and did much harm before driven out by a central Albanian force from Durrës. In the spring of 1916 it was occupied by Austro-Hungarian troops who were evicted by the Italians in July, 1918; but in August they returned and held Berat until their retreat from Albania at the end of September.

Here in Berat we stayed with Major and Mrs. Dodgson (of the gendarmerie), who lived in a shady whitewashed house high enough on the slope to catch any lagging breezes which favoured this hot valley. Its wide-flung windows overlooked half the town, letting in only human and animal noises for wheeled things could not approach very near; but that night the animals made up for the machines and there seemed to be legions of dogs and cocks in the town. A dog barks, his neighbour takes up the cry, and then from all over the town others of his clan join in—and having the last bark seems an affair of honour with these wretched creatures. But the Albanian cocks are worse. They have two peculiarities. They crow at all hours of the night; and they crow as if suffering from violent colds in their throats—and worse still, draw out the eerie, creaking, final note for upwards of a minute! For these qualities they are highly valued, particularly as wedding gifts (and the longer the crow the more valuable the cock), for they have great power against evil spirits.

CHAPTER X

IN THE SOUTHERN MOUNTAINS

"Illyrian woodlands, echoing falls
Of water, sheets of summer glass,
The long divine Peneian pass,
The vast Akrokeraunian walls,
Tomohrit, Athos, all things fair . . ."
(Tennyson: *To E.L.*—Lear.)

AN early start from a town upon a trek may be planned but it is hard to accomplish. *Qiraxhi* and pony owners make one last effort to improve upon your terms with them. Loads have to be adjusted—and the loading reveals deficiencies. Then Ramadan (our *qiraxhi*) stops in the bazaar for oats and a new girth; and Hussein and Qamil (our escorting gendarmes) call for their new-baked bread. So this May 30 we were not clear of Berat until ten; and our four ponies seemed to have forgotten all they ever knew of following in line, straying about the broad track near the town and colliding with laden beasts coming in to market. But at last we found ourselves in meadows where Vlachs camped and flocks grazed.

But we had not gone far when a storm came growling over Tomori's shoulder, and soon a curtain of grey rain swept towards us. We flung up our tent and piled kit inside only just in time to save everything from saturation.

Next morning, when the sun had dried us, we went on down the soft valley. The air lay heavy and the fierce sun made the distances quiver. At every stream Ramadan lay to drink, then bounded forward to overtake his steaming ponies—he was a short, deep-chested man with fair moustache and blue eyes, dressed in baggy linen trousers (cream-coloured once) girded with a long red sash: *opinga* with motor-tyre soles: thick dark blue *dolama* beneath an ancient *à la Franka* jacket: and a round white cap on his head. He had an inordinate appetite for maize bread.

At last, after a long pull upward by scrub-grown spurs and stony paths, we topped a rocky lip and came to Bargëllas, a straggle of stone houses with rare windows high up, standing among walled fields of maize and scattered trees and bounded by rock-strewn slopes. We camped in this stony place; and the *kryeplak* brought milk, eggs, onions and *raki*.

From our stony way next morning we overlooked a hilly country patched with forests and little meadows or strips of plough, streaked here and there by silver streams and fading in the distance to dim shapes through a mist of heat. Over a grassy col—Çafa Gulumak—we came into a narrow green valley where flocks with tinkling bells grazed by a stream; and by an ice-cold spring we halted for midday maize bread and cheese. Then, climbing another col, we looked far down into the Tomorica valley, and across it to another range with steep flanks scored by torrents and dark-streaked by forest. At our level (6,000 feet) stretched a narrow shelf, from which the upper heights of Tomori rose precipitously among gaunt pines, thrusting tusks of rock and cornices of snow into the wild cloud-wisps 2,000 feet above. On this shelf stands the *tekké* of Kulmak, a single storey stone-built house with courtyard and outhouses. There used to be only a two-roomed place here where one *dervish* lived, but in 1914 Greek bands destroyed it. During the war the Austro-Hungarians sat upon Tomori, the French upon the heights beyond the

Tomorica valley, so there must have been many encounters between patrols in this broken country.

Two *dervishes* took us in to Băba Ali Tyrabiu—a tall man of charm and wit, young but bearded, who had taught himself good French. A white turban with green band (a mark of rank) and full white robe girded by a sash were his dress. But we shivered in his room. Every winter the *tekké* is cut off by snow and wolves howl round its walls. Then a bare room with a great fireplace was put at our disposal, and though the fire vomited thick smoke we were most thankful for it and for the strong tea we brewed by it.

As the sun sank behind Tomori and the shadows crept down through the trees from the lonely heights the Tomorica valley's depths lost their greens and browns for soft mauve shades; and the wild white clouds, brooding on the hills beyond, changed to pink, then mauve, then melted into the ink-blue night which flowed over the silent land. I watched this scene, then withdrew from the cold rapiers of wind to the smoky fire for *meze* and *raki*—and afterwards supper of mutton and *kos* and sweetened rice and talk with *Baba* Tyrabiu. There were two Austrians also here to collect bugs from chasms in the limestone—some of their nightmare insects had never been found before. There are many caverns in Tomori, cut by underground water, and by Bargëllas a river gushes forth to a fine fall.

The morning was wet; but later the sun broke through the greyness and the low storm-clouds, torn to tatters, drifted and eddied in confusion between our feet and the valley's bed, clinging to spurs and hiding in hollows till the sun thrust down its shafts and chivvied them away. So we climbed to Tomori's holy summit. An hour's stiff scrambling brought us to the ridge—which is broken on its eastern side by precipices and steep screes but falls away more gently to the west. There was snow in the hollows and 12-foot snow cornices above the eastern precipices; yet the grassy parts were thick with cowslips and forget-me-nots, crocuses and narcissi. Eddying clouds shut out our view, but we followed the ridge easily by a succession of crests to the southern of the two main summits and came to a new-built shrine encircled by a stone wall—the shrine of Abas Ali, mythical saint of the Bektashis.

One August 25 long ago, goes the legend, Abas Ali came from Arabia to Berat; and mounting a great white horse (which has left hoof-marks upon the mountain) he fought the barbarians of the neighbourhood. When he had overcome them he rested for five days on Tomori, then went to dwell on Mount Olympus; but every year he returns on August 25 for five days, when there come Bektashis—and Christians too—sometimes eight or nine thousand people, to pay him homage. They bring their sheep for food, slaughter them on the summit, then take them down to their bivouacs by the *tekké*. So Tomori is a holy mountain and *për Baba Tomorit* a sacred oath. The shrine was built, so *Baba* Tyrabiu told me, on the site of an antique pagan shrine, so Abas Ali probably inherited his supernatural powers from the pagan god he displaced.

Abas Ali was good to us, for as we came to his shrine the bitter wind drove the clouds away down the mountain-sides, unwrapping a land of congealed ink flecked with untidy wisps of cotton wool and streaked with curling silver ribbons stretching to a molten sea. There was the whole coastline with Durrës, black Saseno, and the dark Acroceraunian wall. Nearer, though far below, lay the white houses of Berat like a handful of tiny pearls dropped into a fold of a crumpled green velvet carpet: and the Osum river winding between little moss-green hills mottled by woods and meadows and the sun-splashes. North and south were the snow-patched heights of our range, but east of us the Tomorica valley still held a boiling sea of cloud.

That evening there was *meze* and supper with *Baba* Tyrabiu in his room where he lives and sleeps and prays with his *dervishes*. At one end stood a wooden erection like a broad step-ladder with three steps, on which burnt several candles. On the right of this affair was a low divan, covered with carpets, extending down the side of the room. On this sat the *Baba* in Turkish style, and on his right a servitor—a probationer not yet a *dervish*. Before the *Baba* was a *sofra*, and on the other side of it a low bench for us, covered with a carpet. On the walls hung pictures of men hallowed by the Bektashis (among them St. John the Baptist), a large pendulum clock with the hours in Turkish time, and a ball of little yellow flowers with a musky smell, dried and wired tightly together—they are a common decoration hereabouts and are said to grow only on one mountain near Këlcyra. For *meze* there were little pieces of liver and fat mutton which went down well with Prishtë's celebrated *raki*; then came soup, fried meat, maize bread, *kos* and coffee.

Dawn came grey and sullen. *Baba* Tyrabiu would take no payment until I begged him to accept a small present for poor wayfarers. With his last words he asked me to remember that Bektashism stood between all religions—and in Albania, for mediation and unity between all beliefs in the national interest. But Abas Ali would not let us go. We had travelled barely an hour towards the valley when clouds rolled after us with a muttering of thunder. Just in time we unloaded and pitched our tent, for the storm broke with tropical fury. Crashing peals of thunder echoed and re-echoed round the valley,

"Mali" Skraparit and the Tomorica Valley

(See p. 255)

the rain roared on the canvas, and brilliant flashes of blue lightning rent the heavy grey clouds. Here, truly, we were at the mercy of nature's wild gods—but we were happy in the fug of our tent, dry and content.

Passing next day the scattered houses of Oyanik, we plunged through a deep beech forest and came out upon open hillsides 2,000 feet above the valley, our track often precarious and sometimes dangerous, in places barely six inches wide. Northward, the valley wandered away to lose itself in blue haze. But across it the mountains stood as if cut in cardboard and painted boldly in shades of blue, yellow, green and brown for a stage scene, their flanks scored deeply by the rocky beds of many watercourses which broadened and drew together (as they fell towards the river) like the veins of skeleton leaves. Here and there stood a square stone house by meadows and patches of plough on the flatter places. And over all the woolly clouds, drifting across a blue sky, cast rolling shadows. Southward, bare broken ridges barred the valley; and beyond them rose the heights of *Mali* Skraparit, well snow-capped still, ending in a cone-shaped peak above *Çafa-e-martesë*. There were several pretty villages—groups of houses high on a spur. At Zagori the schoolmaster, proudly wearing a scout's badge, brought water and *lokoum* as we rested beneath a walnut tree. At Milova the women and children were filled with curiosity by us, but they would take no payment for their bread and milk—"We have bread and we give you what we have," they said. At Milova begins the *shkallë* to *Çafa* Devris. We struggled upward, pushing our sweating beasts' loads, slipping and stumbling on the loose stones and choking with the dust stirred by all our feet until at last we passed through a rocky ravine to the large village of Korita which was amused because we brewed tea on a spirit lamp at the fountain. Not far beyond we camped by a well among walled-in cornfields. Eager for the flesh pots of Çerevodë, our gendarmes grumbled they had no bread here, but that is a common complaint which must be ignored or control of movements passes to the grumblers; so I threatened to dismiss them—thereat they stopped their grumbling and soon found bread.

In the morning we reached Çerevodë, capital of the sub-prefecture of Skrapar, a place of thirty houses round a little square by the Osum river. The sub-prefect, the doctor and a lawyer from Berat welcomed us in the office of the district commandant (2-Lieutenant Kemal Borshi) and insisted we should stay a night so that they might show us hospitality. Their wish seemed so sincere that we agreed.

The doctor's dispensary was his bedroom and his living room, a chaos of clothes, bottles, cigarette boxes and a rusty spoon, a crazy ladder outside leading up to it above a ramshackle place of meat and flies which was the butcher's shop. Wild pig, deer, wild goats and smaller game teem hereabouts, we were told; and there are many wolves which ravage flocks and come down to the villages in packs sometimes in winter, but men are rarely attacked unless alone on the hills when the weather is hard. Theft in Skrapar is practically unknown, but not so murder for honour; and a woman who commits adultery is generally killed by her husband, or by her relatives if she is unmarried. But in most ways the people here are more sophisticated than those of the northern mountains, for the war brought foreign troops to all their villages.

Our night in Borshi's house was comfortable. But the latrine presented problems for it was also the charcoal dump, wood store and hen house. Chickens roosted or brooded in the most inconvenient places and a large

IN THE "TEKKÉ" AT PRISHTË   (See p. 257)

ram was tethered to the door. Borshi's wife was a good-looking girl whose age, by her birth certificate, was seventeen, but Borshi was sure she was twenty.

Our rocky path next day lay first through thick scrub on the left brink of a deep canyon, narrow and sheer to the river. The walls, of red and grey sandstone, are buttressed curiously, sombre trees clinging to every crack and ledge between; and from either brink the mountains rise gently at first, then more steeply, their spurs dark with foliage. Presently we bore to our right, climbing through woods and cornfields, our track often a deep ditch overhung by blackberry bushes and thorn trees. At a farm a kind old man spread a gay carpet beneath a walnut tree and set a box (covered by a red rug) for my special honour; then he brought curdled milk, *raki* and eggs, so everyone was happy in this drowsy spot with its wide view and humming bees and soft breeze. Our host's small son gave me the chance to repay all this kindness and I pressed some coins into his little hand—whereat the old man objected till I said my money was only a gift for the child.

Going again, we followed a steep-rising valley where a stream flowed beneath big trees, then climbed heavily to the *tekké* of Prishtë. The approach to the *tekké* is worn across the face of a precipice of clay and shale so slippery that we took off our boots—though the ponies, shod with flat iron shoes, thought nothing of it.

The *tekké* of Tahir Baba was built admirably by *dervishes* in 1921, of stone, with many neat windows. There are two square blocks with two storeys, joined by a single-storey central part which consists of store-rooms and kitchen off a stone-flagged cloister. The kitchen is cavernous, with smoke-blackened rafters and a vast open fireplace beneath an immense chimney-piece on four pillars, its pewter dishes and crockery and tables spotlessly clean. Apart from the *tekké* are the outhouses where vats and kettles for making *raki* are kept: and a fine stoned-up spring in a porch. Below the *tekké*, upon a knoll among dark cypresses, stands a shrine with a dome, where the dead of the *tekké* lie.

A *tekké* was first built here about 1870 but was destroyed by Greek bands in 1914—the Greeks destroyed about forty *tekkés* (apart from shrines) but now there are more than fifty in Albania. All the inhabitants of the district fled to Vlona; but they returned when the Italians came and the *dervishes* were able to continue "teaching the people to be honest and kind." Prishtë has ten *dervishes*, who claim to convert above 500 Moslems annually in their neighbourhood. Their *tekké* stands beautifully upon a spur, below scrub-covered ridges and above slopes under vineyards, maize fields, orchards and vegetable plots. Far beyond the valley towers *Mali* Tomori and Abas Ali's shrine may just be seen.

Through my mind there rushed thoughts of Omar Khayyám, of Hadji Baba, of Druids even, as three *dervishes* came from this modern building to meet us. They wore white hats somewhat like turbans, heavy beards (one red and luxuriant) and full white robes with sleeves, girdled by scarlet sashes: and two had long black gowns like students'. Quietly they bade us welcome, regretting *Baba-i-madh* Kamber Ali had not returned; but they led us to the *Baba* in charge, a placid patriarchal man with flowing white beard and the gentleness of his creed upon his features. With him we drank coffee. Then two *dervishes* showed the way about and plucked sweet-scented roses for us and for themselves. There were cats everywhere—sleek cats, contented as the *dervishes*. Kamber Ali's room had a divan covered by bright cushions down three sides and a gay carpet on the floor—a colour scheme of cherry and

The "Baba" of Prishtë

(See p. 258)

IN THE SOUTHERN MOUNTAINS

mauve—and several cupboards with well-carved doors. Here the people come from nearby villages to pray and be taught. A gong calls the *dervishes* to meditation at dawn and sunset, and between times they work, or study in their rooms. Our room was large, with four windows: mattresses, quilts and gay cushions on the floor: shelves, table and chairs. With *meze* as much of Prishtë's famous *raki* as we dared drink: then supper. We slept thankfully, like the cats.

We were sad to leave, and the *Baba* would take nothing for his *tekké*'s hospitality—not even for the poor. Down to the village of Prishtë we went, then over a high spur through a forest of stunted oaks which the goats keep down; then downward, sometimes by meadows and sometimes by bare scratches across scars in the mountain's flanks to which the ponies held by a miracle of balance. At last we came to Zaborzanë, a poor group of houses by the Osum river. Not far on a grassy glade a hundred feet above the river and shut in by wooded slopes was a perfect place for camping, so here we idled a day, bathing and basking in the sun.

On June 9 we were on our way early, climbing through oak and beech woods beyond the river. Presently we left the cool trees and came out upon barren hillsides patched with scrub and disfigured by ugly scars—a weary, waterless, battered land, shadeless under the high sun which put to sleep the colours. The track threw back the sun's heat till the sweat made a plaster on our faces of the dust from our feet. Only the crickets and ants and large black beetles cared for work. The crickets' ceaseless din seemed to thicken the dust and clog the air: the ants ran in brown hordes by their beaten ways across our track: and the beetles swarmed enthusiastically wherever ponies had left droppings— rolling the dung into balls as big as themselves and going away with them backwards, pushing them between their hind legs at a great rate. We passed more than one shepherd playing on a flute—a wild sad sound. I heard this instrument played only here. South of us was a tragic land, for it has never recovered from the Greeks' ravages in 1914. Frashëri was a small but prosperous town; and Luarasi had about 600 houses before the Greeks came, though now it has only 140.

The country was bare and broken till we reached the head of the Tomorica valley and looked back at our trail from Tomori to *Çafa* Devris. Passing upward from here we came to steep bare slopes, windswept and cut by icy streams from the crags of *Mali* Skraparit, and looked up to snow-choked ravines between black precipices. Then began a long climb by a stony track which traversed the slopes to *Çafa-e-martesë*. Below, the air had been leaden with heat; but up here it was boisterous with a wind which roared down the ravines and swept round the bluffs, piercing every chink in our clothing. Spur after spur promised falsely to be the summit, but at last we were over the bare saddle and dropping towards a big beech forest. We camped by a shepherd's conical hut of branches and thatch, part of which our men took (before we could stop them) for much-needed fires. At dawn the owners came to reproach them for their damage; but somehow the affair ended in smiles and these shepherds set us on our way downhill.

Beyond the forest we came upon a summer settlement of Vlachs—twenty-two men and thirty women in nine conical huts of bent branches well thatched with straw and looking like old-fashioned bee-hives. They were kind folk, anxious to tell all their affairs.

The Vlachs are a distinct division of the Latin peoples, descended from Roman provincials. They speak a

Dina Jano and his Family

(See p. 261)

IN THE SOUTHERN MOUNTAINS

language very close to Roumanian and call themselves Aromani or Romani, though the Albanian Vlachs are known as Farsherots—a name derived from Frashëri which used to be the centre of four or five Vlach villages. There are, scattered throughout south and central Albania, many Vlachs besides those round Frashëri. In Korça there are many—they have a big church which was partly destroyed by an earthquake in January, 1931; and there are two large groups in that neighbourhood, round Plyasa and about Voskopoli and Shipska. Konispoli, south of Butrinto, is another centre. West from Berat there is a big Vlach population estimated at 10,000 in winter, inhabiting thirty-eight small villages. In Vlona there are many Vlachs—and northwards too, by Elbasan, Kavaja and Durrës.

Our Vlachs had come here from Konispoli in twelve days with their flocks for the summer and had built their huts in three days. Their chief, Dina Jano, bade us into his hut for his wife's delicious coffee. The walls were plastered inside with mud for about three feet from the ground and the floor was spread with clean rugs. In the middle was a stone slab serving as fireplace. There was nothing else within but some earthenware lamps of ancient Roman pattern and a bunch of Easter candles. The women spin all the wool—the older women walked about with distaffs from which they wove with dexterous fingers and spinning bobbins. Jano compared his language with Italian, saying how near the two tongues were. His son, though married, was at school in Corfu; his daughter-in-law was a big ugly girl in a sombre costume brightened by gay embroideries and so covered by strings of glittering coins and aimless leather straps thick with metal studs that she looked like an ironmonger's shop. All the women wore round their waists massive leather belts studded with metal; and some had on their foreheads blue tattoo marks—the pattern was a three-pronged fork, either square or triangular, the prongs pointing upward and the central prong prolonged downward like a stem or shaft to the bridge of the nose to join another mark (like a handle) at right angles. It was a decoration without significance, Jano said. On their heads most of the girls wore thick black bands which looked like halos and left their crowns uncovered; but from these bands black scarves hung over their necks and shoulders. Above their halos the elder women wore stiff black caps like inverted buckets which gave them a witch-like air: but they were decorated by no embroideries and straps like the girls. Jano was hatless and simply dressed in thick dark blue cloth—close-fitting trousers, *dolama*, long open jacket, a sash at his waist, and *opinga*.

We went on down a long lean valley, its sides covered with withered grass and boulders. Here and there was a tree with a splash of shade; and to a branch of more than one were tied wisps of straw. The women hereabouts take straw to church one feast day after Christmas, the priest blesses it, then they tie it to their trees or near their property to keep evil spirits away. Sometimes, too, stones are jammed in the forks of trees as resting places for the feet of the dead as they pass through the air. At Gjonbabas, a small Moslem village, the women—unveiled and dressed in red rags mostly— fled from our sight. At last we climbed from this valley between maize plots and over a spur till suddenly we overlooked Gjergjevica—in a hollow between steep hillsides of red earth dotted with box shrubs and stunted pines. Gjergjevica's mosque is a two-storey white house with windows and a minaret at its side. As we dropped through the narrow alleys of the village the women (dressed like those at Gjonbabas) fled indoors and peeped at us through the lattices of their loose-built stone houses.

From here we followed a narrow rising valley filled with the smell of juniper and box, then scrambled from it to a col dotted with pines and came into sight of Voskopoli at the end of a grassy vale. At this stony ruinous place we were met by the post commander (whose idle fingers played with a string of amber beads) and the president of the commune (a youth in white flannel trousers and straw hat who had studied at Bucharest). They said we should stay at the Orthodox nunnery of St. Prodhromos, so there we went all together, up the hill by a good road among pine trees.

The nunnery stands on a stony hillside about 5,500 feet above sea level, a big two-storey place in the shape of an L with a square bell tower above an archway into a courtyard. It was enlarged in 1910. The upper floor has good windows, but below are narrow slots discouraging to marauders. In the courtyard stands an antique church containing a gloomy and idolatrous confusion of hanging lamps, giant candlesticks, sacred pictures, frescos, carved woodwork, and upright seats fixed to the walls. There are forty rooms in the nunnery; and to our surprise we found it was no nunnery at all, for a greasy and bearded priest in the black robe and high black rigid hat of his Church was the head of it (with twenty-four decrepit black-robed sisters under him to do the work) and it was full of visitors. Anyone may have a room there, no charge being made but "presents" being accepted and (unlike the *tekkes*) expected. So the Korça people, young and old, Moslems and Christians, moral and immoral, make it their chief health and week-end resort, bringing their own bedding and food. The Moslems are notably more generous with their presents than the Christians. A girl called down the corridor to my servant Lef, asking him the time. He answered rudely, explaining to me that "she is a bad girl—I knew her in Korça."

Voskopoli is a dreary place with barely 400 inhabitants among the ruinous walls of its past glory. The grass of its meadows hides the stones of from 8,000 to 12,000 houses, and from the ruins of public buildings thorn trees and poplars spring, casting their shadows over ground once trodden by a prosperous Vlach population.

According to Leake all this neighbourhood was once a flourishing Vlach or Wallachian colony; but when the Turks came the people scattered, some remaining in the security of this upper valley where they founded Voskopoli—"the city of shepherds." As time went on the safety of the place attracted many settlers from Greece and other parts who, becoming ashamed of its name as their prosperity grew, changed it to Moskopoli "which, meaning the city of calves, seems no great improvement." But its old name clings and is generally used. With it grew Shipska, a smaller town, probably a kind of residential quarter, up the valley a mile beyond St. Prodhromos. Voskopoli was most prosperous in the first half of the eighteenth century, being the great commercial centre for central Albania and upper Macedonia. Its merchants had branch houses in Venice, Vienna, and Budapest, and frequented the great fair of Leipzic. Locally the town is believed to have held 60,000 people, but Wace and Thompson put the figure at 20,000. It had twenty-five churches (most of them built early in the eighteenth century and elaborately decorated with frescos by the contemporary nuns of St. Prodhromos), twelve different trades, a good school (widely famed), a high standard of living, and two printing presses—one at St. Prodhromos. It is said there was a printing press here when only one other existed in the Balkans—at Constantinople.

But Voskopoli's wealth attracted Albanian marauders. It was first sacked in 1769, by Albanians probably led by Ali from Tepeleni, and it was sacked again in 1788. But its churches were spared, for the Moslem Albanian generally has a certain respect for Christian institutions (probably through superstitious dread of the Christians' evil spirits) and Ali always had as a matter of policy. Ali's harsh rule completed Voskopoli's ruin and the inhabitants scattered widely. Many migrated to their co-religionists in Greece; but religion was not their only bond with the Greeks, for Greek was the only written language in the peninsula, the language of their religion and the language of their culture in an uncultured Moslem world.

When Leake came this way in 1805 he was told there were only 200 to 300 inhabited houses in Voskopolis He was probably the first Englishman to go this way to Berat—he passed by Lavdhari and through a district then thickly populated beyond its powers of production, hearing within a short distance Turkish, Albanian, Macedonian Slav, Wallachian and Greek spoken. He crossed Çafa Guriprerë where he passed a crude fortress on a rock, taken by Ali from the Pasha of Berat in 1798 and held by a dozen dirty half-starved Albanians. A *kula* at Dobrenj had been ruined in the war between Ali and the Pashas of Berat; and he noticed some ruinous Hellenic walls a little to the south of Tomori village.

Voskopoli had recovered little if at all by 1914, though it was a centre of Greek propaganda. But in 1916 another disaster befell it. A Voskopoli man killed the son and nephew of Sali Budka, the famous south Albanian guerilla leader who had thrown in his lot with the invading Austrian and Bulgarian armies; so on October 16 Sali burnt the place—but he, too, spared those seven churches which had not fallen to ruins. He lives still, at his village near Kolonia, like a biblical patriarch, proud of his days.

Then came to Voskopoli troops from the French Salonika Expeditionary Force—Algerian Riflemen, Chasseurs d'Afrique, Indo-Chinese, Zouaves and Senegalese mostly—and in February, 1917, drove the Austro-Hungarians and Bulgarians and Sali's bands from Voskopoli. They used the churches as stables and hospitals and barracks, and badly defaced the lovely frescos, picking out the left eyes of a whole row of saints, scratching their names and chipping off the plaster; but though the Albanians blame the French hotly for the damage, most of the hundreds of names scratched on the frescos are in Greek characters. The troops, they say, lit fires in the churches which blackened the frescos, burnt most of the movable woodwork, and broke into and looted the church of St. Nikola—I was shown the hole they made. Worse, they say, many looted treasures and carvings may be seen in French private collections or museums (though the priests carried off and hid what they could); but in view of the state of what remains, one is inclined to think it a pity the French did not carry off more for preservation than they did.

Close below the nunnery are the churches of St. Venerdi and St. Dionicë, adjoining each other and said to be the oldest in the place. They stand in the shade of big trees, very low, of stone, quaintly built with wooden rafters, and over the doors was the word "Contageux"—a reminder of the French occupation. A fresco in the church of St. Venerdi has a sticky surface which retains coins and it is lucky if your coin sticks

FRESCOS AT VOSKOPOLI   (*See p*. 266)

—lucky for the priest. The church of St. Athanasius dates from 1710 and, like the others, is richly decorated with frescos, many of them beautiful work worthy of care beyond the resources of poor Albania. The churches of St. Nikola and St. Michael have a transverse section at the back which was reserved for women and is connected with the main body of the church—where the men worshipped—by a small door only. In a corner of the church of St. Nikola was a huge pile of human bones and skulls. The Orthodox disapprove of leaving corpses interred, thus wasting good ground; so when they have been buried three years they are dug up again, the bones washed, a service held over them, then they are stored. If a corpse is not entirely decayed it is a bad omen.

At the school sixty-five boys and twelve girls had only one teacher! A Vlach who had been foreman in a factory in America and came from Shipska told me many women of the villages know no Albanian—only their own tongue. He complained bitterly of lack of money and opportunities here.

The next day, in a car, we zigzagged downward by a rough road between spurs of red earth, swung across the plain and were soon at Korça, for I wanted to call at the Kennedys' school. Mr. and Mrs. Kennedy, American missionaries, have gallantly maintained a school here in the face of incredible difficulties for over forty years. When the Greeks attacked Korça, Kennedy stayed at his school while bullets pattered on its walls. Now he had 140 boys and girls in his care.

Back at St. Prodhromos that night the priest had a fine spread for us and his friends. Afterwards, all the other visitors to the place, about a dozen women—including Lef's "bad girl"—were asked to join us. They brought a gramophone and much noisy chatter and one old woman read our fortunes in coffee cups. The "bad girl" giggled apprehensively.

The next afternoon we pushed on again, through a valley thick with firs and oaks and juniper shrubs, and camped by a spring between wooded bluffs, glad to be under the stars again. In the morning we climbed till we overlooked the wild Devolli valley 2,000 feet beneath. Here and eastward the river is pinched between scarped shoulders of red earth bared by the rains of all vegetation but a few firs. At our level these shoulders flattened, each separated from the next by a re-entrant cut deep into the mountain by water-courses. Above the flat places the mountains are steep again to their summits. Northwestward the valley's sides are less abrupt, though water-courses have gashed red wounds in them; but the heights stand further back, their spurs green with trees and little meadows and cornfields.

Leaving Gjinikas high to our left we went down steeply to the river, and climbed beyond to 2,000 feet again in the shrivelling full-day sun which melted the shadows and swathed the colours in a pallid mist of heat. The ponies struggled in a lather of sweat, Ramadan urging them monotonously. Except on the subject of bread Ramadan was not talkative, but once he told me he had fought the Italians in 1920 (and enjoyed it) so I asked him about the Austrian occupation. "The Austrians were not bad," he replied; "but there was too little bread."

Climbing steadily and sometimes stiffly we came at last to a scrub-grown col—Çafa Shinapremtesë; and just beyond, on wide turf by a spring, we camped as the crimson sun sank behind a great cone-shaped hill. Then the night closed in, chill (at 4,600 feet), so we were glad of our fires.

As we passed, next morning, the village of Shinapremtesë (ten stone houses scattered among patches of corn) a stout fellow in lowland dress came up with us. This part, he told, had never paid taxes in Turkish times for the Turks never penetrated it; and in those days there used to be several big feudal families hereabouts, but they have sunk now to peasant level. There are many wolves, which destroy sheep and horses but attack men only at night—though twelve Austrians were devoured here during the war.

Our way to Elbasan lay roughly north-north-east, by the western flanks of a fine range of mountains between 5,000 and 7,000 feet in height. This range begins north of the Devolli and close east of Çafa Shinapremtesë, running almost due north to the Shkumbini. A third of the way northward is the highest peak, and here the range puts out an arm, eastward first, then northward along the eastern side of Lake Okhrida to Çafa Thanës, enclosing in its loop the sources of the Shkumbini. Two-thirds of the way northward the range puts out another arm, *Malit* Shpatit, this time north-westward and not so high or rugged, which ends by the Shkumbini close east of Elbasan. The summits of the main range are very rugged, their gulleys choked with snow till late in the year; but below these summits lie dark forests of beech and pine and oak. Here, too, are rich pastures where the men of the valleys take their flocks in summer. Below the forests and pastures are, often, outcrops of rock from which the mountain-sides fall away sharply to the heads of short valleys drained by tributaries of the Devolli; and the valleys are divided by irregular spurs, bared of trees by ruthless felling, the ravages of goats and the labour of farmers. Our way led in and out, up and down these spurs and valleys, and in the next three days we were wearied of its hot monotony. Of all this region our staff map had ideas far from realities.

Beyond Shinapremtesë we climbed a bare ridge into

a wide basin drained by a narrow valley to the Devolli. As we went down we followed a straight furrow made, without doubt, by an earthquake—the earth had swelled up till the crack was like pouting lips. Passing Ormasi (a collection of stone houses with rough tiles and high windows) we climbed then dropped again, always in scorching sun-heat, to Kukëri, a place of perhaps thirty houses dotted about gentle slopes among neatly walled patches of plough and meadows and full fields of corn and scattered trees between precipitous rocky spurs. At the store we bought *raki* and *lokoum* and other provisions —the old storekeeper was genial in spite of all his flies which buzzed in swarms from our faces to his sugar. Then, by a little mosque in a grassy place among olive trees by a stream we camped, with a view of grand Tomori to delight us.

The new sun, when it burst over the mountain tops, was as hot as full day's, and the olives' shade seemed to stifle us. In this heat we climbed stiffly to the bed of a gently rising valley, its sides harsh with scars between shadeless scrub in clumps apart. At Rashdani post we lunched on bread and onions by a trickle which a rock gave grudgingly, then laboured onward to a pass at our bare valley's head, hoping for trees beyond; but beyond was as bare as before, though the ridge opposite, which enclosed between us a basin drained by the Holta stream, was dark with trees.

The track we chose now became more and more difficult, passing through thickets and over water-worn clefts until it petered out in the scrub high above the Holta. The guardian dog of a house rushed at us savagely, being driven off by stones. "Oh lord of the house," cried our gendarme Nexheb to the seemingly deserted shack, "where is the path?" "Oh gendarme," replied a voice from within, "your way lies below my field."

And the man came to show us, pausing to drink at his spring from a gourd. So at last we got down the steeps to the Holta's summer trickle which was lost, almost, in its wide stony bed. Here we camped by the edge of the stones. Not far down the river was pinched between two abrupt wooded spurs, each topped by a pillar of rock which seemed ready to bear the arch of a gateway between them. In the evening this was a pleasant place, but we had no shade against the dread morning sun. There was a plague of beetles, moths and mosquitoes, which came to their destruction by scores in our candles' flames after dark—but the mosquitoes do not often carry malaria in these high parts, nor did they bite me, though it was so warm I sat late in my accustomed state of shirtlessness (my shirts being in the river) and slept (as always) in the open.

Beyond another bare ridge we came next morning to Zavalina, a place of ten scattered houses among soft grass and trees. The store-keeper, who sold us sugar, was full of apologies for having nothing but a cigarette to give in hospitality. Up and down again in the heat we went until we reached the spur over which Pashtresh is scattered. Here we found the women and girls in their best clothes, for it was their feast day. The most striking part of their costume is a crimson cap like a fez, completely covered by gold and silver coins; and they wear sleeveless jackets like undersized waistcoats, richly embroidered, over embroidered shirts with long white sleeves: and aprons, coloured in stripes, or white and embroidered with a red pattern.

We had promised to visit at Pashtresh a peasant girl who had been servant to the Hills in Tirana. She was overjoyed that we kept our word. Proud in her *alla Franka* clothes which were odd and ugly to see among the native dresses, she bade us to her home for coffee. Her grandmother, a wizened crone in a flowing robe of dirty white homespun, sat on the floor in a corner, silently, smoking a large briar pipe with a glowing ember on the tobacco. Her mother, with bright-hennaed hair, crawled on the floor, part-mad and shrill, asking indecent questions. Then we camped in a meadow as the sinking sun drew long shadows from the soft hills, touched the distant Shkumbini to a silver streak, and set Tomori's mass against a golden glow.

Next midday we came into sight of Elbasan, spread beautifully on the flat beyond the Shkumbini with the wooded bluffs of the Krraba mountain behind. As we went down through the pine trees and bracken Nexheb killed a snake—black-backed, with black and white checked belly and forty inches long—which held a huge and still-living bull frog between its wide-stretched fangs. In three more hours, going by deep-worn tracks, like ditches, overhung by bushes, we reached the town and off-loaded at the "Hotel Europa." Then I paid off Ramadan, and dismissed our two escorting gendarmes with a tip they took with a big show of reluctance. It was a sad parting, for the mountains make enduring friendships. Ramadan's emotion was hardly concealed. He brought me a farewell gift of three cucumbers and a bottle of beer, bade me long life and a good road with nervous haste, and firmly refused payment for the two extra days he and the ponies would take for their return to Berat. The last I saw of him he was sleeping heavily, with other *qiraxhis*, in a doorway off the street.

Elbasan was close as an oven between its hills, the valley's sun-baked air lying astride the town as a pall of heat. We replenished stores and engaged a fresh *qiraxhi*—Ali Haxhi—with three ponies. Ali was a little man with wild black moustache and twinkling eye, proud possessor of a much-tattered umbrella. Our fresh gendarme, Prenk Noi, a Catholic Mirditë, was a little man too but with less than half Ali's spirit and a passion for Ali's umbrella against the sun.

Threading our way through streets thronged with peasants and their laden donkeys, we shepherded our ponies between all these feet and loads (which seemed to boil in the heat) until Ali led away along the dry bed of a stream and up a spur to Godalesh, a lovely village shaded by mulberry trees, which embraced Islam in 1898 to escape the oppression of local Turkish authority. Looking back we saw Elbasan as an enchanted city of minarets and red roofs among its trees, the silver river beyond it winding away into the plain's mist of heat which shut the sea from sight.

Half an hour above Godalesh we came to a grassy knoll and camped only just in time to avoid a wetting. The rain drifted across the valley and glittered like a silver curtain as it came to us slowly across the turf, leaving the sweetness of rain-washed grass in the air when it passed. Down through the oak scrub Prenk led us next day to Lyabinoti-*poshtme*, near the road, then up again to Lyabinoti-*sipërme* (Lower and Upper Lyabinoti), this unnecessary detour because the poor fellow had not understood we preferred rough mountain ways to the good road. Our track wound from scattered house to house, cobbled and hedged mostly, with water running in the ditches by the side and cooled by the shade of fig and pear and chestnut trees and overhanging vines. There were children with charms of coins tied to their fair locks. In Elbasan women were hard to see, but here they came forth as openly as their men, gay in their local dress—white scarves over their heads and their hair hanging in two plaits tied at the ends with red strings: *opinga*: white socks pulled over the ends of white baggy trousers which were held up by red sashes:

white shirts with sleeves: and over them sleeveless white jackets of thick wool, open, trimmed with red wool: and square grey homespun aprons at their waists.

Going up a shallow valley our track was unusually good, almost a road (with a military telephone wire on the trees); but it gave out upon a col of red earth carved curiously by water—*Çafa* Shëmeil. Here we looked down the valley of *Llumi* Shëmeil, a steep-sided place, its bed entirely covered by the boulders of spring torrents. Away to our left was Shëmeil village, a cluster of stone *kulas* high up with loopholes for windows.

Going down steeply we followed the stony river bed, shut in by steeps of bare red earth dotted with stunted oaks, though we could see forests of great trees and pastures above which looked rich and cool. At last we reached Floç, a village of about seventy *kulas* scattered among meadows and trees within perhaps three miles. Fording a full stream—Ali bearing Prenk and me over on his back—we camped upon a low ridge covered by big oak trees and bracken. A woman brought good sheeps' milk and a great disc of maize bread but would take no money for them. Ali took the ponies to a house for the night, fearing wolves. Here we stayed a day and found the plague of flies, with us always, rose at this place to a torment. They bit and pricked mercilessly. And there were other pests too—mosquitoes and ants—which took their share of making us uncomfortable. A dumb idiot boy, stark naked and grimacing, crept up to camp; but Prenk chivvied him away harshly. In a field nearby a woman hoed, her baby in a wooden cradle slung from a bough near her.

There are many wolves and wild goats here and wild pig too, said a man who came to talk with us—more pig than the villagers have sheep or goats. There are bears too, in the forests of Martanesh, but the peasants have no guns now for hunting. When the Italian surveyors were here "they put flags on the mountain tops"; and they were liked because they behaved well and above all "paid for everything with money, much money." Lef and I went with our informative friend to his house on the hillside above a hay field and sat under a mulberry tree to eat the fruit. The house was curious. From within the stone-built barn beneath, a rickety ladder gave to the second storey. This upper part was built out upon beams far beyond the stone walls, so the house looked top-heavy. The upper walls were of handsawn planks, the roof of rough tiles heavily weighted with stones. There were no openings in the barn's walls; and in the upper part, on one side, only five narrow holes close together, with sliding squares of stout wood as shutters. We went in for hot milk and sat in a carpeted recess by the five holes which gave light to a cavernous room with smoke-blackened rafters, bare save for a big wooden chest and a stone hearth. Our host had helped to defend this *kula* in his father's time, but it had not been attacked lately. I proposed photographing him and his wife (whose dress made it up for her want of looks); but he would not bring his wife, saying we would laugh at her, that it was not their custom, and finally that she would not come even if he called her. But he added that if I could take her unawares I might—which I did not attempt, however.

Two women in their gorgeous costumes came past our camp but when I tried to photograph them they fled. Here they wear white headcloths flowing over their shoulders: scarlet jackets, short, like double-breasted waistcoats but open, richly faced with black and gold thread and black lozenges on the scarlet sleeves: sometimes a scarlet blouse beneath the jacket: and beneath that a white robe, almost to the ankles, girdled by a red and white sash. From beneath the robe peep the ends of white baggy trousers, gathered into multi-coloured *çarapi*. Sometimes they wear also a long grey or black homespun surcoat, sleeveless and open in front, reaching to the ankles: sometimes an apron of the same material, hanging behind from the waist: and sometimes an apron hanging loosely in front from well below the waistline—almost from the knees. Then there are necklets and bracelets of coins, or perhaps of beads, or metal-studded straps.

We moved a short way the next day to escape from the flies, climbing upward through a cleft in a ridge of red earth which seemed to hold from slipping down the mountain-side the little fields and scattered houses of Zdransha. Behind Zdransha rises a rugged mountain which has shed its spare rocks all over the slopes in which the Sunni Moslems of the place have scratched maize plots. We halted by a small white mosque which stood beautifully against the bare red earth scarps. By the mosque was a tiny school; and all the flat space round about was so taken up by thousands of untidy graves that a place for our camp was hard to find—elsewhere being rocks or corn plots or steep places. There was a store selling rice, coffee beans and cigarettes; and the villagers brought bread and milk, but they were (exceptionally) surly folk, disinclined to be helpful, so we got eggs and wood with difficulty. There are not many trees here, and every particle of dry stick is picked up by the women.

Having breakfasted well on *kos* and mulberries and coffee we went forward again on June 24. Up another sharp-rising ravine and through a cleft in another ridge we passed into a still higher hollow, this one uncultivated, carved and scarred and bared by the rains. The day was dull and dead, the breath gone out of it, the shadows grey smudges without edge and the veil of heat over the sun a bilious yellow. Climbing steeply through stunted oaks and bracken we came to Neshta (which showed only two houses). Across several spurs drained by half a dozen streams rose the great heights of *Malit* Privalit and Kaptin, broken by rocky outcrops among their trees, with a high pass between them. In a field worked two gangs well apart, one of men and the other of women. Soon the oaks gave way to beeches which were ever bigger as we rose higher; and the track, never good, became execrable, littered with rotting timber, at last petering out altogether in a great silent forest. But, following a telephone wire hung from the trees, we came eventually to a grassy summit near an icy spring flowing from a rocky cliff.

We were guided over the summit and down again through forest by three little shepherd boys, Bektashis, who had cattle up here. The eldest, aged twelve, said with pride that he was in the fourth class at school in Martanesh and could read and write. All three wore flat white caps, *opinga*, baggy brown homespun trousers, white shirts with sleeves, and thick white *dolama* heavily braided in black at the edges. They were lithe as cats, their feet light on the leaves, with all the good manners of their creed and mountain blood.

Prenk now declared firmly, looking warningly at the boys, that there was no spring nearer than Martanesh village, far away in the valley; but I told him he lied, for the whole place was damp. Then I asked the boys, upon their honour as Albanians and as mountain men, where there was water and place for the ponies. Near, they replied, ignoring Prenk, was good water, a fold for the ponies, and as for food they would sell us a lamb for 4 shillings. So we went with them. We crossed a pretty stream where one of them pointed to a mark in a rock, saying solemnly it was a hoof-print made by Skenderbeg's horse. Soon we came into a little valley shut in by rocky sides of limestone covered with beech and fir trees. The valley's bed was soft with rich grass, a carpet of flowers, and the evening sun cast long shadows across it from the trees. There were curious frogs in the damp places whose cry sounded like distant gulls. At the end a spring gushed from the rock, so cold that its water numbed our lips; and the stream from it flowed away through a deep cleft, rocky and dark. At the mouth of this cleft, between the water and the trees, was a turfy ledge in the shade, just wide enough for our camp. It was a cool, mysterious, silent place, fragrant with woody smells and the scent of flowers, holding a hint of the wolves and bears of childhood's story books.

Prenk and the boys took our ponies to the fold and came again, as night was closing down, with a lamb ready skinned and an invitation from the boys' father to his fold to eat another he would provide "without money"—an invitation it would have been unfair to accept. Lef threw the lamb's black fleece at my feet, saying I could sell it for ninepence in Tirana. I gave it to Ali, who was hugely pleased.

Close beside a great fire which cast riotous shadows about the ravine our men and the boys drove in two forked stakes a yard apart. Then they thrust a sharp-pointed rod through the lamb from vent to neck and out through the mouth. The legs were spitted across the rod, the inside salted and sewn up. Then the ends of the rod were rested on the upright forks and the meat turned slowly before the blaze for an hour. It was a wild scene in the firelight. Black shadows wrapped us round, blacker for the moon which lit the little valley and the rocks beyond it and caught the slow pillars of smoke as they climbed above the trees. Here and there fireflies flashed like fairies on their way from bough to bough. In the night-quiet the only sounds were the men's mutterings and the burble of water on the stones. As the moon crept higher, shortening the shadows, touching the dark stream's ripples to molten silver, glinting on the leaves and drowning our fires in its full light, the lamb was ready—and we were glad, for it was our first meat since Elbasan and before Elbasan we had eaten meat only at Voskopoli and Prishtë. Lef brought me the head, all teeth and eyes, and was puzzled when I preferred a leg, for the brains and eyes are the best parts and the head always given to the chief man or guest.

We left this enchanted place sadly and went up the valley to *tekké* Balim Sultan where *Baba* Xhafer, white-bearded and stately, came out to greet us. He had heard we were nearby and why had we not come to stay at the *tekké*?

A *tekké* was first built here about 1870, and at the same time another in the valley near Martanesh; but in 1921 the Serbs burnt the one here, though they did not harm the lower one which was strongly defended by local people. The lower *tekké* was threatened in 1914 by rebels from Tirana but was saved after some fighting. The new *tekké* here is strongly built of stone to the height of its single storey, surmounted by a very high roof with wide eaves, very steep to throw off snow, made of handsawn planks. It stands in a courtyard with high arched entrance gate. Within was dark and cavernous. In the *Baba's* room the floor was spread with white fleeces by the walls and two gaily embroidered saddlebags hung from pegs. We sat for coffee in the shade of the arched gate.

In the two *tekkés* there were only eight *dervishes* and *Baba* Xhafer—who was *Baba* of both; but there were several probationers, one a well-educated young man from Korça who spoke French. He led us by a narrow path up the shady hillside to a little door in a white stone wall which hid the mouth of a cavern. We went in—it was like stepping into a refrigerator. Inside, close to the door, were several mugs and a petrol can holding holy water collected from the drippings in the cave (and having perhaps, medicinal value); this water is given to sick children whom it cures—but of what it cures them our friend did not say. Further in are two shrines, one that of the holy man Balim, a contemporary of Mahomet. Beyond the shrines a passage led into the mountainside, and this we followed for some paces. The air became, if possible, colder, till it rattled my teeth and the passage narrowed till it was hard to go on. Here our guide stopped, saying no one could go further— —one *dervish* who tried was overcome. In the cold I felt unheroic and came out. The sun-heated air was like a blast from a furnace as we passed back into the open. *Baba* Xhafer explained the cave is sacred. The legend is that Mahomet himself made the passages which may not be defiled by man; and they lead underground, so he said with solemnity, to the top of Tomori and to the *tekké* on the crag above Kruja.

Baba Xhafer wished us a good road, first giving us provision of bread and cheese. Now we headed direct for Tirana, descending towards the wide Martanesh valley, a densely wooded place broken by rocky outcrops, then climbing among tall beeches to the top of a pass vaguely marked upon the map as *Çafa* Tuglaver—though a local commune guard had never heard that name for it nor any other. Over this pass we entered a shallow valley, the bed of it covered by luxuriant grass and flowers, with clumps of trees apart and its gentle sides heavily shaded by magnificent beeches. Parts of it were like an English park, except that we saw crags above the tree tops. Then we came upon two or three shepherds' huts and folds, a place called *Stan* (fold) Bica Shëngjerçit. Its rich grass was alive with big grasshoppers of all colours. Leaving these meadows as the valley pinched together we came out at the top of a bare mountainside and saw far below us the upper valley of the Arzen, stretching away to *Mali* Dajti and *Çafa* Priskës. Here we dropped sharply to Shëngjerçe, a stony place scattered over a spur round a little mosque and surrounded by a waste of bare mountains, rugged and treeless. We scrambled down to the river bed and went along to a clump of plane trees, a stuffy sandy place but there was none other for camping between the stones and the steeps.

June 27 was our last trekking day. We wandered on down our bare valley, the unbeaten way hard for all our feet among so many stones, and a mask of heat, reflected from the rocks and sand, burning our faces. At length we climbed to *Çafa* Priskës, the track steep and shadeless and our throats parched for the lack of water. Crossing the *Çafa's* narrow col we descended by a scrub-choked ravine to *han* Krana where we came into sight of Tirana and refreshed ourselves at a brackish spring with insects in its pool. Then we went on downward through Dajti's scrub-grown foothills, passing farms and hayfields and olive groves; and we came into Tirana as the shadows drew out and the colours revived for their twilight glory, the orange of the sun's last light behind the minarets outshone by the glow of the moon, full and immense, a golden ball, creeping from the purple hills we had lost.

During my last days the heat was terrific—so fierce it was unwise to stir a yard with head uncovered. The high sun beat down mercilessly upon low-lying Tirana, bleaching the colours and cutting the town into hard blacks and whites. The streets, muffled by inches of powdery dust, were choked with baked air and reflected the harsh rays which burnt the skin and dazzled the eyes and drove the sweat from the pores in streams. The representatives of other Balkan states pined for their own capitals where it was never so hot; and the British said the worst Indian heat was more supportable with India's provision for it. In the midday hours nobody stirred. At nights I lay (in the porch of the tiny house where I stayed) beneath a mosquito net, under a moon which lit beautifully the green leaves and flowers of the garden shrubs—the stuffy flower-scented silence broken only by the sad cry of the night bird calling "Gjon, Gjon" for her lost mate, the ticking of a cricket, the slow deep tones of Albanian talk next door and the plaintive sound of a native banjo.

· · · · ·

On July 14, as the *Lussino* ploughed through the blue water southward from Durrës, I stood at her stern to watch her lengthening wake—my last visible link with Albania. Then I went to the saloon to write the last page of my Albanian diary. When I had laid down my pen the fresh breeze caught and turned the written page. My Albanian days were done.

APPENDIX

CIDNA: probably Cidna village near Dibra.

DAYNA: (or *Dayno* or *Dagno*) no longer exists. Between 1361 and 1491 an independent bishopric, it was then merged with *Sappa* and *Sarda* (diocese of the Zadrima plain) under the Archbishop of Durrës. *Sappa*, of which no trace remains, was fifteen miles south-east of Shkodër and became a bishopric in 1390. There are few traces of *Sarda* which was on the Drin eight miles from Shkodër and became a bishopric in 1190. The last bishop, William, of *Sappa*, *Sarda* and *Dayna*, appointed in 1590, was a French Dominican sometime Vicar-Bishop of Winchester.

DIOCLEA: (or *Dukla*) its ruins lie two miles north of Podgorica.

DRIVASTO: once a prosperous fortress town on a hill seven miles north-east of Shkodër, it largely shared Shkodër's vicissitudes during the thirteenth to fifteenth centuries. Sold by the Balshas in 1396 to the Venetians, the Turks took it by storm in 1478, impaling the heads of its officers beneath the walls of unsubmissive Shkodër. It became a bishopric in 877 and there were thirty-five bishops in all; but about 1640, the place having degenerated, the bishopric was merged with Shkodër. The Moslem village of Drishti now stands among its ruins.

DURRËS: (anc. *Dyrrhachium* is probably a corruption of a local name). Near the mouth of the Shkumbini river is a small ruined fortress called Turrezë—in Albanian *turrë* (-*a*)=heap of stones, enclosure, fortress; and *trujë* (-*a*) is an alternative word with the same meaning.

GRADISHTA: Slavonic, meaning little (or ruined) town.

KRUJA: (sometimes Croia)—*kruë* (def. *kroni*, *krôi*)=spring, fountain; *kryë* (-*a*)=head, chief (hence *kryeqendrë*=headquarters); *trujë* (-*a*)=heap of stones, enclosure, fortress—which Albanians suggest may be the origin of *Troja*, Troy.

MODRISSA: (Knolles mentions)—was Gur-i-Pishkashit, north of *Çafa* Thanës, according to Tirana authorities. When he lost *Sfetigrad*, Skenderbeg fortified *Modrissa*.

APPENDIX

ORONYCHIUM: (Knolles mentions)—was Dibra, according to Baron Franz Nopsca. Near Dibra is a flat place called Fusha e Toranikut. Thus, the nearby town being *Toranik*, Byzantine historians would Hellenise it to *Toronichion*—then, stretching a point to give it meaning (as was often done), *To Oronychion=Oros Onychion*=mountain nail.

PALACHIENSIS: (or *Balleacensis*)—was on the Drin. It had eight bishops, the last appointed in 1478. Records of it seem to be scarce.

PETRA ALBA: (Knolles mentions)—was evidently Guri Bardh, both names meaning White Stone; and Guri Bardh would be on Skenderbeg's route from Petrela into Mati.

POLAT: (or *Pulti* or *Pulati*)—was thirty miles north-east of Shkodër but is now obliterated. It had a bishop in 877: and between 1345 and 1520 the diocese was divided into Upper and Lower Pulati with two bishops whose quarrels once provoked Skenderbeg's intervention.

POLOGUS: believed to have been Tetovo, or near Tetovo, in Yugoslavia.

SFETIGRAD: (Knolles mentions)—Slavonic, meaning Holy Town—was evidently Koxhaxhik, near Dibra. The Turks re-populated *Sfetigrad:* and Turkish is the language of Koxhaxhik to-day.

STELLUSA: (Knolles mentions)—was Gjytet-i-Skenderbeut in Mati, according to Nopsca.

SVACIA: (or *Scias*), was a district north-west of Shkodër. After the death of its twenty-second bishop the bishopric was merged with Shkodër.

VALCAL: valley of: (Knolles mentions)—was evidently Fusha-e-Domusdovës, west of *Çafa* Thanës.

BIBLIOGRAPHICAL NOTE
Chief authorities consulted:

BALDACCI, ANTONIO. *L'Albania.* Rome, 1930.

BOURCART, JACQUES. *L'Albanie et les Albanais.* Paris, 1921.

BROWN, H. A. *A Winter in Albania.* London, 1888.

BYRON, LORD. *Childe Harold's Pilgrimage.*

DESCOINS, GÉNÉRAL. *Six Mois D'Histoire de L'Albanie.* Revue d'Histoire de la Guerre mondiale. Oct. 1929 and January 1930.

DODWELL, EDWARD. *A Classical and Topographical Tour Through Greece During the Years 1801, 1805 and 1806.* Vol. I. London, 1819.

DURHAM, MISS M. E. *High Albania.* London, 1909; *The Struggle for Scutari.* London, 1914; *The Burden of the Balkans.* London, 1905; *Some Tribal Origins, Laws and Customs of the Balkans.* London, 1929.

HOBHOUSE, J. C. *A Journey Through Albania and Other Provinces of Turkey in Europe and Asia, to Constantinople, During the Years 1809 and 1810.* Vol. I; London, 1813.

HOLLAND, SIR HENRY. *Travels in the Ionian Isles, Albania, Thessaly, Macedonia, etc., During the Years 1812 and 1813.* London, 1815.

HUGHES, REV. T. S. *Travels in Greece and Albania.* 2 Vols. London, 1830.

KNOLLES, RICHARD. *A Generall Historie of the Turkes.* London, 1603.

LEAKE, WILLIAM MARTIN, LT.-COL., R.A. *Travels in Northern Greece.* Vol. I. London, 1835.

LEAR, EDWARD. *Journals of a Landscape Painter in Albania, Illyria, etc.* London, 1852.

MENEGHETTI, N. T. COL. DI COMPLEMENTO. *Quel Che Cesare Non Dice Nel Suo Capolavoro.* Milan, 1931. (79 pp. and 10 plans).

PEACOCK, WADHAM. *Albania: The Foundling State of Europe.* London, 1914.

POUQUEVILLE, F. C. *Travels in the Morea, Albania and Other Part, of the Ottoman Empire.* 1813.

REY, LÉON. *Guide de L'Albanie.* Paris, 1930 (158 pp.).

SPENCER, EDMUND. *Travels in European Turkey in 1850.* 2 Vols. London, 1851.

SWIRE, J. *Albania: The Rise of a Kingdom.* London, 1929 (560 pp., full bibliography and maps).

Albania—section in the Near East Year Book, London, 1931 (108 pp. general information).

UGOLINI, LUIGI M. *L'Antica Albania.* Rome, 1927; *Albania Antica.* 3 Vols. Rome, 1927.

WACE, A. J. B. and THOMSON, M. S. *Nomads of the Balkans.* London, 1914.

(NOTE: The above supplements the extensive bibliography contained in my *Albania: The Rise of a Kingdom.* The above are authors mentioned or consulted or quoted in this book.)

INDEX

INDEX

Abantes: 157
Abas Ali, Bektash saint: 253-4, 258
Abatë (Shala): 126
Abduction: 107
Abdulla, *qiraxhi*: 62-3, 69, 97-9, 110
Abyssinian crisis: vii
Accursed Mountains: 98, 118
Achaea: 33; Achaians, 182
Achmet Pasha: 55
Achris, lake: 38, 42, and *see* Okhrida
Acroceraunian (Akrokeraunian) Mts.: 48, 160-1, 250, 253
Acropolita: 70
Adilé, Princess: 201
Adrianople: 71, 75, 78
Adriatic (Sea): 142; key to, 151; hotel at Himara, 167; hotel at Vlona, 148
Æmathia: 72, and *see* Mati
Æneas: 177, 179
Aeropus, Mt.: 229
Ætolia: 232; Ætolians, 181-2
Afranius: 31
Africa: 31
Aghas: 46
Agricultural reforms: 144, 195, and *see* Beys
Agrit, pass: 120-1
Agron, King: 48, 181
Ahmed—Ali Pasha's servant: 192; Hill's orderly, 111, 116, 119
Air service: vii, 197; port at Vlona, 157
Akrokeraunian Mts.: *see* Acroceraunian
Alaric: 145-6
Albania: advertises for a king, 15; autonomy of, 103; business in, 206; corruption in, 198, 203, 205-6, 220, 223, 244; crown of, 185-6; crown property, 177; defence of, 151-3, 204; foreigners in, 208; government, viii, x, 18-9, 23, 86-7, 92-5, 105-7, 110, 118-9, 122-3, 144, 162, 198-200, 203 *et sqq.*, 215 *et sqq.*, 244; independence of, 19, 92, 154-5, 198, 201, 203, 235; kingdom of, 106, 200, 215; partition of, 150, 154-5; political dan-

Albania—*continued*.
gers of, 218; population of, 204; princes of, 81, 83, 89-90, and *see* Skenderbeg; principality, 104; relations with Italy, 151, 200, 203-4, and *see* Italy, Italians, Tirana; revolts in, rebels, 23, 27, 33, 42, 94, 104, 119, 122-3, 158, 200, 243, 248-9, 279; roof of, 121; Serbian policy towards, 23, 49, and *see* Serbs, Serbia, Yugoslavs, Yugoslavia; throne of, 15, and *see* Wilhelm, Zog.
Albanian(s): army, 19, 60, 151-3, 194, 204-5, 217 (General Staff, 167-8, 205); attitude towards advisers, 205; budget, 204, 221; cocks, 249; courtesy, 27; dogs, 39, and *see* Dogs; farm, 36; flag, 17, 112; fleas, 114-5; goats, 117; hospitality, 156, 175, 255, 257; illiteracy, 68; irredentist dreams, 174; language, viii-ix, 166, 183, 265, 267, 283; League, 103, 235, 248; lethargy, 64; lowlanders, 111; mercenaries, 164, 166; officials, 208-9, 223; province of Korça, 40; Provisional Government, 34, 94, 104, 155; Republic, 95; sovereignty, 41; trade deficit, 144; types, 198; workmen, 28
Ali Pasha, the Lion: x, 36, 56, 85, 147-8, 150, 165-6, 169, 171, 178, 181-92, 224-5, 231-9, 243-8, 265; appearance, 187; army, 102, 189; character, 188; physician, 114; besieges Shkodër, 56; takes Vlona, 154; Himara coast, 161; Himara, 167; Nivica, 176; negotiates with the French, 180; receives British visitors, 225; at Tepeleni, 226-8; vengeance, 230-1; takes Berat, 247-8; sons, 185-6, 188, 190, and *see* Mukhtar, Sali, Veli; mother, 230-2, and *see* Khamko; sister, 230-3, and *see* Shainica; wife, 185, 192, and *see* Ermineh; life story, 183-92.

INDEX

Albanopolis: 70, and *see* Kruja
Albanorum Oppidum: 246, and *see* Berat
Albinoes: 27
Alexander (the Great): 70; King of Yugoslavia, 123, 219
Alexandria: 169
Algerians, Algerines: 154, 266
Ali Haxhi, *qiraxhi*: 272-4, 278
Alphonso, King of Naples: 78-80, 151
Amantes: 157; Amantia, 158, 181, 224
America: 40, 236, 240, 267, and *see* United States; emigrants to, 26, 165, and *see* Emigrants; Americans, 16, 18, 35, 145, 210; American enterprises, 34, 209; American spoken, 40, 160, 165, 170; Quota Law, 40; missionaries, 267; Americans killed, 42; warships bombard Durrës, 34
Amesa, Skenderbeg's nephew: 74, 79-80
Amurath: 71, 73, 75-8, and *see* Sultan Murad II
Anastasius, Emperor: 33
Anchiasmus, bishops of: 177
Anchises: 177; lake of, 179
Andromache: 179
Andronicus II, Emperor: 153
Angevins: 156, 179, 246
Anglo-Persian Oil Co.: 144-5
Anjou, Charles of: 32, 70, 153; John of, 32, 81
Ankara: 244
Anthony, Mark: 30-1
Antigonea: 181-2, 225, 229, 232, and *see* Tepeleni
Antipatria: 48, 246, and *see* Berat
Antivari, Archbishopric of: 48
Aoos, river: 145, 224, and *see* Vjosa
Appius Claudius: 232-3
Apollo: 145, 148
Apollonia: 29-30, 32, 145-8, 158; Apollonians, 158
Apollonius, bishop: 32
Apsus, river: 245, and *see* Osum
Apulia: 32, 79, 81
Apustius: 246
Arab: 90; Arabia, 16, 253
Aranitas, General Xhemal: 205
Aras: 25
Archæologists: 146, 178-9; work, discoveries of, 180-2
Architecture, styles, etc.: 17, 20-3, 35, 89, 91, 100, 115-6, 124, 127-8, 134, 193, 214, 224, 234, 236, 246, 257, 275, 279

Ardenica, monastery: 146-7
Armistice, the (1918): 19, 93
Aromani: 261, and *see* Vlachs
Arzen, river: 66, 197, 212, 281
Asia: 85; Pasha of, 52, 55
Asnaus, Mt.: 229
Asparagium: 30, and *see* Muriçiani
Aspri Ruga: 30
Atanasia, Mt.: 159
Athens: 29, 181; Athenian Peninsula, 187
Athos, Mt.: 250
Attintanes: 48
Aulon: 145, 153, and *see* Vlona
Austerlitz, battle: 186
Austria, Austrians: *see* Austria-Hungary.
Austria - Hungary, Austro - Hungarians: 33, 36, 41, 43, 55-9, 93, 103-4, 124, 128-9, 138, 141, 143, 147, 150, 154, 159, 202, 205, 219, 249, 251-2, 266, 268
Automobile Association: vii, 220

Bailey: 225
Baizë: 141
Bajram feasts: 197, 215
Balabanus Badera: 82-4, 213
Balim Sultan, *tekké*: 279-80
Balkans (Peninsula): 18, 56, 69, 73, 175, 265; Albanian claims in, 174; capitals, 210; governments, 222; states, 33, 282; wars, 92, 104, 150, 152
Ballsh: 147
Balsha Princes: 33, 69, 88, 149, 153, 156, 247, 283; Balsha II and George, 49; Balsha III, 49, 153; Rugina, 153
Barbarians: 48
Barbary Corsairs: 170, 179
Bardanjolt: 59
Bargëllas: 251-2
Bari: vii, 27
Barletius, Marinus: x
Bartholomeus: 53
Battler Smith: 201
Bayazid, Sultan: 231
Bears: 98, 106, 167, 274, 278
Bektashis, Bektashism: viii-x, 15, 209, 234-5, 239, 241-2, 252-4, 277, 279, 280; account of, 240; assembly of, 244; introduced, 242; mysteries of, 241. *See also Tekkés*
Belgrade: 94, 200
Belica, river: 233; valley, 231, 235
Beligrad: 246, and *see* Berat
Bença, stream, village: 225

INDEX

Benedictine Abbey: 104
Berat: viii, 49, 82, 143, 145, 147, 150, 153, 189, 190, 237, 245-50, 253, 256, 261, 265, 272; Ali Pasha escapes from, 184; Ali takes, 247; history of, 245-9; Pashas of, 56, 154, 166, 183-4, 189, 245-7, 265, and *see* Kurt Pasha; Ibrahim Pasha, 187, and *see* Ibrahim; Skenderbeg besieges, 78-9, 247
Berdelecit, pass: 134
Berisha: 115, 117, 121
Berlin, Treaty of: 103
Berthier, General: 180
Besa: ix, 89, 94, 98-9, 000
Bexhill: 137
Beys, landowning: 94, 143-4, 199, 201-2
Bib Doda, Prenk: 102-5; family home, 110
Bibulus, Admiral: 30
Bica Shëngjerçit, *Stan*: 281
Bijelopavliç: 57, 101
Bistrica, river: 179, 181
Bitolje: 41, 57, 92
Bitumen: 148, 156
Boea: 48
Bogë: 129-31
Bohemund, son of Guiscard: 32
Bojana, river: 45, 48, 50-2, 55, 152
Bombay: 103
Borshi: 171; Lieut. Kemal, 256-7
Bosnia: 117, 120
Bourcart, Jacques: 91 (*see* bibl.)
Bregumatit: 104, 152
Brigands (Bandits): 47, 50, 96-9, 113, 116, 127, 129, 130, 185, 239-40, 248; in Tirana, 198
Brigjë: 141
Brindisi: 29, 30
British: 59, 166, 187, 222, 282; in Albania, 208; adviser, 145, and *see* Stirling; aid, Ali seeks, 186; bombardment of Durrës, 34; comfort, 18; evacuation of Parga, 186; government, 60, 145, 205, 219, 233; gypsies, 196; inspectorate of gendarmerie, 60; intervention against Yugoslavia, 105; journalists, 222; khaki, 124; legation, 17-8, 201, 206; ministers, 16, 204, and *see* Eyres, Hodgson; n.c.o., 126; officers, 60, 135, 195, 205-6, and *see* Church, Dodgson, Hill, Leake, Nelson, Percy, Smith, Stirling; representatives, 222, and *see* ministers; ships, 169, 172, 180, 191;

British—*continued*.
tourist agency, 219; vice-consul in Bari, 27. *See also* England
Bronze Age: 180
Bubesit, pass: 245
Bucharest: 263
Buda (Pest): 72, 264
Buddhism: 240
Budka, Sali: 265-6
Budua: 48
Buffaloes: 173, 197
Bugs: 20, 163, 172-3
Bulçizë: 21, 25-6; pass, 152
Bulgaria, Bulgarians: 32, 35-8, 41, 49, 70, 93, 143, 166, 179, 222, 266
Bullis: 147, and *see* Byllis.
Buonerba, Lieut.: 134
Burelë: 89, 90, 92, 96, 152-3
Burgejet: 90-3
Burney, vice-Admiral Sir Cecil: 59
Bushati: 55, 58; Pashas of, 55-8, 85, 187, and *see* Shkodër; Kara Mahmoud, 243, 247
Buthrotum: 29, 158, 178-9, and *see* Butrinto
Butrinto: 178, 180, 186, 191, 261, and *see* Buthrotum
Byllis (Bullis): 147, 181, 224
Byron, Lord: x, 157, 187, 225-6 (*see* bibl.)
Byzantines, epoch, influence, remains: 32, 38, 49, 51, 70, 146, 153, 155-6, 177-82, 224-5, 233, 238, 246, 284

Caesar: x, 43, 145, 153, 157, 162; fights Pompey, 29-32; his legionaries, 179
Caliph, the: 190
Camarilla, the: 206, 208, 215-7, 221
Cami, Aziz: 219
Campo Formio, Treaty: 176, 180
Candavian range: 42
Cangon, pass: 41
Caretto: 191-2
Catalans: 246
Catholics: *see* Roman Catholics
Cattaro: *see* Kotor
Celydnus, river: 157, and *see* Dukatit
Cem, river: 137, 139
Cepo, monastery: 233
Çerevodë: 256
Četinje: 42, 57, 60
Chamber: 206, and *see* Parliament
Chamberlain, Sir Austen: 200
Chamois: 106
Chaon: 179; Chaonia, 155, 162, 179; Chaonian towns, 166, 225
Charms: 97, 120, 262

INDEX

Chasseurs d'Afrique: 266
Chesti, Lieut.: 42, 216
Children, survival of: 68, 126
Chimaera, Chimariot: 157, 161, and *see* Himara
Christ: 73, 88, 241, 245
Christians: 53–8, 72–3, 120, 127, 161, 169, 176, 187–8, 190, 197, 209, 233, 242, 245, 253, 263–5, and *see* Orthodox Christians, Roman Catholics, Religion; fanaticism, 243; head shaving, 120; Christendom, 66, 85; Christianity, 71, 81, 88
Church, Col.: 186
Cicero: 178
Cidna: 83, 283
Ciganes: 196, and *see* Gypsies
Cigarette holders: 17–8, 22
Cika, Nebil: 215
Cikës, Mt.: 159
Çiroçaf: 245
Citrons: 163
Civil Code: 87
Clevas: 232
Clodiana: 35, 158, and *see* Pekinj
Communes, organisation of: 86–7; guards, 86, 98–9, 119, 133, 280; officials, 116, 119, 133, 172–3, 263
Communications: 144, and *see* Air service, Roads
Communists: 155, 222
Conference of Ambassadors: 39, 136
Congreve Rockets: 186, 191, 247
Constantinople: 48, 52, 54–5, 58, 79–84, 92, 103, 185, 190, 192, 194, 228, 237, 265
Contarenus, Franciscus: 85
Copper: 114
Corcyra, Corcyreans: 29
Corfu, island, straits, town: 165, 169, 173, 176–7, 179, 180, 183, 186, 191, 229, 242, 261
Corinth: 29, 187; Corinthians, 29, 145
Corvenus, Matthias, King: 51
Crnoievic, Prince Ivan: 72
Croat: 158, 205
Croia: viii, 61, 283, and *see* Kruja
Crusaders: 32, 82
Cuni, Lec: 137–8
Curi, Bajram: 118
Curzon, Hon. R.: 248
Cynoscephalae, battle: 230
Cyriacus of Ancona: 43
Czechoslovakia: 67

Dajti, Mt.: 197, 211, 281
Dalmatia: 62, 186; Princes of, 83; Dalmatians, 161

Damesi: 229
Dardani: 182
Dayna (Dayno, Dagno): 74, 88, 283
Deabolis: 41–2, and *see* Zvezde
Decauville railway: 17, 143, 156
Deer: 256
Deliani, Mehmed: 187
Delvina: 182, 187, 190; Pashas of, 182, 185, 187; plain, 176
Delvinaki: 183
Dema, Father: 138
Dervish At: 25
Dervish Pasha: 103
Dervishes: ix, 186, 197, 240–4, 251–4, 258–9, 279–80, and *see* Bektashis
Desnica, stream: 237
Despots: of Epirus, 179; George of Serbia, 73
Devolli, river, valley: 152, 268–70
Devris, pass: 255, 260
Dhirmi: 173, and *see* Zrimadhës
Dhrynopolis: 233
Dibra: 25, 50, 69, 71, 75, 78, 152, 201, 283–4; district, 72, 78–9, 133; Lieut. from, 128; road to, 20; Dibrani, 74–5, 168, 172
Dibrri, *bajrak*: 101
Dioclea (Dukla): 47, 283
Dionysius the Elder: 43
Djakova: 101, 103
Dobrenj: 265
Doçi, Primo: 100, 103
Dodgson, Major and Mrs.: 249
Dodwell, Edward: x, 149, 161, 166 (*see* bibl.)
Dogs: 22, 65, 189, 196, 249; danger of, 39
Dragoti village: 229
Dress. native: ix, 16, 18, 21–2, 34, 40, 45–6, 63–4, 67–8, 96, 100–1, 113–6, 126, 133, 143, 146, 236, 251–2, 261–2, 271–7
Drin, river: 22, 24–5, 38, 42–3, 45, 50, 70, 87, 116–7, 120–1, 283–4
Drinasa, river: 45, 70
Drishti: 283
Drivasto: 47–50, 54, 83, 283
Druids: 258
Duck, wild: 29, 42, 180
Dukagjin, district: 122; revolt in, 119, 122–3, 200; Dukagjini, 43, 87–8; Lek Dukagjin, 74, 88, 101; descendant of, 124; laws of, 87–8, 92, 107
Dukati: 158; river, 157
Dulcigno: 169–70, and *see* Ulcinj
Durazzo: viii, and *see* Durrës

INDEX

Durham, Miss: x, 119–20, 146 (*see* bibl.)
Durrës: vii, viii, 16–8, 30, 35, 48–50, 66, 70, 81, 83–4, 92–4, 143, 155, 177, 187, 195, 197, 211, 216, 222, 249, 253, 261, 282–3; archbishop of, 48; battles of, 31; bombarded, 34; description, 28; history, 29, 32–3; king at, 200; military importance, 151–3
Dyrrhachium: 29, 283, and *see* Durrës

Earthquakes: 28, 32, 146, 149, 156, 158, 160–3, 174–5, 226, 261, 270
Eden, Morton: 19, 20, 24, 104–5
Education: 68, and *see* Schools
Egypt: 58, 163, 190, 196
Elaeon, plain: 232; Elaeus, 233
Elbasan: 29, 31, 36–7, 59, 84–5, 93, 146, 152–3, 191, 195, 201, 212, 247, 261, 269, 272–3, 279; description and history, 35
Elders: ix, 86, 88, 115, 119, 120, 131
Elections: 207
E—martesë, pass: 255, 260
Emigrants: 26, 40, 165, 174, 234, 236 267, and *see* America; in Yugoslavia, 216
England: 135, 186–7, 236; English language, 26, 40, 103, 164, 172, 174, 240; similarities, 108, 112, 141, 148, 170, 281; Englishmen, 112, 201, 206, 225, 247, 265; English company, 148; frigates, 154; newspaper, 149. *See also* Anglo-Persian, British
Epicaria: 114, and *see* Puka
Epidamnus: 29, and *see* Durrës
Epirots: 82, 177, 181–2; (mod.), 235; bands, 233, 237
Epirus: 74, 78–9, 181–2, 212–3, 232, 237, 246; despot of, 179; king of, 80; kingdom of, 78; provisional government of, 235; prince of, 81
Epirus Nova: 32
Erebara, Col.: 205
Ermineh, wife of Ali Pasha: 185, 188
Ersek: 240
Essad Pasha: 33, 59, 92–3, 104, 207; assassination of, 26
Ethem Bey, mosque at Tirana: 193
Euboea: 157
Euenius: 145
Europe: 85, 135, 190, 203, 227, 233; feudalism, 106; hotel at Elbasan, 272

Evil Eye: 68, 88, 97, 168
Eyres, Sir Harry: 17

Fadlullah, mystic: 240
Fani, *bajrak*: 101
Fani Gojanit, valley: 113
Fani-i-vogël, river: 100, 112
Fano, island: 173
Farsherots: 261, and *see* Vlachs
Fauces Antigonenses: 229, and *see* Këlcyra gorge
Ferdinand, kings of Naples: 81, 166
Ferises Pasha: 73
Ferries: 116–7, 142–3
Feud, blood: 21, 46–7, 71, 88–9, 96–7, 104, 107–8, 115–6, 126, 130, 166–7, 181, 201, 225, 231, 275; rules of, 47, 88; victim of, 131; feudal families, 106, 269
Fieri: 143–8, 154; rising at, viii, 158
Fierza: 116–7
Filigree work: 17
Finance, Ministry of: 199, 221
Flamininus, Consul Titus Quinctius: 229
Floç: 274
France: vii, 103, 186–7, 248; pact with Yugoslavia, 200. *See also* French
Franciscans: 43, 127, 138
Frasheri, Mehdi: viii, x, 203, 209; village, 172, 260–1
French: 18, 26, 40–1, 59, 81, 94, 105, 125, 145, 148, 154, 170, 176, 180, 186–7, 229, 251, 266; archæological mission, 146; consul at Janina, x; language, 27, 252, 280. *See also* France.
Frescos: 263–7
Frontier: with Greece, 181–3, 238–9; with Yugoslavia, 19, 23, 25, 38, 59–60, 94, 105, 118, 123, 128, 130, 135–41, 199, 216
Fusha Arshit: ix, 114
Fusha e Domusdovës: 37, 284
Fusha e Toranikut: 284
Fustanella: ix, 46, 146, 248

Galata Serai: 92
Gallic mercenaries: 181
Gardiki: 184, 231–2
Gendarmes, gendarmerie: 19, 20, 23, 25, 36–7, 60, 68, 86, 90, 96–9, 111, 114–39, 165, 168, 172–3; posts, 68, 87, 96, 113, 116–21, 126, 133–5, 139, 165, 169, 205, 212, 235, 239, 249, 256, 263, 270, 272; British officers, 60, 205–6, and *see* Dodgson,

INDEX

Gendarmes—*continued*.
　Hill, Percy, Smith, Stirling; Mirditë, 108, 273; Hussein, 250; Nexheb, 270, 272; Qamil, 250; Prenk Noi, 273-4, 277-8
Gentius, King: 145
George, Despot of Serbia: 73
Gheg Laz: 140
Ghilardi, General: viii, 150, 158-9, 162-3, 205
Gibraltar: 150
Gjana, Mt.: 98
Gjarpenit, pass: 134
Gjeloshi, Ndoc: 219
Gjergjevica: 262
Gjinikas: 268
Gjinokastra: viii, 49, 146, 187, 190-1, 229-36, 243; description of, 234; Italians proclaim Albanian independence at, 235; valley of, 176, 182-3
Gjonbabas: 262-3
Gjoni, Marka, family: 102, 105-6, 110; Gjon, 100, 106-9, 112; Mark's wedding, 109-10
Gjytet i Skenderbeut: 284, and *see* Stellusa
Glaucias, King: 29
Godalesh: 273
Goranje: 234
Goths: 32, 146
Grabom, *Han*: 128-9, 136, 139
Gradishta: 147-8, 283
Grand Hotel at Shkodër: 59
Grava Bay: 170
Great Britain: vii, 150, and *see* British, England
Great Mountain Land: ix, 121, 140, and *see* Malcija e madhe
Greece: 57-8, 62, 150, 153-4, 173-4, 190, 233, 235, 239, 243, 248, 264-5; Greeks (anc.), 38, 145, 147, 149, 178-82; (mod.), 40, 104, 154, 161, 165, 167, 182, 187-91, 226-7, 232-5, 239, 243, 258, 267; bands, 40, 230, 249, 251, 258, 260; characters, 266; colours, 40, 173; language, 166, 183, 265; propaganda, 40, 162, 265; revolt, 192; War of Independence, 186; Grecophiles, 173
Grittus, Admiral: 51
Gruda: 140
Guiscard, Robert: 32
Gulumak, pass: 251
Guri Bardh: 284
Gur-i-Pishkashit: 283
Guriprerë, pass: 265

Gusinje: 127, 134-6
Gylacia: 145, and *see* Apollonia
Gypsies: 28, 120, 155, 195-6

Hadji Baba: 258
Hadrian, Emperor: 233
Hadrianopolis: 181, 233-4
Hashi, district: 101
Hasluck, Margaret: x
Haxhi Bektash Veli: 240
Haxhi Seret: 230, 245
Hecatompedon: 48
Hector: 179
Helen (legend.): 229; bride of King Manfred, 153; Hellenic walls, 265, and *see* Greeks
Helenus, son of Priam: 179
Helicranum: 182, and *see* Delvina
Heraclius, Emperor: 49
Herapit, Mt.: 127
Hertzegovina: 49, 186
Highgate: 16
Hill, Oakley, Major: 111, 116, 126, 130-1, 138, 201, 271; Mrs. Hill, 111, 271
Himara, coast: 16, 158, 173; village, 160, 164-71, 187; Himariotes, 166-7
Hobhouse, J. C.: x, 183, 227, 233 (*see* bibl.)
Hodgson, Sir Robert: x, 222
Holidays, national: 214-5
Holland, Sir Henry: x, 147-8, 183, 231 (*see* bibl.)
Holta, stream: 270-1
Hormova: 185, 230
Hospitals: 197
Hot springs: 22, 36, 42, 148
Hoti: 140-1, 152
Houroufi sect: 240
Hughes, Rev. T. S.: x, 39, 102, 167, 183, 227-8, 231-2, 237, 247 (*see* bibl.)
Hungary: 51, 72, 129
Huniades: 71, 73
Hushuf, family of Ali Pasha: 183
Hussein Riza Bey: 59
Hyssejnagoll, Emin Bey: 201

Iacup Arnauth: 82
Iballja: viii, 114-6
Ibex: 106
Ibrahim, governor of Tepeleni: 227
Ibrahim, Pasha of Berat: 150, 154, 187, 247-8
Illyria, Illyrians: 29, 48, 145, 153, 157, 181-2, 232, 246, 250; kings of, 48, 181; princes of, 83, 181; remains, 70, 114; wars, 29, 48

INDEX

India: 282; Indo-Chinese troops, 266
Infant betrothals: 89, 107; mortality, 68, 126
Interior, Minister of: 220, and *see* Juka
International Boundary Commission: 40
Ipek: 136, and *see* Pec
Iron Castle at Janina: 189, 192
Isaacke Pasha: 80
Ishmi river: 31, 43,
Iskender: 71, and *see* Skenderbeg
Islam: 44, 240, 273, and *see* Moslems, Mahometanism
Ismail Pasha of Berat: 247
Ismail Pashou Bey: 190, 192
Israelites: 163
Ionian islands: 150, 180, 186; coast, 176
Italian(s): 16, 18–20, 33–4, 36, 41–2, 59, 60, 65, 79, 89, 91–4, 104, 108, 113–4, 143–5, 148, 150–1, 153–5, 158–9, 169, 170, 178, 191, 193, 195, 203, 206, 209, 216, 218, 220, 222, 229, 235, 249, 258, 268; in Albania, vii, 203–5; archæological mission, 178; language, 166, 261; military mission, 151; officers, 42, 125, 203–4, 216; surveyors, 134, 275
Italy: 41, 67, 93, 110, 123, 136, 150–1, 154, 158, 177, 199–204, 216, 218, 248; loan to Albania, 95, 203, 210; pact and treaty with Albania, 200; relations with Albania, vii, 95, 123, 150–5, 204; strategic considerations, 79, 90, 109, 150–3, 204–5

Jackals: 148, 171, 180
Janina: 32, 102, 183–92, 229, 231–2, 237, 243, 248; Ali Pasha's capital, 183 *et sqq.*; bishop of, 180, 190; Pashas of, 183–4, 190, 192, and *see* Ali Pasha
Janissaries: 52, 75–6, 243
Jano, Dina: 261–2
Japan: vii
Jaundice: 142
Jesera massif: 127
Jesuits: 113
Jews: 163, 187, 190
Jonuz, Turkish commander: 84
Joseph II, Emperor: 56
Jubani: 69
Juka, Musa: 220–2, and *see* Interior
Justinian, Emperor: 38, 166, 182, 195 233

Kalivo: 181
Kamber Ali: 240, 258
Kanina: 150, 155–6, 191
Kaplan. Pasha of Delvina: 185
Kaptin, Mt.: 152–3, 277
Karaburun Mts.: 149
Kara Mahmoud: 56, and *see* Bushatis
Karl Viktor, Prince of Wied: 41, 202, and *see* Wilhelm
Kastoria: 32
Kastrati: 141
Kastriota, family: 69, 70, 73, 81, 156, 247; Pal, 69; Gjon, 69, 70, 81; George, 70, 73, and *see* Skenderbeg
Kavaja: 30, 34–5, 195, 261; Pashas of, 195
Kavakia: 182
Kefali, Cape: 176·
Këlcyra: 32, 190, 237, 240, 254; gorge of, 229, 237
Kennedy, Mr. and Mrs.: 267
Khalivare: 113
Khamko, Ali Pasha's mother: 184, and *see* Ali
Khurshid Pasha: 192
Kingdom: 200, and *see* Albania, Zog
Kirchner, Baron von: 167
Kiri, river: 45, 50
Kjorë, Mt.: 159
Klementi, clan, district: 105, 120, 123, 129, 135–6, 138; migration, 140
Knolles, Richard: x, 44, 51, 71, 91, 212, 283–4; quoted, 51–5, 71–85, 212–3 (*see* bibl.)
Kodra monastery: 230
Kodrion: 48
Kolkondasi monastery: 147
Kolonia district: 237, 240, 266
Kolshit, pass: 117–20
Komani: 114
Komnenus, Emperor Alexius: 32, 41, 156; Michael, 246
Konica: 184, 243
Konispoli: 181, 187, 261
Korab Mts.: 23
Korça: viii, 32, 37, 40–2, 119, 209, 240, 243–4, 261, 263–4, 267, 280; description and history, 40–1
Korita: 255
Kosova, district: 118, 121, 133; battle, 49, 101; Kosovopolje, 56
Kotor: 136
Kotta, Prime Minister: 244
Koxhaxhik: 284, and *see* Sfetigrad
Kozhni: 131–2
Krana, *Han*: 281
Kranje, Mt.: 84

INDEX

Krasniç, clan: 120
Krosi, Abdurrahman: 207–8, 216–7, 221, 223
Krraba, pass: 31, 84, 212, 272
Kruja: viii, 32, 62, 65–77, 80, 83–6, 90–3, 136, 191, 213, 242–3, 280, 283; description, 65–9; fortress, 70 *et sqq.*; siege, 75 *et sqq.*; *tekké*, 242
Kryezezë: 114
Kryeziu, Cena: 201–2, 216; Gani, 216
Kthela, clan, *bajrak*: 101, 108
Kuç: 167
Kuçesi, Mt.: 224
Kukëri: 270
Kukës: 116, 118, 152
Kulas: ix, 21, 89, 90, 95–8, 115–6, 124, 265, 274–5
Kulmak, *tekké*: 251
Kurt Pasha of Berat: 36, 56, 184–5, 246–7
Kurvelesh, district: 225
Kushneni, *bajrak*: 101
Kypero: 170
Kyrias school: 164, 209

Lalës, Mt.: 31
Laos, river: 224–5, and *see* Vjosa
Latin peoples: 260
Laurettano, Antonio: 51
Lavdhari: 265
Lawrence of Arabia: 16
League, of Nations: vii, 145; of Albanian People, 72. *See also* Albanian League
Leake, W. M., Lieut.-Col.: x, 41, 154, 160, 166–7, 169, 171, 182, 186, 195, 214, 227, 247, 264–5 (*see* bibl.)
Lear, Edward: x, 158, 160, 165, 195, 250 (*see* bibl.)
Lecci, Antonio da: 52–5
Lef, author's servant: 264, 267, 275, 278–9
Legends: 43, 50–1, 91, 116, 170, 196, 213, 229, 242, 253, 280
Leipzig: 264
Lek Dukagjin: 74, 92, and *see* Dukagjin
Lepanto, Pashalik of: 186
Lesh: 31, 42–5, 48, 50, 54, 72, 80, 83, 85, 87, 104–6, 136, 153, 213; history, 43; Skenderbeg's bones, 44; Skenderbeg dies, 85
Leskovik: 239–40
Lezha, Miss: 164–5
Liaperia: 224
Libohova, village: 185, 233; Ekrem, Minister, 217, 219

Librash: 152–3
Lichnis, lake: 38, and *see* Okhrida
Lichtenstein: 202
Lin: 38
Linguetta, Cape: 149–50
Linxhë: 36
Lion of Janina: 192, and *see* Ali Pasha
Lissa, Lissus: 43, 77, and *see* Lesh
Literica, fortress at Janina: 192
Livy: 48, 51
Ljuma, district: 24, 103
Llana, stream: 195–6
Locri: 157
Logara, pass: 30, 149, 154, 159, 171, 224; village, 159
London: 21; pact, 150, 154; periodical, 201
Lovçen, Mt.: 66
Lowlanders: 35, 46, 118, 142 *et sqq.*, 198
Luarasi: 260
Lurja, district: 100, 102
Lushnja: 147, 154, 247; description, 142
Lussino, s.s.: 282
Lyabinoti: 273
Lykova: 175

Macedon-ia, Macedonians: 38, 41, 50, 72, 74, 77–8, 82, 226, 229, 230, 246, 264–5; language, 37, 265; war, 182; villages in Albania, 37
Madame Tussaud's: 16
Mahmoud, grandson of Ali Pasha: 191
Mahomed II, Sultan: 33, 35, 51–5, 76–84
Mahomet, Prophet: 82, 241, 280; Mahometan priests, 53; Mahometanism, 240, and *see* Islam, Moslems
Maize bread, qualities of: 96
Malakastra: 224
Malaria: 29, 42, 155, 195, 246, 271
Malcija e madhe: ix, 60, and *see* Great Mountain Land
Maliq, lake: 39
Malisin, Mt.: 239
Malit, pass: 113, 152
Mamic, Skenderbeg's sister: 82, 91
Mamuras: 42
Manfred, King of Sicily: 32, 70, 153, 179
Mann, S. E.: x, 196, 201
Map, deficiencies of: 131, 269, 280
Margellic: 147

INDEX

Maria Angela, wife of Bib Doda: 102
Marmont, Marshal: 186
Martanesh: 152, 274, 277–80
Massena, Marshal: 186
Mati district, river: 21, 42–3, 67, 69, 72, 89–93, 103–4, 126, 136, 153, 207, 243, 284; Zogu bridge, 153
Mborja: 41
Mecca: 241
Mecovo: 32, 243
Medua, gulf of: 66
Megzes, pass: 131
Mehemet Ali of Egypt: 58, 190–1
Mehmed, Pasha of Berat, 247; Reschid, 57, and *see* Reschid
Melçani, *tekké*: 243
Melisopetra: 32
Meneghetti: x (*see* bibl.)
Merlera, island: 171, 173
Merturi: 117
Mesopotamo: 178
Metohiçës, pass: 137
Mexican army: 158
Michael, Emperor: 70, 246
Midhat Constitution: 104
Military School: 193; militia, 158–9. *See also* Army
Milosh, Prince of Serbia: 58
Miloti: 90, 152–3
Milova: 255
Mirashi, Pal: 124–5
Mirdita, Mirditi: 56, 58, 87–8, 100–12, 123, 232, 273; abbot of, 100, 112; history of, 110 *et sqq.*; wedding, 109
Mitrovica: 174
Mnela, Mt.: 98
Mocenicus, Admiral: 51
Modrissa: 78, 283
Mokra Gora: 73
Molossian dogs: 39, and *see* Dogs
Monarchy: 200, and *see* Zog
Mondragone College: 110
Montenegro, Montenegrins: 23, 49, 56–9, 72, 92, 101, 103, 129, 138–40, 152, 154, 191; besiege Shkodër, 58–9
Moors: 187, 226
Morea: 192; Pashalik of, 186
Moses: 163; Golemus, 72, 77–9, 82
Moskopoli: 264, and *see* Voskopoli
Moslems: 15, 39, 43, 46, 48, 56–7, 64, 70, 91, 101–3, 120, 127, 143, 150, 162, 169, 173, 182, 188, 196–8, 201, 209, 214–5, 220, 224, 226, 231–4, 240, 242–3, 258, 262–5, 283; community, world, 244, 265; fanaticism, 198, 209, 241–3; feasts,

Moslems—*continued*.
215, 241; rebels, 36; relations with Bektashis, 244; Sunnis, 198, 276; women, 27, 209, and *see* Women
Mountaineers: 21–6, 46, 71, 86 *et sqq.*, 251 *et sqq.*; amusements, 119; characteristics, 125, 144, 198; hospitality, 124, 133, 137; laws, 88–9, 107–8; neglected, 110, 123
Muharem (Bajraktari): 118, 133
Mukhtar, son of Ali Pasha: 85, 183–91, 248
Munich: 202
Murad II, Sultan: 71, and *see* Amurath
Muricës, pass: 20, 26
Muriçiani: 30–2
Mussolini: 110, 145, 200, 219; boulevard, 193
Mustafa Pasha: 74; of Delvina, 182, 187
Myrdacz, General Gustav von: 205
Myzeki: 79; Myzekija plain, 143

Nafié, Princess: 201
Nakos, George: 172–3
Naples: 80; kings of, 78, 151, 166
Napoleon Bonaparte: 166, 186
National Bank: 95, 204, 210
Neapolitans: 32; influence, 164; service, 166
Near East Foundation: 34
Near East and India: 220, 222–3
Near East Year Book: 208
Negropont, Pasha of: 184
Nelson, Lord: 186, 248
Nemerçka range: 233, 238
Nermandjesh, pass: 120
Neshta: 277
Newfoundland: 103
News transmission in the mountains: 71, 131
Nicephorus, Emperor: 32
Nikaj: 118, 121
Nikol, shepherd: 120
Nikopolis: 158
Niksh, *bajrak*: 129–30, 138
Nish: 57, 71, 213
Nivica Bubarit: 175–6, 180; Nivica Lovës, 225
Noli, Fan, bishop: 41–2, 90, 94, 199
Nopsca, Baron Franz: 284
Normans: 32, 38, 42, 49, 153, 156
North Channel, Corfu: 177, and *see* Corfu
Nymphs: 148

Oath, the: 98–9, and *see* Besa
Octavius: 145; Pompey's general, 153

INDEX

Odysseus, Ali Pasha's officer: 191
Oil in Albania: 144–5
Okhrida: 29–30, 37–9, 42, 47, 56, 82, 152, 190, 269; description, history, 38–9
Okol: 127–30
Old Mosque, at Tirana: 194
Olympus, Mt.: 253
Omar Khayyám: 258
Onchesmus: 177, 181, and *see* Saranda; Onchesmites, 177
Oracle at Selenica: 148
Oricum: 30, 157–8
Ormasi: 270
Oronychium: 74, 82, 284
Orosh: 98, 101, 103, 105
Orthodox Christians: 15, 215, 243–4, 267, and *see* Christians; Easter, 60; faith, 162; monasteries, 146; nunnery, 263; Vlachs, 239
Osman, Legation kavass: 201
Osum, river: 245, 253, 256, 259
Otranto: 79, 151
Outlaws: 96, 113, 130, and *see* Brigands
Oyanik: 255

Pact with Italy: 200
Palachiensis (Balleacensis): 48, 284
Palasa (Palaeste): 162
Palestine: 163
Pal-i-bardh: 101
Pan: 38, 148
Panormos: 158, 170
Parga: 186–7, 190
Pariani, General: 151, 153
Paris: 26
Parliament, at Tirana: 193, 206
Pashou: 192, and *see* Ismail Pashou
Pashtresh: 271
Paul Emilius: 158
Paulus Angelus, Archbishop: 81
Pavla, river: 179–80
Peace Conference: 155
Peacock: x (see bibl.)
Peç: 136
Pekinj: 35, 158
Peloponnesian War: 29
Penal Code: 87
Peneian pass: 250
Penkova: 224
Perati bridge: 239
Percy, Major Gen. Sir Jocelyn: 60, 201, 205
Perduci, Balthasar: 83
Pericles (at Piqeras): 172–4
Perlat: 87, 96; *bajrak*, 101; Peter, 74–5
Permeti: 190, 233, 237–8, 240

Perseus: 232
Persian: 240
Pes, pàss: 127–8
Peshkepijë: 22–3
Pestriku Mts.: 101
Petra Alba: 71, 284
Petrela: 71, 82, 211–3, 284
Phanote: 181, 232, and *see* Gardiki
Pharsalia, battle: 32, 41
Philip V of Macedon: 43, 145, 158, 182, 229
Phillips, General: 19
Philostratus: 233
Phoenice: 177, 181–2
Phrosini, the case of: 188
Pikernion: 171, and *see* Piqeras
Piperi: 57
Piqeras: 171–4
Pirro Pallas hotel at Saranda: 176
Pistum: 43, and *see* Ishmi
Pliny: 161
Plomer, William: x
Plotsça: 158, 224
Plyasa: 261
Podgorica: 60, 141, 283
Pogradec: 39
Pojan monastery: 146
Poland: 72
Polat (Pulti, Pulati): 47–8, 284
Pologus: 78, 284
Polygamy: 201
Pompey: 29–32, 41, 145, 153, 162
Ponies, mountain: 25–6, 61–4, 69, 90, 98–9, 111–5, 129–30, 250, 257, 272–4, 277–8; accident to, 99; habits of, 19, 63, 115, 120
Poniküt, pass: 134
Pope Paul II: 83, 88; Pius II, 82
Porta Romana: 29
Porte, The: 56–7, 103, 138, 144, 148, 176, 185–7, 247–8, and *see* Turkey
Porto Palermo: 167–8, 170, 176, 186, 190
Postenani: 240
Pouqueville: x, 154, 161, 179 (see bibl.)
Powers, Allied: 15, 94; Central, 143; Entente, 150, 154; European, 180; Great, 23, 33, 140, 189, 199
Prague: 201
Praying Mantis: 174
Pregonati: 225
Preloci: 134–5
Prenka, Kol: 102
Presba, lake: 38, 152
Press: 15–6, 149, 201, 208, 219–23; Albanian, 215; Viennese, 202; Bureau, 195

INDEX

Prevesa: 167, 174, 186, 190–1, 232
Priam: 179
Prifti, Tsans: 230
Prilep: 58
Prishtë, *tekké*: 240, 254, 257–9, 279; village, 259
Prishtina, Hassan: 201
Priskës, pass: 281
Privalit, Mt.: 152, 277
Prizren: 50, 105, 108, 114, 152
Prophet, The: 241, and *see* Mahomet
Puka: 114
Pulato, Pulati (Polat, Pulti): 88, 284
Pulcherie, sister of Theodosius: 146; Pulcheriopolis, *see* Berat
Pyrrhus: 39, 237

Queen Mother: 217, and *see* Sadié Toptani
Qykës: 37

Radohina massif: 127
Ragusa: 43, 47
Railway: 197, and *see* Decauville
Raja: 117
Raki: ix; manufacture, 168, 258
Ramadan, *qiraxhi*: 250, 268, 272
Rapsh: 130, 139–40
Rasbul hills: 17
Rashdani: 270
Rayahs: 57, 143
Red Cross, Albanian: 201, 210; American, 209
Regents: 15, 27
Religion: 209, 214–5, 240–4, 252–4, 263, 265, 279–80, and *see* Bektashis, Christians (Orthodox, Roman Catholics), Moslems, Islam
Reschid Pasha: 36, 57–8, 85
Revolutionary Union: 218
Ried: 219
Rijeka: 45
Roads, building: 90, 106, 125, 158
Rodoni, cape: 69, 84
Roman Catholics, Catholicism: 15, 44, 48, 56, 100, 102, 106, 123, 138, 162, 215, 219, 243, 273
Romani: 261, and *see* Vlachs; Romanies, 196
Rome: 83, 113; Romans, Roman remains, etc.: 29, 35, 37–8, 42–3, 48, 50–1, 114, 145, 147–9, 153, 158, 161, 179–80, 182, 224, 229–33, 246, 260–1
Rosafa: 50, and *see* Shkodër castle
Roumanian language: 261
Roumelia, Derwend-Pasha of, 185; Vali of, 186

Royal Guard: 200
Russia, Russians: 56–7, 91, 102, 169, 180, 185–7, 199, 248
Russo-Turkish War: 57
Rustem, Avni: 26–7

Sabel Pasha: 71
Sajakaj, Father: 127
Salih, son of Ali Pasha: 185, 190, 228, 235
Salonika: 29, 33, 40, 50; Expeditionary Force, 266; Gulf, 187; Metropolitan, 47
Samosraki, island: 173
San Stefano, Treaty: 37
Sappa: 283
Saranda: viii, 174–7, 181–2, 190
Sarandaporos, river: 239
Sarda: 283
Sari Salik, *tekké* at Kruja: 242
Sari Sallteku: 242
Saseno, island: 148–51, 253
Saso: 149, and *see* Saseno
Sasso Bianco: 31
Scampa: 35, and *see* Elbasan
Scarfica, pass: 182
Scerdilaidas, Prince: 181–2
Schools: 34–5, 110, 142, 164, 173–4, 206, 208–9, 248, 264, 267, 276–7; need for, 110; children, 41
Scoea, gate of: 179
Scorpions: 125, 138, 208
Scot, similarity to: 108
Sebalias Pasha: 79
Selasforo: 41, and *see* Zvezde
Selati, *bajrak*: 101
Selcë: viii, 105, 129–31, 135–9
Selenica: 148, 156, 161
Selim, Sultan: 43; Agha, 225–6
Semeni, river: 30, 142–3, 146
Senegalese troops: 266
Senije, Princess: 201
Serbia, Serbs: 22–3, 33, 36, 38, 43, 49, 58–9, 70, 73, 91–4, 103–4, 124, 141, 152–6, 179, 243, 246, 279; origin of *bajraks*, 101; retreat, 33, 113, 152; policy, 23, and *see* Yugoslavia
Sergius and Bacchus: 50
Seton-Merriman: 210
Sevaster: 224
Sfetigrad: 72, 74–5, 78, 82, 284
Shainica, Ali Pasha's sister: 184, and *see* Ali
Shala, district, clan: 88, 101, 120–1, 126–7, 137; *Llumi* Shalës, 126
Shëlbuem, Mt.: 43
Shëmeil, pass: 274

INDEX

Shëmija: 113
Shëmin, *Baba:* 243
Shëngjerçë: 152, 281
Shëngjin: viii, 31, 103
Shëngjon monastery: 146
Shën Ilia, Mt.: 159
Shenjt, Mt.: 98, 100
Shënkolli church at Lesh: 43
Shën Naoum monastery: 38-9, 136, 152, 242
Shëntriada fort: 233
Shën Vasili: 175-6
Shëpal: 112-3
Shinapremtesë, pass, village: 268-9
Shipska: 261, 264, 267
Shkodër: viii, x, 42-60, 74, 83, 94, 101-4, 107-8, 113, 116, 119, 122-5, 135-7, 140-1, 152-3, 164, 216, 243, 283-4; archbishops, 47-9, 283; description, 45; history, 47-9; sieges, 47, 52-5, 58; lake, 45, 60, 140, 152; Pashas of, 55-8, 85, 183-4, 187, 189-91, 195, 247
Shkrelë: 130-1
Shkumbi, Shkumbini, river: 30-1, 35-7, 55, 66, 142, 269, 272, 283
Shoshi: 101
Shpatit, Mts.: 269
Shtegut të Dhenvet, pass: 129
Shulemburg, Marshal: 180
Sicily, Kings of: 32, 70, 153, 179
Simeon, Tsar: 47, 70, 166
Simois, stream: 179
Sirocco: 211
Skenderbeg: vii, x, 38, 44, 51, 53, 61, 64, 66, 70-85, 87-8, 91, 101, 151, 162, 209, 212-3, 237, 242, 247, 278, 283-4; Skenderbeut, Mt., 77
Skivovik, Mt.: 167
Skrapar(it): 255-6, 260
Slavs, Slavonic: 41, 51, 56, 93, 104, 265, 283-4, and *see* Bulgarians, Serbs, Montenegrins, Yugoslavs
Smith, Major Coleman: 235
Snakes: 138, 272
Snipe: 29, 180
Sofia: 185
Soko brothers: 104-5
Sokrat (of Piqeras): 172-4
Sola, Italian Minister: 200
Solyman Pasha: 51
Sophie, Princess of Wied: 17, 202
Sopot: 171
South Down: 121
Spaç, district: 113; *bajrak,* 101
Spain: 30, 187
Spata, Gjin Bua: 234
Spencer: x, 248 (*see* bibl.)

Spilio monastery: 234
Spilja: 176
Sts. Athanasius, Dionicë, Michael, Nikola, Venerdi, churches at Voskopoli, 266-7
St. John the Baptist: 254
St. Mark, standards of: 53, 70; lion of, 164
St. Nikola bay (Saseno): 149
St. Paúl: 32, 238
St. Prodhromos nunnery: 263-4, 267
Stefan Dushan: 49, 153, 179, 246
Stellusa: 72, 284
Stirling, Lieut.-Col. W. F.: 16-9, 60, 109, 201, 208, 219-21
Stone Age relics: 180
Strabo: 161
Struga: 38, 152
Sturdza, Prince: 43
Subashi, bridge: 230
Suka, *tekkë*: 240, 244
Sulejman Pasha: 247
Suli: 186; Suliotes, 157
Sulpicius, Consul: 42, 246
Sultans: 48-9, 57-8, 70-5, 85, 101, 103, 177, 186, 190, 198-9, 213, 243, 248; Sultan-Mother, 195. *See also* Amurath (Murad), Bayazid, Mahomed, Selim
Suma, Angjelin: 218
Sunni Moslems: 276, and *see* Moslems
Sushica, valley: 171
Svacia (Scias); 47, 284
Sveti Naoum: 38, and *see* Shën Naoum
Swiss Alpine Club Journal, 128; Swiss hotel manager, 148

Tamarë: 132, 138-9
Tarabosh, Mt.: 59
Taranto, princes of: 32, 170
Tartars: 187, 226
Taut Gaiola: 52
Tekkés: ix, 240-4, 251-4, 257-9, 263, 279-80, and *see* Bektashis
Tennyson: 250
Tepeleni: 181-5, 189-91, 224-30, 235-6, 243, 247, 265; Ali's court at, 226-9
Tetovo: 284, and *see* Pologus
Teuta, Queen: 48, 181-2
Thanës, pass: 37, 152, 269, 283-4
Theodoric, Theodorus: 32
Theodosius the Younger: 246
Thessaly: 31, 167, 230
Theth: 122, 128
The Times: 109
Thronium: 157-8
Thunderstorms: 123, 211, 254-5

INDEX

Tilsit, Treaty of: 180, 186
Tirana: vii, viii, 17–8, 25–7, 42, 47, 64, 69, 87, 92–5, 105–6, 112, 123, 125, 136, 153, 158, 162, 167, 173, 178, 193 *et sqq.*, 243–4, 271, 278–81, 283; Albanians of, 125; bazaar, 193–4; chosen as capital, 59; comedies, 210; conditions in, 197, *et sqq.*; development of, 34, 193; holidays, 214–5; life in, 208, *et sqq.*, 281–2; officialdom, 208; Pact of, 95, 123, 200; plain of, 62, 66, 82, 85, 143, 211–3; Treaty of, 95; rain in, 142
Tirana, *qiraxhi*: 111–2, 118, 141
Tojari: 245
Tomori, Mt.: 66, 142, 225, 242, 245–6, 250–3, 258, 260, 265, 270, 272, 280 (Tomohrit, 250)
Tomorica, valley: 251–4, 260
Topallaj, Major: 217, 219
Topia family: 33, 70, 92, 156, and *see* Toptani family; Charles, 146; George, 33
Toplana: 126
Toptani family: 92, 195, and *see* Topia family; Ahmed and Kaplan, Pashas, 195; Sadié, 92
Tosk chieftain: 237; Toskeria, 247
Tourists: vii, 219–20
Trade routes: 50, 108, 114
Trajan, Emperor: 147
Trekking, provision for: 62–3
Tres Tabernae: 37, and *see* Qykës
Tribuçi monastery: 230
Trieste: 166
Trikkala: 176, 185
Trouées, military: 151–2
Trout, at Okhrida: 38; bombed, 119; poisoned, 132–3
Troy, Trojan: 157, 178–9, 283
Tuberculosis: 40
Tuglaver, pass: 280
Tumenist, Mt.: 77
Tunjan, *shkallë*: 19, 20, 26
Turkey, Turks, Turkish: vii, 17, 21, 28, 33, 36, 38, 44–58, 69–74, 77–85, 88, 91–2, 98, 101–4, 107–9, 114, 117, 129, 138, 141, 150, 153–6, 161–2, 166–9, 171, 177–93, 198–9, 201, 206–8, 212–3, 226–7, 231, 236–9, 242–4, 247–8, 254, 264–5, 269, 273, 283–4; besiege Kruja, 75; besiege Shkodër, 51; objection to education, 68; Prince, 198, 201; roads, 197; republican government, 201, 244; Turkophiles, 33, 93, 243

Tuzi: 60
Tyrabiu, Ali: 242, 252–4
Tyrant of Syracuse: 43

Ugolini: x (*see* bibl.)
Ulcinj: 55, 170
United States: 174, and *see* America

Valçal, valley of: 82, 284, and *see* Fusha e Domusdovës
Valerius Maximus: 147
Valiare, *Han*: 230–2
Valjevo, battle: 129
Valmes: 35, and *see* Elbasan
Vanista: 234
Varna, battle: 73
Vashu, bridge: 21
Vaudoncourt, Col.: 186
Velbuzhd, battle: 49
Veli, son of Ali Pasha: 185, 187, 191, 237; Ali's father, 183
Venice: 43, 55–6, 88, 176, 180, 264; Venetian bridge, 196; fort, 180; republic, 72; Venetians, 32–3, 48–51, 69–70, 74, 77, 80–5, 88, 92, 148–9, 153, 156, 164, 166, 171, 176, 179, 184, 283
Verlaci, Shevket: 201
Vermosh: 128–30, 134–8
Vero: 234
Vezirit, bridge: ix, 116
Via Ægnatia: 29, 35, 37, 158
Vibullius: 30
Victoria, Queen: x
Vidin: 185
Vienna: 93, 202, 205, 216–9, 264
Virgil: 179
Virpazar: 45
Visits to Monasteries of the Levant: 248
Vistrica, valley: 32
Vivari, lake: 177–9
Vjosa, river: 142, 145–8, 153, 224, 229–30, 237–8
Vlachs: 37, 176, 181, 236, 239, 250, 267; account of, 260–4
Vladislaus, King: 72–3
Vlona, Vlora: viii, 49, 91–2, 142, 145, 148–58, 166, 171, 178, 187–91, 224, 246, 258, 261; earthquake, 149, 156; importance of gulf, 150–1; Italians occupy, 154; Italians evicted, 94, 155; family, 150; Edhem, 19; Ismail Kemal, 19, 148, 150, 154
Von Hahn: 120
Vonica: 232
Vorra: 42
Voskopoli: 261, 263–6, 279

INDEX

Vrakë: 141
Vranacontes: 74, 76
Vrioni, Omer: 191–2, 247
Vuklë: 129–34, 138
Vuksanaj: 124–6
Vuna: 164, 166–7

Wace and Thompson: 264 (*see* bibl.)
Wallachians: 264–5, and *see* Vlachs
Water, importance of: 97, 213; supply in Tirana, 214
Wied, Prince of: 15, and *see* Wilhelm
Wild goats: 106, 256, 274; wild pig, 62, 171, 180, 256, 274
Wilhelm, Prince: 15, 17, 33, 36, 41, 92–3, 95, 104, 154, 158, 162, 198, 202, 222, 243
William, King of Sicily: 32; bishop, 283
Winchester: 283
Windischgraetz, Prince Ludwig: 93
Wolves: 21, 39, 98, 106, 110, 127, 141, 167, 252, 256, 269, 274, 278
Women: 17–8, 27, 37, 51, 67, 79, 87, 89, 96–7, 101–2, 107, 113, 117–20, 126, 128, 131, 137, 140, 143, 164–75, 188, 194–7, 209, 241–2, 255–7, 262, 267, 271–7
Woodcock: 180
World War: vii, 17, 41, 104, 114, 143, 147, 150, 159, 169–70, 198, 205, 235, 249, 251–2, 256, 269

Xanthus, stream: 179
Xhafer, Baba: 279–80

Yorkshire farm: 240
Yssuf, Elez: 23–4
Yugoslavia, Yugoslavs: vii, 38, 59–60, 95, 105–6, 121, 123, 127, 136–9,

Yugoslavia—*continued*.
141, 151, 153–4, 199, 200, 216, 218–9, 222, 284; relations with Albania, vii, 59–60, 94–5, 105, 123, 135–6, 203, 205, 218–9; relations with France, 200; with Italy, vii, 60, 200, 218; Italian military dispositions against, 151–3; acquires Shën Naoum, 39; invades Albania, 94, 105; Zogu's flight to, 27, 94–5

Zabiache: 54
Zaborzanë: 259
Zadrima: 87–8, 104, 283
Zagori: 233, 239, 255
Zavalina: 271
Zdransha: 276
Zinai od Bosna: 58
Zog (Zogu, Amet, King): viii, 23, 27–8, 41–2, 60, 64, 87, 89–95, 100, 106, 112, 118, 122–3, 127, 162, 194 *et sqq.*, 200–5, 210 *et sqq.*, 243; Abdulla, Amet, Mahmoud, Xhelal, Pashas, 91; Xhemal Pasha, 92; Xhelal, Prince, 89, 92; King, attempts to assassinate, 16, 216–7, 221; birthday, 215; description of, 95; domestic affairs, 201–2; home of, 91; message to, 123; mother, 91–2, 201; origin of, 91; palace, 194; policy, 199; President, 95, 122, 202; Prime Minister, 16, 94; proclaimed King, 95, 200; sisters, 91, 201; story of, 92 *et sqq.*
Zographos: 235
Zoroastrianism: 240
Zouaves: 266
Zrimadhës: 162–4, 171, 173
Zrinos, river: 229, 233
Zvezde: 41